ONLINE DATING
for
SENSITIVE WOMEN

∞∞∞

A proven system to build your
confidence, protect your
energy, and attract your
perfect partner

Michelle Gibeault

ISBN: (Ebook) 978-1-7375085-0-2
ISBN: (Paperback) 978-1-7375085-1-9

Cover design by: Michelle Gibeault

Happy Healthy Her Publications
Printed in the United States of America

This book is for all the women who have been called "too sensitive."
Beautiful women, your sensitivity is your greatest strength. Someone will
love your tender heart. I know I do.

For Ilia, who has supported me, loved me, and healed me unconditionally.
You are the yang to my yin. I love you indubitably.

For Chelle, my compass, my cheerleader, my dearest friend, thank you for
reminding me of my worth. Without your support and encouragement, I
would not be where I am today. I am eternally grateful.

For Mom, the strongest woman I know. You led by example, even if I
wasn't always quick to follow. I am grateful for all you have taught me. I
am a strong woman because an even stronger woman raised me.

For Dad, who continues to watch over me. Thank you for sending such a
supportive partner. He reminds me of you in so many of the best ways.

Contents

Introduction

Have you been told you are "too sensitive?"

Are you committed to being kind and considerate; what society calls a "good girl?"

Are you afraid to date, but you also don't want to end up alone?

Have you been through a devastating divorce or a challenging break-up, and you are not sure you can love again?

If any of these apply, this book is for you. As a sensitive woman, you care deeply about others and always try to do what is right. You have made a life out of putting others' needs before your own, which often meant you ended up in one-sided relationships that left you depleted. Perhaps you have protected your sensitive heart by avoiding romantic relationships altogether. You may even be like me, a mix of these experiences, having lived through a draining marriage and then a period of lonely solitude following divorce.

Whatever your personal life challenges have brought, there is a common thread that all sensitive women share — a hunger for a meaningful, loving connection. We are wired to share deep love with others. It is a natural part of our lives.

However, we live in a world that feels foreign. People can be so insensitive and cruel. As interactions move increasingly online, it feels even harder to experience the deep connections that we crave. The world of online dating is especially challenging for sensitive women, who often feel more comfortable with the energetic exchange of interacting face-to-face.

Personally, I developed a love/hate relationship with online dating over the nearly two years I explored its rocky waters. Diving in headfirst six months after my divorce, I was naïve and vulnerable. I didn't understand the unreal world that I was swimming through, and the sharks always seemed to be lurking. Quickly, I found myself confused, insecure, and lonelier than I had ever been.

Sounds awful, right? It could be.

It was also exhilarating! As I realized I had far more power than I ever imagined, and that I could still be loving and kind on my own terms, a whole new world opened up. I experienced fun dates, met interesting men, discovered how brave and resilient I was, all while falling in love with my life and myself. This ultimately led to meeting an amazing partner!

From one sensitive woman to another, I truly want you to experience the joys of online dating without the awkwardness, frustration, and disappointment. Please learn from my mistakes! Think of me as a trusted friend who whole-heartedly wants you to find the love you deserve. If I can do it, you can too. I have your back every step of the way.

My Story: The Bad Side of Being Good

I am the typical "good girl." I have always lived by the Golden Rule. In fact, I have lived by lots of rules in my life, mostly aimed at doing what is right. I am also an empath who feels others' emotions and energy, often deeply connecting to their pain and sadness. Likewise, I am a highly sensitive person (HSP) whose nervous system is easily overwhelmed. Furthermore, I am the INFJ personality type, known as "The Advocate" or "Counselor," who is drawn to serve others. These inherent aspects led me to put others' needs and wants before my own.

It took me until my late 30s to realize that this focus on others was actually codependency. Since then, I learned that the root of codependency is a lack of self-love that fuels a strong need to please others and gain their approval. Looking to others for validation and love is unhealthy, yet it is the natural inclination of many sensitive women.

To fulfill society's expectations, we believe we must be kind, smart, funny, pretty, considerate, and happy. ALL. THE. TIME. It is exhausting and unrealistic. Not to mention, the outward focus on pleasing others primes us for manipulation.

For most of my life, I did not even believe that toxic or manipulative people existed. I had an overly optimistic belief that everyone was doing the best they could in life, and that people only take or abuse because they don't know any better. The truth is, many people manipulate, lie, cheat, and steal. These toxic people know exactly what they are doing. They seek sensitive women because we are easy targets.

I don't regret being good, kind, or sensitive, but I do recognize that my focus on doing so above my own needs has caused me to lose out on a lot of joy and shared love. In addition, it has led to a great deal of emotional abuse and illness throughout my life, as I have attracted an overwhelming number of narcissists and energy vampires.

It took me a whopping 46 years to learn the hard lessons I am sharing with you here. No matter where you are on your life journey, I hope you will gain knowledge and support from this information.

Love Came Walking In

My story has an incredibly beautiful ending. After nearly two years of being on and off the online dating apps, I hit my limit. I met and dated several seemingly nice men, but they all turned out to be disappointing. They just could not meet the intensity of my heart.

As 2019 started, I set my intention on doing things differently. No more hiding myself or lowering my expectations. I had written a powerful affirmation in my journal:

I will no longer settle for less than I deserve!

That first week of January, a man reached out to me from a dating app I had forgotten I was on. Our coffee date went well. He was quiet, but seemed nice, a safe match even if there wasn't much of a spark. I felt hopefully optimistic that it was going to be my year for love. Driving home from the date, Van Halen's "Love Walks In" came on the radio, one of many signs from the Universe that things were looking up.

Two weeks later an eagle flew in front of my car as I was getting onto the highway near my home. Eagles symbolize freedom and personal power. It reminded me I was in control of my life.

The following week, a powerful full moon eclipse occurred in my sign of Leo. At that point, I had been trying to maintain friendly connections with men I had met online. However, I realized I could no longer give my energy away to people who didn't fully support me. The Universe will not allow positive new opportunities to arrive if old attachments are still lingering, so I cut ties completely in a full moon release ceremony and vowed again to reclaim my power and freedom.

That night I reconnected with an acquaintance I knew almost 20 years before. He felt comfortable, safe, and familiar. Furthermore, he was a solid catch with a beautiful home. We dated for several weeks, but like the prior man, there was just no spark. Despite this, he started making plans for me to meet his family the following weekend. I felt as though I was again giving away my power, getting swept into a safe, yet boring pattern I had known before.

Feeling anxious and energetically blocked, I booked an appointment with a trusted energy healer. As she worked on my body, a pronounced heaviness lifted. She reminded me I couldn't ignore my inner knowing. My spirit was always talking to me.

As I was driving home from the appointment, I received a text from the man I had been seeing. He said he didn't think things would work out. I felt blindsided and confused. Just then, a hawk swept down from a nearby tree and flew in front of my car. Hawks are my sign of validation and support. I knew things were happening for my highest good. Yet I couldn't quite shake the feelings of frustration. *Would I ever meet the right one?*

At the beginning of February, I pulled my energies away from the online dating world and focused more attention on the self-love efforts I had been working with for months. I knew deep down that I was better off alone than settling for someone safe. Not sure I even wanted to keep my dating profile active, I boldly changed my description to state that anyone who wanted my attention needed to read my entire profile and be prepared to ask me out for coffee or dinner. I was just so tired of all the games.

In the meantime, I got back to living my life. I met up with an intuitive friend with whom I always had a strong connection. We hiked to the top of a nearby mountain and settled in on some rocks. As we spoke of how oddly peaceful both of our lives seemed to be, a large turkey vulture kept circling overhead. Vultures had been showing up around me ever since my dad passed nearly five years before. My friend and I thanked Spirit for joining us. I told her candidly that I was craving more passion in my relationships. I wanted someone who treated me well, while also truly lighting me up. She validated my request, stating that she believed I would have both.

The following afternoon, I put on my most empowering playlist and headed out for a walk in my neighborhood. I ended up at the swing set of a nearby park. As I settled onto a swing, it started to drizzle. I didn't care. I felt so alive and free. I said aloud, *"I love myself. I love my life. I have built what I wanted. I have all that I need. I am so blessed and lucky. I am grateful. Thank you. Thank you. Thank you."* As a final surrender to the anguish I had been experiencing in online dating, I threw in, *"I don't need anyone else to complete me. I am whole as I am."* I continued to swing higher and higher, letting the rain clear the tears that had come to my eyes. It felt like years of grief and self-doubt were washing away.

When I returned home, I flipped open my laptop to find a message from a man from Match.com. I hesitated before opening it, feeling so good with my newly declared freedom. The man assured me he had read my very long profile right to the end and he would like to take me out for dinner or coffee at the location of my choice. He asked if we could talk on the phone first to get to know each other better. We spoke on the phone that night for nearly four hours.

It is cliché to say, but it truly felt like we had known each other our entire lives. When I first got divorced, I had a strong sense that my dad would send someone to watch over me. The man I was speaking to on the phone had a laugh that reminded me of my dad. He even used a silly expression that Dad used to say that I had never heard anyone else use. He told me that as a first-generation Greek, family was especially important to him. I share that same value. I tried to stay grounded in reality, but it blew me away how comfortable I felt.

During the call, I revealed that my love languages were gifts and words of affirmation. I mentioned that my ex-husband had always told me I didn't need flowers and refused to honor my request for even a single rose to show me he cared. This new man assured me he would never be so thoughtless.

I had the following Monday off from work, so we planned to meet for an early dinner at a diner halfway between our homes. Driving to dinner, I tried to stay calm. I tended to get my hopes up for first dates. I wanted this time to be different. However, my horoscope had been eerily predictive stating that, "a cross-cultural connection will thrive." A hawk again flew in front of my car, and I saw the number patterns 222 and 333 on license plates of passing cars, followed by 4:44 flashing on the clock. I knew these positive signs from Spirit well, because they had been happening for years.

My date arrived early and had already asked the wait staff if they could recommend some gluten-free menu items for me. When I walked in, he was standing beside a corner booth, a single pink rose in his hand. I immediately felt at ease in his welcoming energy. Throughout our dinner conversation, I continued to feel so comfortable. We had many things in common, including an interest in astrology and the spiritual synchronicities of life.

Toward the end of the date, he reached across the table and took both of my hands in his. A feeling of warmth radiated through my body. We both got teary-eyed as he shared something amazing that had happened to him just a few weeks prior. His tenant, who lived in the third-floor apartment of the childhood home he now owned, had been hearing noises. She requested the services of an energy clearer/medium.

The medium shared that there was a female Spirit present. This Spirit, likely his Aunt who had passed in 1996, was tired of how poorly women treated her nephew. She promised that if he cleared the space in front of the window in the back hall that she liked to look out of, she would send him a kind woman to love. He was happy to honor his Aunt's request and felt amazed and excited to be meeting me, the woman she may have sent.

We spent hours chatting in that corner booth, oblivious to the world around us. When we got up to leave, it stunned me to see my ex-husband in a booth near the door. I hadn't seen him in two years. I couldn't hide the wash of joy that was surely on my face, a beautiful rose clutched gratefully in my hand.

In the parking lot, as I reflected on such a strange chance meeting given that I had never even been to that diner, my date leaned in and said, "He had to see what he lost." He then asked if he could kiss me. I felt a rush of emotions as we had our first kiss, a super full moon shining brightly in the clear sky above our heads.

Between my mountaintop confession and his Aunt's promise, after over two years together there is no question in our minds that we were meant to meet. All the challenging times we had spent in past relationships and in online dating proved to be worth it. Those experiences enabled us to find one another.

Every moment together is fun. We can talk about absolutely anything. He makes me feel completely at ease. His unconditional love has healed me in ways that I never thought possible. Our growing love story emboldens me to share what I have learned on this wild dating journey.

No Going Back

There have been moments in writing this book that I considered not discussing the most painful details of my failed marriage or aspects of my current partnership. I thought, *"What will people think? It is all too personal."* I want to address my own concerns, if only to make an important declaration. I will not go back into hiding.

When we hide the most painful pieces of our lives, they fester and grow under a blanket of shame. However, when we share the pain, we release and transform it into a powerful lesson. Likewise, sharing stories of joy and love gives others hope. Both outcomes can help to heal, which has always been a powerful piece of my life's purpose.

If I am ever single again, it will not negate the value of the information I share here. Nothing is permanent, but once you love yourself fully, and then welcome in the joy of being with someone who loves you fully too, you accept nothing less.

The sensitive woman who writes to you today is much more courageous, self-assured, and certain of her worth. This book is not just about finding your perfect partner. It is about finding the best version of you — the woman who chooses herself first.

I made a promise to the Universe and myself that once I made it through my divorce I would reach my hand back to pull other women forward with me. I am grateful that I can finally honor that promise. I don't want any woman to struggle with the self-doubt, shame, or guilt that I needlessly carried. I want all sensitive women to recognize and honor their inherent strength, beauty, and enduring light, so they can shine fully.

About This Book

If you're like me, you like to be prepared. I always skim through the "Table of Contents" before tackling a nonfiction book. Oftentimes, there are sections I can't wait to dive into.

I broke this book into three phases that I feel should be followed sequentially to achieve the best result. You are certainly welcome to jump around to the different sections, but I highly suggest that you fully review the "Phase 1: Prepare for Connection" section.

This first section is the "tough love" portion of the book. It is much longer than the subsequent phases because I believe it is the most important. If you liken dating to painting a house, the prep work of buying the supplies, putting down tarps, and taping the walls, takes longer and is more tedious than the painting itself. Yet, that preparation is vital for a successful project. Consider this your support so you don't get paint on your beautiful hardwood floors, or that sweet, sensitive heart stomped on!

The information covered in Phase 1 represents the knowledge that I was clueless about when I started out online. We are going to get real about the challenges of dating so you can avoid all the confusion, embarrassment, and heartache I experienced. What we cover there can help you not only navigate a successful relationship, but also gain clarity around the manipulation that sensitive women often encounter in all areas of life.

I want you to be prepared mentally and emotionally, so that when you are ready for "Phase 2: Put Yourself Out There," you will feel confident and at ease. In that section, we talk about the basics of online dating and the realities of dating in general. We will review the various online dating platforms, cover what to include in a captivating profile, and tackle how to approach first dates with excitement rather than dread.

Once you are out there in the dating world, "Phase 3: Get Serious About Love," gives you practical tools for fully healing your heart, living a vibrant life, and calling in your true love. This section taps into the spiritual principles of the Law of Attraction and the power of intention. I hope you will embrace this with an open mind and open heart, because I believe these alchemical efforts maximized the love in my life, including my own self-love. Once I loved myself fully, the Universe sent me the truly loving partner who was right for me.

Throughout this journey, I suggest keeping track of your thoughts and feelings in a journal. You can do that on your computer in a Word document, in a notebook, or in a print journal. Whatever format you choose, make it your own. Use fun fonts, bold colors, and a favorite pen. During my dating progression, I found it incredibly helpful to process my feelings and emotions through writing. I kept an online journal, along with a Wonder Woman notebook that made me feel powerful.

I wrote this book from my personal perspective as a white, heterosexual woman. I welcome individuals of all races, sexual preferences, and genders to learn from my experience. I believe the core messages shared around dating, confidence, and self-love are pertinent to all sensitive people. However, I recognize I can only relay my experiences from my unique lens, which may differ from yours. Please use what works for you and leave the rest.

You'll notice that throughout the book I share my personal experiences with the men I met. I don't refer to these men by name and have obscured most of their identifying details to protect their privacy. I appreciate the men I met, even the manipulators. I believe we were all doing the best we could with the tools we had. I don't want to vilify any of these men, even if they hurt me. I have forgiven them for any perceived wrongdoings, as I hope they have done the same for me. They ultimately helped me grow into the stronger, more resilient woman I am today.

One of the most beautiful gifts of finding your ideal partner is that you realize all of those other people were doing you a favor by not meeting your expectations. They gave you clarity and the freedom to find your best match. On an even greater level, the people who hurt you help you recognize a powerful truth — you are always better off alone than settling for someone who doesn't honor and support you fully.

The Keys to Finding a Loving Partnership

I truly want you to find a genuine, happy, healthy partnership. Therefore, right up front, I'm going to share the most critical pieces of information I uncovered through my dating experiences. If you can accept these principles, you are well on your way to a loving partnership.

1. You are worthy of love and happiness! You must recognize your worth and make your needs a priority if you want to draw in a healthy relationship based on reciprocity and mutual respect.

2. Good men exist. I hear women all the time saying that there are no good men. What you believe and say carries powerful energy. If you don't believe you can meet a kind, loving partner, then your chances of doing so are very limited.

3. If a man is interested in you, he will do everything in his power to be with you. Men are not that complicated. Genuine love is not complicated either. When a man wants to get to know you better, he will make it happen. PERIOD. If someone is playing games with you, delaying responses, or putting you low on his priority list, he is not your person. We are told that relationships require work and anguish. The truth is unhealthy relationships are difficult. Healthy partnerships are easy and filled with joy.

4. Dating should always be fun! If it stops being fun, game over. Take a break. Give yourself some time to regroup and then try again when you are ready. The only reason to date is to expand the joy in your life. If dating is causing you sadness, self-doubt, or even inconvenience, it is not worth the effort.

5. You only need to meet one person. Online dating can feel overwhelming and competitive. With all the focus on the "likes" and the messages, it can feel like a numbers game where you need to garner as much attention as possible or you are losing. That is not true. You only need to connect with one quality person to win at love.

6. Actions speak louder than words. There are loads of men who will tell you everything you want to hear. However, very few men will consistently display integrity, honesty, empathy, and accountability. Watch for behaviors to match a person's words. When they do, you know you have met a genuine person. It takes at least a month for a person to show you who they are, so give everyone you meet time before you commit to them.

The keys to successful online dating are the same keys to success in life. Be confident, know what you want, stay true to yourself, and have fun. Once you know how to navigate the unique challenges of online dating, having a successful partnership takes very little effort.

Phase 1: Prepare for Connection

Here's where we get real about how ready you are for an online dating experience. It is fine to decide that you aren't ready, especially if you've been through a recent breakup or divorce. It is a wise and healthy decision for many of you reading this for the first time to process this information without jumping online.

You may need to read through this section carefully, establish a support system, and even commit to a period of solitude or further healing before you're ready to move on to Phase 2. Please take your time!

You can't rush love. Sometimes we need time and space before we can fully accept a loving partnership. In the meantime, enjoy yourself and live your life fully. Being single provides a wonderful time for savoring your freedom and falling in love with your life. That kind of enthusiasm and self-love are the very things that draw in a healthy partnership.

Chapter 1: Assess Your Readiness

I thought I was ready for online dating. I was incredibly excited to get back out into the world. I had spent all of 2016 with my head down, focused solely on rebuilding my life. I had a very busy job at a hospice center with an hour-long commute. On my days off, I focused on all the draining tasks of my divorce. Although I worked with some wonderful people, I had moved to be closer to the job, which meant I was further away from all of my long-term friends. As a result, I was lonelier than I had ever been.

The divorce was final in September 2016. With that pressure no longer lingering over my head, I got brave enough to approach my managers. I was struggling with fatigue and I needed a break. Their response was shockingly cold. They ultimately forced me to quit, giving up my health benefits and all my earned vacation and sick time. I dutifully stayed on part-time as they attempted to hire for my position. After several months, no one would agree to the low salary I had accepted. I was driving to an interview for a contract position when a bald eagle flew over my car. That was my sign. I was FREE! I quit my job that afternoon.

That was in January 2017. I am always optimistic at the beginning of a new year. There I was totally on my own, an odd mix of elated and terrified. I thought I was fully aware of my codependency issues and even my propensity to attract narcissists and energy vampires. I was confident that the awareness was enough to protect me. Nevertheless, I was still a "good girl" at heart, believing that most people were kind and had good intentions. That was very naïve, especially for someone who was about to throw herself into the world's weirdest cocktail party.

Although I was eager to make new connections, I was not

fully prepared mentally and emotionally to set the appropriate boundaries. What I now understand is that the online world is not as transparent as the real one. It is harder to read cues or trust your intuition. Likewise, manipulative men who seem perfect are poised and ready to fool sensitive, trusting women.

My hopeful heart believed that the men I met were going to give me the love and attention I desperately craved. What we desire can often skew our perception. The reality of online dating is that no one is quite who they seem. You must recognize that in order to protect your heart.

Some Tough Love Is Necessary

It is also crucial that you realize that while you may want a partner, you do not need one. This powerful shift in mindset keeps you grounded and confident. Partnership is nice, but we are all whole and complete on our own. We do not need a romantic partner in our lives. Too often, we settle for someone because we believe we need them, and, as was true in my case, we are struggling with the pain of loneliness that drives us to disregard our intuition.

It is best not to date when you are lonely. It is like the nutrition advice I give as a dietitian, which is to not grocery shop when you are hungry. In both situations, your judgment is impaired. It is better to spend time with friends, enjoy hobbies, or work on your self-love before attempting online dating in a lonely, vulnerable state.

Questions to Consider Before Dating

That being said, finding a partner to share your life with is an exciting endeavor. Love and companionship are truly wonderful experiences. It is absolutely worth putting yourself out there once you are prepared.

However, you must put in the effort and energy that a successful relationship demands. It is important to be completely honest with yourself about where you are emotionally. Following are some tough questions that can help guide you in knowing if you are truly ready to put yourself out there.

Am I OK with being alone? Do I have a support system outside of a romantic partnership?

I mentioned earlier that I felt very lonely right before I tried online dating. I have wonderful friends and family. However, during my divorce, I was so consumed by my day-to-day survival that I was not maintaining my personal relationships. I had not been reaching out appropriately for support and had cocooned myself. That meant that when I got the impulse to date, I did it with a bit of desperation. I felt like I needed a companion to do things with, and even someone to help me heal the broken heart I had amassed through my empty and loveless marriage.

Manipulative, toxic people can sense loneliness and desperation. They have uncanny radar for agreeable women who will accept less than they deserve. The first man I dated seriously was a narcissist who love bombed me for the first three months of our relationship. I will talk more about that later. The bottom line here is that I needed to be nurturing my existing social connections, so I had the confidence and reassurance that I did not need a man to be happy.

If you realize that your support system needs work, make a list of all the friends and family members you can count on and start actively contacting them to catch up. Make plans for coffee or meet for a hike so that you can work your social muscles. If you were like me and had been in a long relationship, you may have to relearn how to socialize. There is no shame in that. It is a natural by-product of the busyness of life. If your social connections need work, consider trying Meetup.com, joining a church, or signing up for classes that will put you in contact with like-minded people.

It is also extremely helpful to have at least one friend who is experiencing (or has experienced) online dating. That person can be a sounding board for you to pose questions or address any strange behaviors that are sure to arise. I started a new job just after I joined online dating. After a few months of working in that predominantly female office, I learned a colleague was also online dating. She offered a great deal of information, validation, and comic relief. It was comforting to feel less alone.

There are online forums on dating or designed for sensitive women. They offer a place to ask for advice or support. I am also available as a resource. I offer compassionate coaching from a place of true knowing. You can find my contact information at the end of the book.

Do I love myself enough to give love to someone else?

This one is painful. I thought I loved myself. However, I was harboring a tremendous amount of guilt and shame from having to leave my marriage. Despite not doing anything wrong in asking for a divorce from someone who had been dismissive, cruel, and unloving, I felt like a bad person. I did not have good health insurance throughout my divorce, so I had not been through therapy to address all the pain, disappointment, and resentment that was hiding underneath my "I'm fine" persona. Not to mention, it had only been six months since my divorce was final. I do not think time is always the best indicator of readiness, but in my case, six months was too soon.

If I knew then what I know now, I would have worked diligently on self-esteem with a focus on self-love, even if that meant using therapy, coaching, or hypnosis. It would have been worth the effort to gain greater confidence and emotional strength. I have since done that hard work, and I feel like an entirely different person.

Self-love is hard for many sensitive "good girls." We tend to pour our love outward in a selfless manner. Even the phrase self-love used to make me cringe because it sounded like selfishness to me. Nothing is further from the truth. We all have to love ourselves to offer healthy, unconditional love to other people. If you just focus on outward love, you ultimately end up depleted and resentful. Take the time to do some self-love work. We will explore this more in Phase 3.

Do I have a desperate need to find someone quickly?

You can't rush love or connection. If you focus on needing someone now, you are setting yourself up for disappointment. Men will show up who will quickly proclaim that you are the only one for them and that they immediately want to get off on-line dating to commit to you. While that is flattering, it should also raise some red flags.

Speed is not what you are after in creating a loving partnership. Slow and steady is a much healthier approach. Those that speed up the connection tend to be narcissists. It is a primary tactic for that type to sweep you off your feet. Once they believe they have you, they treat you with disrespect.

Many of the men I dated seriously moved quickly, sweeping me up in a rush of attention that made it hard for me to find my center. If I had slowed things down, it would have been easier to get my footing and assess if those relationships were actually what I was looking for.

Do I feel good about my life?

People who love their lives have a positive energy that draws good things to them. Being happy and positive is an addictive energy that most people crave. If you are not feeling good about any aspects of your life, you will not give off the positive energy that will draw in a positive person.

Make a list of the things you like about your life and yourself. Add to that "love list" regularly. Even though I was in a bad place emotionally, I appreciated my life and the freedom I had earned by being brave enough to leave my marriage. I loved my little townhouse and the community where I was living. I loved that I had greater autonomy, peace, and the opportunity to rebuild my life. I was more positive than negative. I think that made a big difference in my online dating experiences.

What values do I want in a partner?

We do not think that much about values in our society. We tend to focus more on surface issues like money, appearance, career, even hobbies or shared activities. However, a solid partnership requires a shared sense of values.

I had not initially spelled out the values that were most important to me. I'm not sure I even recognized what mattered most to me until I experienced behaviors and attitudes that didn't resonate. It is now easy for me to clarify my ideal values as honesty, integrity, open communication, kindness, deep love of family and friends, intellectual curiosity, an open mind, and an excellent sense of humor.

Take some time to think through the values you look for in your relationships. This effort will assist your dating success, while also positively shaping the way you approach your life.

Where did I go wrong in past relationships?

Self-awareness is incredibly valuable. You can't learn from your mistakes if you don't acknowledge them. If you are feeling as though all your past relationship issues were due to your partner, then you need to check yourself right now. You are the only common denominator in all your relationships.

I know that stings. As a "good girl," I never really wanted to rock the boat. I would assert myself with my husband, then immediately feel bad and backtrack to smooth things over. Over time, I allowed him and his family to walk all over me.

I have to accept that, as a people-pleaser, I enabled people to treat me poorly. I was more concerned about how they felt than how I was feeling. That is a recipe for resentment and sadness. I was setting myself up for unhealthy and unfulfilling relationships by not speaking up for my needs.

Try to uncover the blind spots of your relationships. If you are having trouble pinpointing where you need to make changes, consider asking a trusted friend for advice, or even better, look to a trained therapist or coach who can give you an objective perspective.

If you are sensitive and empathic, you may not be putting up firm enough boundaries and pushing back when people take too much from you. This is incredibly common. Do not beat yourself up over it, just accept it, and start thinking about ways in which you can curb the tendency to squash your own needs and over-give in relationships.

What will I do if someone disrespects me?

Since boundaries rarely come naturally for sensitive women, you need to strategize and plan how you will set them when the time comes. First, consider what you feel is disrespectful. Men who catcalled me in our first interaction repulsed me. They would say things like, "Hey sexy" or "You need to come out for a drink with me." Those comments may seem innocent, but I found them to be objectifying. I took time in creating my profile to be a strong reflection of who I am and what I was looking for. That kind of empty attention made me feel cheap, as if my appearance was all that was important to them.

I tried to respond to most men who contacted me in any meaningful way (i.e., commenting directly on something written in my profile). However, when men just came at me with physical compliments, I rarely responded. There were some instances where I did reply. Those men always turned out to be disrespectful of me, disregarding any future boundaries I set.

The lesson here is that you must be firm and clear right away. Do not waver or feel bad for anyone. As soon as you do, you are showing them you are a pushover. Good men do not catcall women online. They understand empty compliments do not work for most women. The men who do it are fishing for women who need praise.

I do not mean to be harsh here. It is just the truth. It takes a man absolutely no time to flip through photos making comments, hoping to see if it will get attention. Men who are genuinely interested in a connection will take the time to read your profile and contact you with thoughtful comments.

Can I reject someone lovingly without feeling bad?

Rejection is inevitable in online dating. Men will reject you and you will have to reject them too. You need to make peace with that quickly to preserve your energy, time, and heart. Initially, I decided I would respond to everyone who took the time to reach out to me. I thought it was bad karma to avoid messages or dismiss someone who tried to connect.

Over time, I realized that for many men, the messages and interactions are highly impersonal. Some men send form-letter-style communications or just say things like, "Hey, what's up?" They put so little effort into the interaction that it was silly for me to give them one ounce of my energy.

It is certainly fine to communicate in brief messages when first connecting with someone. However, the messages should have some substance. In most cases, empty one-liners will not be worth your time. There is nothing wrong with ignoring them. You will need to get clear with yourself that doing so is not cruel or rude. It is self-preservation.

From what I came to understand from many of the men I connected with, most women do not respond at all. A good number of men become disheartened with the dynamics of online dating and lose interest in trying to establish a genuine connection. Realizing this made me sad. However, it was not my job to make those men feel better. My job was to protect my energy and interests — always. The same is true for you.

Most men in online dating are not sensitive in the ways we are. They expect a lack of response. You should never feel bad about ignoring someone who does not feel like a good fit. Get clear on your gut instincts. It might help you to establish a meditative practice or use divining tools to help guide you in selecting which men are worthy of your efforts. We'll go into this more fully in Chapter 9.

As a warning, the risk of engaging with a man you are feeling questionable about is that once you give an inch, he will try to take a mile. That happened to me several times. In one particularly difficult interaction, shortly after I joined Match.com, a man started looking at my profile daily and messaged me several times saying I was attractive. He was older than my desired age range, which I had defined as eight years older than I was, and he lived outside of my ideal geographical range.

While age didn't matter to me, location did. I struggle with fatigue. Juggling a long-distance relationship alongside work would not fit my lifestyle. The man changed his age on his profile and continued to message me. I didn't realize I could block him. Instead, I sent what I thought was a kind message saying that I didn't think we were a good match and that I wished him well. He shot back a message saying I looked like I was in my 50s anyway. I was 42 at the time. His cruel words stung. Even though I knew the man was just being childish and petty, I had a hard time letting it go. I asked every man that I dated after that point if I looked my age. They all laughed and said I looked much younger than my pictures and that I could not take what people said online personally.

The trouble is, as a sensitive woman I do take words personally. At least I did much more at that time. I share this as a warning that worrying about hurting a man's feelings could ultimately backfire, leaving you with the hurt feelings. Keep reminding yourself that most men don't have a heart like yours. They don't feel things the way you do. There are, of course, empathic men, but they are quite rare. Additionally, a truly sensitive man will understand that you have every right to honor your own needs.

Please commit to yourself right now that you will not accept less than you deserve, and that you will trust yourself over anyone else. You are always in control. If at any point someone makes you feel uncomfortable, unworthy, or otherwise unhappy, you are always free to tell that person you are not a good match and cut all communications.

If you are unhappy with what you have uncovered through the previous questions, don't give up on your dating potential. We will uncover ways to build your confidence, self-awareness, and boundary-setting abilities so that you will be closer to putting yourself out there comfortably.

Chapter 2: Plan for the Pros

It is always good to assess the pros and cons when facing a new challenge. I knew so little about online dating when I started that I was overly optimistic. I believed I could scroll through profiles and easily find the person who shared my common interests. The only initial con for me was that I had to put myself out there in a manner that felt very vulnerable — my pictures and personal information would be online for the world to see! Now that I have experience, my pros and cons list is much longer. It contains many surprising bonuses I would never have imagined. I share this with you so that you have a greater sense of what is in store for you.

Let's start with the pros. Despite how challenging it can be to navigate, there are many positive aspects of dating online. Following are the highlights that I found to be true.

Greater Opportunities

There are more men online than you could ever meet in your personal life. This goes without saying, but it is certainly a major pro of the online world. I tend to work in nonprofit organizations with very few men. Likewise, my regular activities revolve around self-help practices like yoga, meditation, and Qigong, all of which have very few men. It wasn't hard to see that my chances of meeting a man were slim. The probability of finding your perfect match requires exposure to a wide variety of people. Online dating has that covered.

More Specific Choices

You can sort your potential matches by very specific factors like location, education, age, personal interests, even astrology. I knew I wanted a connection who lived within a 30-minute drive so that we could see each other easily. Also, even though I have a master's degree, I grew up in a blue-collar family, so I found myself more drawn to men who had life experience and not necessarily formal education. It was exciting to meet men already knowing pieces of their story.

A Chance for Clarity and Growth

Creating a dating profile and actively seeking a relationship forces you to learn about who you are and what makes you unique. This type of deep reflection is valuable work that we rarely take the time to do in our lives. Getting clear on your hobbies and what you enjoy enriches your life far beyond just meeting men. As I uncovered all of my unique traits, continually honing my profile so that it was the truest reflection of me, I grew to genuinely like the woman on my computer screen.

Being married to someone who devalued me regularly had taken a toll on my self-esteem, which I had not recognized. Uncovering who I was opened my eyes to how interesting and fun I am. It did not happen right away, and it was not easy, but I am grateful to have had such a major growth opportunity.

You Are Always in Control

Some experts suggest that sensitive women not venture into online dating because of all the potential predators lurking. While I agree that you will probably encounter those negative, manipulative types, I don't think you should allow them to ruin your chances of connecting with someone great.

Even though I met many manipulative, unhealthy men, I also met quite a few fun and interesting men, including the wonderful man who is now my partner. I am grateful that I never let the jerks drag me down.

The important thing to embrace is that you are always in control. That thought alone is very empowering. It is tempting for sensitive, empathic women to protect themselves by hiding away from the world. If you are in healing mode, that is appropriate. However, if you are ready to get out there and meet someone new, don't limit your potential.

Everything is New!

Meeting new people is fun. It exposes you to new hobbies, new music, and new perspectives. Going on dates also enables you to try new restaurants, bars, and coffee shops, or explore parks and hiking trails you didn't even know existed. My life immediately became richer with new experiences once I set up my online profile and started connecting with men who I would not normally have met.

My partner rides a motorcycle. While he didn't pressure me to ride with him, he eased me into the idea, assuring me we could turn around at any point. Turns out, I love riding on the back of his bike! It is exhilarating and breathtakingly beautiful to take in all the panoramic sites of the back roads near my home. I never imagined that I would enjoy the thrill of riding on a motorcycle, and I am grateful for having the opportunity.

Greater Confidence

Most of us are not inherently confident about our dating and communication skills. Initially, you may feel incredibly nervous and insecure. However, as is true for anything we practice regularly, putting yourself out there, chatting with and meeting new people, helps you gain confidence and improve your communication skills.

My communication style is very inquisitive. As an introvert who can be shy at first, my focus is often on asking questions and then actively listening. This takes a lot of pressure off me. Most of my dates were long, lasting three to five hours. When you give someone your full attention, the conversation just takes on a life of its own. Over time, I noticed that my dating experiences were helping me gain confidence at work as well.

Deeper Connections

As an INFJ personality type, I crave deep conversation and

connection. My marriage lacked true intimacy. My ex-husband never wanted to talk about the kinds of deep, personal topics that excited me. After a while, I came to believe that was just how men are. It thrilled me to learn that such a closed-off state is not the norm. Introspective, deep men exist!

Many of the men I met also wanted depth. During our long dates, we chatted about life, family, and past hurts. It was heart-warming to realize that my perception of men had been wrong. I met one man on OkCupid who said right up front that he had just been through heartbreak and was only looking for friends. I had recently broken up with someone too and was not quite ready for a new relationship. We sent each other messages of encouragement and support over a couple of weeks. In one, he said something especially profound relating to the dating experience, "Disappointments shouldn't sway the authentic self, but rather strengthen our character in this uphill battle." If I had not been brave enough to explore online dating, I never would have gleaned that piece of wisdom.

Many Chances at Love

Love is the most powerful force in the Universe. There is nothing better! Love may seem like a long shot when you first enter the dating world, but the risks (especially when armed with the advice you are learning here) are worth taking. I can honestly say I fell in love with several men along my journey. They weren't all the right fit for me, and it hurt to realize that, but it was as if I was exercising a muscle. When I found my ideal match, I was far more ready for that partnership than if I had not loved and lost before.

FUN!

More than anything, dating should be fun. Always keep that in mind. As soon as it becomes too draining or unenjoyable, take a break. Most dating sites allow you to hide your profile. Don't be afraid to exercise that right at will.

Although it is rare to find lasting friendships through online dating, some men are open to the idea. Even if you don't hit it off romantically, there is an opportunity to develop a friendship or even just a pen pal. A few men never became actual love connections. Still, I had a lot of fun exchanging funny emails with them.

∞∞∞∞

Of course, your positive outcomes and opportunities are going to differ from mine. Take some time to think about your potential pros of online dating. Perhaps online dating will help you live in a bolder, braver way, or it will give you a chance to try out a new hobby. There are many reasons meeting new people can benefit your life. Focusing on the positives will help you feel more confident and excited about dating.

Chapter 3: Consider the Cons

Just as with the pros, your cons are likely to differ from mine depending on your comfort level and your lifestyle. I do not have children, which made arranging dates much easier. I recognize that if you have children or other personal demands in your life, your resistance to online dating may be greater.

Please do your best to assess the cons of dating for you. Many very busy parents can successfully date, so don't get hung up on your circumstances. Here are some of the negative aspects of online dating I uncovered that are worth considering.

It Takes Time

You must put in consistent time and energy to be successful. This includes updating your profile, scrolling through your matches, and answering messages from men who pique your interest. This could take several hours a week.

At the very least, you will spend many evenings reviewing the day's matches. This is a fun process once you realize what to look for. Nevertheless, if your life is already overbooked, you probably want to get real about whether you can handle another daily "to-do."

I met an INFJ man who I thought might be my perfect match. He was sweet, thoughtful, successful in his career, and we had a great conversation on our first date. However, he had a teenaged son and a very busy work schedule. After our second date to the movies, his texts dwindled to every few days. That just wasn't enough of a commitment for me, so things ended abruptly. If you can't dedicate time to dating, texting, or otherwise communicating with a potential partner, you will waste their time and yours.

You WILL Get Rejected

Until I understood the dynamics of online dating, the rejection, or perceived rejection from not getting a response to messages, really hurt me. I mean "dagger to the heart" level of hurt. My self-esteem was already low and my expectations were, as I now recognize, ridiculously high. I believed I would get at least some response from everyone I reached out to. It does not work like that.

Some of the profiles you see online are not actually active. Meaning, that handsome man with the perfect profile is not even online anymore. Perhaps his subscription expired, or he met someone and never deactivated his profile. You are getting your hopes up for nothing!

We will dive into this heartbreaking reality in the section that follows. For now, just know you have to accept and even expect rejection. It is an essential part of the process. It is actually in your best interest that not every man "likes," responds, or reaches out to you. If they did, it would be overwhelming and unlikely to lead to a genuine connection.

You Have to Reject People

I am not sure which is worse for a sensitive woman, being rejected or having to reject someone. Both feel awful, especially if you grow to know and like someone. There were men I liked, but I just couldn't see myself with for the long-term. Perhaps if I was younger, I would have been willing to date multiple people to see how things went. However, at 42, I wasn't looking to spend my energy on anyone who didn't have solid potential.

I had to end several connections, sometimes quickly. I learned that fast and firm was the best way to go. There was no sense in trying to drag it out. That only made things worse. I think it is best to end an actual relationship, where you have had several dates, via an in-person or phone conversation.

One man I had been seeing for several weeks ended things via a short text. He had just told me a few days before that he wanted me to meet his parents the following weekend. Even though I didn't feel we had true potential, I found the text to be jarring, as there was no explanation for his change of heart. I would never want someone to feel as confused as I did. Once you have had several dates, I think you owe it to the person to have an actual conversation around why you think the relationship should end. Anything less feels cowardly.

It Is a Competition

As a sensitive woman, I shy away from competing with other women. When you are online dating, you have no choice. This can be especially unnerving when you realize other women are more aggressive and better at the dating game than those of us who are more shy and reserved.

You must step outside your comfort zone a bit. If you are serious about finding a partner, put aside any fears of competition and accept that it is all part of the process. Try not to think too much about other women. Keep your focus on the end goal of the loving partnership meant for you.

So Much New Energy Can Be Draining

As a sensitive person, you are likely very reactive to other people's energy. Even if you are meeting fun, energetic people, all that new energy can be exhausting. Likewise, if the interactions are negative at all, you may end up feeling emotionally drained. It is important to realize how much your energy may be affected and to put protective measures in place.

For instance, while I loved long chats on my dates, you may decide that an hour is all you can handle. It is perfectly appropriate to set an end time for dates so that you have an out. It is also a good idea to establish a grounding practice or some means of clearing the energy before and after dates. I always keep crystals in my purse and often wear them as jewelry. We'll cover other ways to protect your energy throughout the book.

You Could End up Feeling Jaded

If you encounter a string of negative interactions or game-playing men, it is very easy to lose your enthusiasm. I have been in forums for sensitive women where women have lamented that they never want to date again. It is common for both women and men to conclude that online dating is just not worth their time.

Please don't let yourself get into that headspace! There are always going to be negative or nasty people in the world. It may seem like they are all hanging out on online dating apps. That does not mean there aren't kind, thoughtful, and even sensitive men on there too. Mindset is everything.

It Can Be Scary

The number one comment I got when I told my girlfriends that I was trying online dating was, "Wow! You're so brave. I don't think I could ever do that." The funny thing is I get nervous about many things, but I wasn't that nervous about dating. As I mentioned earlier, my excitement and desire to get out into the world again far exceeded any fears I had. I think that is a strong gauge of how well you can succeed online. If you are feeling brave enough to try it, then you are likely ready. If you are still a little leery, then keep working through this book. There is much more advice to uncover. I hope that by the end your courage will be soaring.

It Is Addictive

It is worth noting that being online can be addictive. This can be both a pro and a con depending on how you look at it. Once you have received the positive reinforcement of online dating — the "likes," the messages, the excitement of new faces popping up daily — it is hard to disconnect. Sometimes I felt like I had two distinct realities, the online world where I could chat freely with strangers and the actual world where I was still sensitive and introverted. It was almost like being two different people, which was exciting yet confusing.

Not fully understanding the online world made that more of a negative in the beginning. I felt very insecure, needing the praise and positive attention, while also fearing rejection. It is a very uncomfortable and unnatural place to be if you don't recognize the pitfalls. Nevertheless, you are going to be armed with all the inside information. Hopefully, this won't turn out to be a con for you.

This is your life. You must be sure that the pros and cons of online dating work for you. Sit down now with your journal and create two columns for your "pros" and "cons." In each column get as detailed as you can about what you currently believe are the most positive and negative aspects of online dating. Date your entry so that you can return to this list later to track what has changed for you.

Chapter 4: Realize It Is Unreal

I have alluded to this several times already so it probably won't come as a surprise when I tell you the online dating world is not like actual life. The rules of common decency and social norms are not in play. You must keep your guard up and your intuition strong at all times. If someone feels off to you in even the slightest way, honor that feeling.

NEVER let being nice supersede honoring your instincts. This is something I did far too often in subtle ways — by responding to people I didn't feel were a good match, by giving men my phone number when I wasn't fully ready, by texting back-and-forth for weeks when it was obvious the relationship wasn't going anywhere. In retrospect, I can see how silly I had been worrying about the other person's feelings when they did not care about my feelings or needs at all.

As a sensitive woman, you must constantly remind yourself that saying "no" or avoiding someone to protect yourself is not malicious or mean. If your intentions are positive and loving, then you can't go wrong, even if you ultimately disappoint someone.

Healthy men understand boundaries and the realities of rejection. Unhealthy and manipulative men, on the other hand, are likely to push back. If that happens, it is a blessing because it shows you quickly who to avoid.

Following are some concepts that are important to understand about the unreal nature of the online world.

Lying Is Common

When you are an honest person, it is hard to fathom why someone would lie or misrepresent themselves. I still don't understand it myself. If you ever meet that person, their lies are going to come out.

As a sensitive person, you may naturally give people the benefit of the doubt. Your tendency is likely to look for the good in people. In online dating, it is best to question everything.

My partner always says, "Trust, but verify." I feel like a safer approach is to question, verify, and then monitor. Never give anyone the full benefit of the doubt online. Many men are playing by different rules. There are men who are married, those who are dating many women at the same time, and even those who are using a false identity.

For instance, when I first joined OkCupid, a man sent me a message that had terrible grammar. Since I am a writer, clear communication is important to me. Still, I didn't want to be a snob, so I responded. He quickly asked for my phone number. Against my better judgment, I gave it to him, just as he gave me his.

As I always did, I immediately Googled his phone number and learned that he wasn't who he said he was. Upon further digging, I learned he had been arrested for driving through the stop sign on a bus, endangering children. I felt sick when I learned that. He was not at all the kind of person I was looking to date. My desire to not be a snob could have gotten me into a lot of trouble.

The bottom line is, until you have researched someone, met them in person, and established a genuine connection, you must assume that everyone you meet online is potentially not who they say they are. I realize that sounds dramatic, but you can't be too careful.

People Are Unusually Brazen and Uncomfortably Bold

I have never really been one to frequent bars. However, I went to a college where frat parties were the norm every weekend. As such, I am no stranger to pickup lines and drunken flirtations. What happens in the online world is far more unfiltered than anything you will experience in real life. People feel a sense of

35

anonymity when they are online that gives them a false bravado. This can be uncomfortable for a sensitive person. I can read someone's energy at a party and recognize that they are drunk or feeling nervous, but online those nuances go away leaving only aggressive and bold words.

I was feeling especially lonely one Friday night after a difficult week of work. I ended up mindlessly scrolling through my Match.com picks. Suddenly, I got a message from a man with a boat. That was his entire persona, "Man with a boat." He had loads of pictures of himself on his expensive-looking boat. The message said, "Come have a drink with me right now." It felt so invasive. I mean, who are you? It is bad enough to have someone approach you when you are at a bar for a night out with your girlfriends. But in my home? I felt oddly violated. I can only assume that was his big move. He probably sent the same message to a dozen other women, hoping one would bite.

This is an uncomfortable reality of the online world. Once you realize how readily it happens, you can laugh it off. Just ignore those types and keep focused on finding a loving partner who won't be a creep!

Predators and Scammers Are Lurking

This is the scariest and most unbelievable aspect of being online. Some men are seeking to swindle unsuspecting women. They will share sob stories about being in financial trouble, and will then ask for money. Never send anyone you meet money or personal information (like credit card numbers or your social security number). Even if you have met them in person, please be leery of anyone asking you for assistance. Consider how strange that is to ask a stranger for help, even if you have been texting or on a date or two. Healthy individuals do not ask strangers for anything.

Although I never had anyone ask me for money, a few men who messaged me through the apps immediately shared very personal details of their "supposed" lives, presumably to evoke my pity. When I didn't take the bait, their profiles mysteriously disappeared. For instance, one man whose pictures looked like a chiseled supermodel had a profile gushing about being a widower and longing to have someone to heal his heart. Like a sucker, I sent him a message saying that I was sorry for his loss. He messaged back with something short and impersonal. Then his profile disappeared. I think the OkCupid admins might have actually taken it down.

This primarily happened on the two free sites I was on — Plenty of Fish and OkCupid. It makes sense that when there is no paper trail (i.e., a paid membership that can be tracked to a credit card) or a monetary commitment, you are more likely to encounter scammers. As an example, the first time I joined Plenty of Fish I was quite nervous about even setting up a profile. All I included were the basics — a screen name, my age, and location. I had no actual description or pictures. Still, within minutes I had men liking my profile and messaging me about how beautiful I was! It was odd. It felt as though they may have been bots sending out automated messages. It is almost like the spam requests we get via email. In these cases, there isn't an actual human being on the other end looking for love and connection. What a disappointment.

Over a decade ago, a coworker I was friends with was blindsided by her husband unexpectedly asking for a divorce. He was cheating on her with someone he met at work. My friend was so devastated and out of sorts that she felt the need to find someone fast. She set up a free profile online. Within a few days, she met an incredibly handsome man, or so she thought, based on his pictures. He told her he was stuck in Florida and couldn't get back to the Northeast because his ex-wife had stolen his bank accounts. My friend ended up sending him hundreds of dollars to get him a plane ticket. She never heard from him again.

She met other men who told her she was the woman of their dreams and that they would take care of her. Yet, they were really just interested in sex. In her fragile emotional state, she trusted these men and got herself into some very dangerous situations, meeting one at a hotel in another state. This points again to the importance of really being emotionally ready to date. If you are still harboring resentment from a past relationship, or are looking to make an ex jealous, you are likely to get harmed.

I know what you must think — why would I want to willingly step onto such a minefield of lies and deception? The answer is simple. You can find love. Couples find each other all the time through online dating. Don't be discouraged by the negativity. Rather, use what you have learned to empower and protect yourself. You are always in control. You never have to respond to or interact with anyone who seems shady or makes you feel uncomfortable.

Chapter 5: Learn the Games

I was incredibly naïve to how frequently people manipulate and play games online. It is hard for my sensitive spirit to understand why anyone would intentionally play with another person's heart. I would never do that, but I had to accept quickly that it happens all the time. I suspect some people forget there is a human on the other end of the digital connection.

In addition, some men have read misguided books or watched videos on how to pick up women. Sadly, much of the dating advice for men focuses on luring and manipulating a potential partner rather than creating loving, long-term relationships.

Furthermore, some men are online just looking for an ego boost or a purely physical relationship. They play games just to feel better about themselves without regard for how they are making others feel. It is frustrating and disheartening to have to navigate such childish behavior. However, once you are aware of the games, you are empowered to avoid them. Be on guard for the following games and manipulative behaviors.

Ghosting

Ghosting is when someone that you have been communicating with suddenly disappears, like a ghost. They stop texting, messaging, or otherwise interacting with you. They may even block your number so that your calls and texts don't get through.

Ghosting is probably the most common game that you will encounter in online dating. In terms of the online dating apps, I would guess that at least 50% of interactions in the app end with one person ghosting the other by just not responding. Sometimes it happens because the conversation wasn't going anywhere, other times it is simply because one person started talking with someone else that they like better. It could even be that the person's subscription ended, and they dropped off the site.

The maddening part of being ghosted is that you have no idea why it happened. There is no closure, which means you are left wondering if they might come back at some point. It is demoralizing to put effort into a connection to have it disappear without warning.

For that reason, you have to learn not to assume and not to take things personally. You must detach from the outcome when you are first chatting with someone, knowing that nothing is real until you have met in person and directly discussed where your relationship is going.

People who ghost are cowards. It is easy to say, "I'm sorry, but I don't think we're a great fit," or "I just met someone else who I feel a strong connection with." I received messages like that many times and appreciated the candor. I also delivered many messages like that and received grateful responses. Apparently, those types of honest messages are rare. Women are especially likely to leave men hanging.

I will always advocate for a woman protecting herself first. However, please be respectful of others. I believe in karma and the Golden Rule. It felt awful to be excitedly talking with someone for several days, only to have him suddenly disappear without an explanation. I never want anyone else to feel that way. I hope you don't either. Everything that goes around comes around, so please try to avoid ghosting others.

Zombieing

When someone who ghosted you reappears, they are zombieing you, or coming back from the dead. They will just suddenly text or message you as if nothing ever happened, often without a logical explanation for their disappearance.

The worst case of ghosting I experienced was with a man that I had been dating for three months. After our first date, we both agreed to see each other exclusively, and the relationship moved quickly. We texted daily and went out every weekend. Still, he hadn't connected with me on social media and didn't introduce me to any friends or family. Furthermore, he lived only ten minutes away and had never invited me over to his house. My friends thought he was married, which was not the case. However, it certainly felt like he was hiding something.

When I expressed my disappointment and confusion about not being included in his life, he was shocked by how I felt. He couldn't understand my perspective and said that other women he dated never had a problem with that. His lack of accountability and understanding was surprising. He seemed to disconnect from the conversation completely, offering little explanation for his behavior. Around ten minutes into the discussion, he just got up from the picnic table on my back porch and quietly left my house.

The lack of closure was incredibly difficult for me. I texted him the next day seeking clarity. He responded with a nice, but generic text wishing me the best. The following day he blocked me, refusing all texts and calls. At that point, he was a ghost.

I had never experienced anything like that. It devastated me. I didn't think we were the best fit as a couple, but the lack of closure hurt as my imagination ran wild. I had every negative thought you could imagine. *I wasn't attractive enough. He was ashamed of me. He was dating other women all along.* The painful consensus from my friends was that he was just using me for sex.

Oddly, with all of those negative thoughts swirling through my head, what made me most upset was the idea that I might have hurt him. As an empath, I couldn't get past the look on his face when he left my house. He looked distraught. In reading his energy, it felt as though I had ripped his heart out. However, nothing he said implied that was true.

The therapist I started seeing thought I was silly for having feelings of guilt. This is one challenge of dating as an empath. We feel the emotions and energy of others. Yet, if we don't have words to confirm those feelings, we end up frustrated and confused.

Around two months later, my ghost reappeared as a zombie. He sent a sweet and simple message. I immediately felt a sense of relief knowing that he didn't hate me. We ended up meeting for a drink, and our relationship slowly rekindled.

He explained why he had been so uneasy about inviting me to his home, and it was plausible. He also justified his ghosting by saying he was so hurt that it felt easier to avoid me. While I felt some relief being able to apologize for my role in any misunderstandings, it was clear over the few weeks that we reconnected that we didn't communicate well. I think we both feared being honest. That ultimately led my zombie to go back to the dead.

The moral of this story is that when someone ghosts you, it is a clear indicator of their character and their inability to communicate directly. Honest, considerate people don't avoid communication. That is hurtful and immature. Furthermore, if a man does it once, he will probably do it again.

Pocketing or Stashing

Being pocketed or stashed means that your relationship is kept secret or on the DL (down low). The person doesn't introduce you to friends or family or acknowledge you on social media.

Although not everyone is active on social media, most people in their 20s-40s do have some presence online. When someone you are dating doesn't acknowledge you in this realm by avoiding your friend requests, or never liking or interacting with any of your posts, that can be a sign that they are afraid of having your relationship be public.

It could be because they are dating other women. However, it isn't always for a sneaky reason. Some people are just very private. It can also be a timing issue. If a man dates a lot, he may be leery about sharing details about a new relationship for fear of it not lasting. People with kids are also more likely to want to keep their dating quiet until they are ready to introduce their new partner to their children.

Regardless of the reason, being pocketed or stashed does not feel good. As I explained to my former ghost/zombie date, I felt like I was his "dirty little secret." I wanted him to want to show me off. The fact that he didn't recognize that hurt my already fragile self-esteem. His very unapologetic response was that no one had ever accused him of that. That is never a good excuse. I suspect that if he had exhibited that kind of secretive behavior in the past, and he didn't get called out on it, those women simply weren't that interested in him.

The antidote to the pocketing/stashing game is to be very clear about your expectations. If you want someone to be all-in with you, you have to let the person know. Honesty is crucial for a healthy relationship. If someone wants to date other women, they should be clear about that. If they aren't sure how they feel about your relationship, they should be clear about that too. You should ask directly if you are unsure about where things are going. This is something I was afraid to do. It was the reason I ended up feeling played. I failed to recognize at the time that the games don't work if you refuse to play.

Breadcrumbing

When someone breadcrumbs you, they subtly string you along through online communications, yet they rarely, if ever, meet you in person. You might get daily or weekly texts or messages that lead you to believe they are interested, yet they never actually ask you out.

The hallmarks of a breadcrumbing relationship are inconsistency and a lack of clarity about the relationship's direction. You can't trust that the person is going to always respond, or you feel unsure about their intentions.

I found this to be a common technique with men who weren't emotionally available. Meaning they weren't ready to have a true, vulnerable, in-person connection. This could be for a variety of reasons. Perhaps they were dealing with a broken heart, or they were feeling insecure about their dating skills. Maybe they were already seeing other women, and they were just keeping a connection with me in case things didn't pan out with that relationship. It could also be because they didn't have the actual time to date. This seemed to be especially common for men with kids. It was as if they wanted to have the illusion of dating someone, even though they didn't really have the availability.

Regardless of the reason, being strung along amounts to a frustrating waste of your time. When you are a sensitive woman, all the energetic connections, even just via texts, can drain your energy.

When I first started online dating, I didn't mind the mindless texts back-and-forth. I was just getting a sense of what I wanted and it was nice to have the attention. In the first three months, there was a rotation of at least six men who messaged me regularly for weeks at a time, yet never asked me out. At first, I felt that their ongoing attention meant they were into me. However, over time, the texting seemed canned with the same cheesy lines. The lack of interest in meeting was also a clear sign they weren't motivated for actual connection.

I had so many men breadcrumb me throughout my time in online dating that I changed my Match.com profile to say, "All the back-and-forth texting is exhausting. If you think we might have a connection, please contact me to grab a coffee or a drink." As you know, just days after making that change, the amazing man who is now my partner contacted me and asked me out to dinner.

I've said it before, and I will keep saying it over and over. Men who are genuinely interested in you will communicate regularly and will want to see you in person as much as possible. Save your time and energy for that kind of dedicated man.

Negging

Negging is making a negative comment in a playful or flirty manner. The person is trying to get a reaction and subtly put you down so they feel in control. It takes you by surprise, leaving you feeling rejected and confused. You think you're starting a friendly conversation with someone, and suddenly they insult you? It disarms you, which is exactly the intent.

I previously mentioned the older man who told me I looked like I was in my 50s when I was much younger. He was negging me so that I would feel bad about myself. Unfortunately, it worked. I responded to him, feeling as though I had to explain myself. It was just a way for him to get me to react. It clearly didn't work out in his favor, but some manipulators don't care if they get a negative or positive reaction, as long as they get some response.

There was a show on VH1 years ago called the "Pickup Artist." In it, a man named "Mystery" taught a group of men how to pick up women. One of his favorite techniques was to walk up to a woman in a bar and neg her by delivering a backhanded compliment like, "I don't usually buy drinks for a woman like you, but I guess I'll make an exception." It was shocking how effective this awful tactic was. Many women would immediately respond, wanting to prove their worth.

Negging is a favorite passive-aggressive form of communication for narcissists and sociopaths. Those types of people have low self-esteem, even though they seem arrogant and overconfident. They put others down so that they can feel superior. Oftentimes, they degrade their target so much that the individual feels grateful for even the slightest bit of kindness.

If you are already struggling with low self-esteem, you are particularly at risk for this demoralizing technique. Your mind is focused on proving your worth rather than realizing what a jerk the person is. It is crucial to detach from any insults you receive. Once you internalize them, it primes you for more abuse.

If this happens to you, try to see it as a compliment. Men use this technique when they feel that their targeted woman is out of their league. It is a weak, last-ditch effort to get your attention when they know they don't deserve it.

Snarky or Sarcastic Communication

Snark and sarcasm are like negging's less hurtful cousin. They are indirect forms of communication that are slightly mocking by nature. In my opinion, they are passive-aggressive and leave you a bit off-kilter wondering what the person meant.

One of the first men I met online texted using sarcasm constantly. In addition, he was too cool to use emojis, so he had to end almost every sentence with "LOL" so I knew he was kidding. I constantly felt like he was insulting me, but then I would see the "LOL" and I'd give him a pass. Communicating with him was much too confusing. I put up with it for far too long because I thought he was charming. He also seemed to be breadcrumbing me, texting even though he had no interest in a relationship.

Sarcasm and snark have become very common forms of communication in society. They can be funny if delivered well. However, when you're first meeting someone and trying to establish a connection via text or message, clear communication is best.

In addition, if you are a sensitive woman, sarcasm comes across as threatening and mean. Personally, I don't want to be around anyone who is mean to me or others. Those who are genuinely funny don't need to resort to sarcastic comments or put-downs to get a laugh.

Bragging / Provoking Self-Doubt

We all tend to brag a bit. I know I fell into that mode on first dates because I wanted to prove my value right away. In some regards, that is a basic rule of the online dating game. If you want to gain someone's interest, you need to share all the most flattering information about yourself.

The true bragging that falls into the manipulative, "game-playing" territory goes a step too far. One example is when a man talks nonstop about all the women that are interested in him, leaving you feeling like a number. Another instance is when a man keeps bringing up his ex, making you feel like she is still an important part of his life.

Men who talk about their exes, or how popular they are with other women, are trying to increase their value in your eyes. By evoking a feeling of competition, they encourage you to work at winning them over. Sometimes they will offer a sense of success by telling you how much better you are than those other women.

Men who use this tactic are also prone to flirting in front of you (i.e., with the server) or looking at other women when you are out with them. They are constantly trying to evoke your jealousy. This can be a powerful means of gaining your attraction if you don't recognize what is happening.

One man I was attracted to bragged incessantly about how hot his prior girlfriends had been. He went into detail about the gorgeous young woman who had everyone in the bar staring at her. At first, I found the stories amusing. After a while, I thought he was telling me I was not hot enough for him. I felt dejected and not good enough.

I was sharing my feelings about the situation with a friend when she explained that I was likely misinterpreting the intentions of the bragging. Her husband had done the same thing to her when they first met. She called him out on it immediately. Since she was brave enough to confront him, he admitted he had only shared about his former attractive dates because he wanted to impress her. He thought doing so made him seem more valuable.

Regardless of the intention, when a man brags by bringing up other women, it is confusing and potentially deflating. It typically backfires when used on a sensitive woman because it is so insincere.

Again, detaching from the stories that someone tells you is important. You are trying to establish a connection that requires actions more than words. They may brag just to feel better about themselves, or they could be trying to manipulate you. You don't know which it is until you've gotten to know the person better and observed their patterns over time.

Love Bombing

Love bombing is essentially the opposite of negging (provoking self-doubt). The person bombs you with a constant supply of compliments and praise. They tell you everything you want to hear. *You're the best thing that ever happened to them. You're beautiful and intelligent, so much better than all the other women they've met.* The flood of feel-good chemicals you experience from a love bomber, who is often a narcissist, is intoxicating. If you have been negged by other potential dates or have been in a toxic relationship, you are especially vulnerable to this form of false flattery.

The question to ask yourself is, "Does this feel too good to be true?" If the person just met you online and you have only communicated via phone or text, there's no way he could know how amazing you are.

My ex-husband had love bombed me before our marriage. He gave me wonderful, thoughtful gifts for our first Christmas together and told me within a few months of dating that he wanted to marry me. It was overwhelming, yet felt wonderful since I hadn't dated much and never experienced what I thought was genuine romance. However, there was always a piece of me that felt like something was off. It didn't become apparent until after we were married, and he stopped all efforts at pleasing or complimenting me. The rest of our marriage was heartbreaking. Love bombers build you up and then set you up for a terrible emotional fall.

It had been so long since I experienced love bombing that I didn't initially recognize the pattern when it showed up in online dating. The first man I started a serious relationship with love bombed me steadily for three months. He started immediately, telling me after our first phone call he was going to want to kiss me as soon as he met me. That intention shocked me. I even asked him how he knew he would feel that way in advance. He gushed about how beautiful I was, and how he could just tell.

On that first meeting, he was totally over the top with his enthusiasm for our potential. I liked him, but I felt overwhelmed. That was a powerful sign that something was off. I disregarded my gut instincts and honestly enjoyed the love bombing. It felt so wonderful to have someone showering me with praise after not having that throughout my 13-year marriage.

The blissful feeling lasted until I said, "I love you." It was the eeriest feeling. At that very moment, I felt his energy shift. A strange sneer came over his face. In retrospect, I later realized that as is the case with narcissists, he had "dropped the mask." He felt that he "had" me. Afterward, he changed, withdrawing his attention and behaving in thoughtless and arrogant ways.

Most love bombers can't keep up the facade for very long. It is best not to give them the time or space to do so. You must find your own source of validation so that you don't need compliments or praise from anyone else. When someone love bombs you, simply say, "Thank you." Don't give them much of a reaction beyond that, because the reaction is ultimately what they are looking for.

Cushioning / Benching

In both cushioning and benching, you're essentially the person's backup plan. With cushioning, the person is being flirtatious and giving you the idea that they are interested. All the while, they are already in a relationship with someone else. They are essentially having an emotional affair with you. They aren't telling you about their partner and vice versa. It is an ego boost and power play for the man to keep a connection with you. They see you as someone to turn to if their active relationship doesn't work out.

Benching is a little more drastic and is similar to ghosting. It is when someone is being wishy-washy about a relationship. They are with you, and then they aren't. It is like in sports when you are taken out of the game. They bench you, yet leave you waiting to be called back into play. There is no actual closure in this type of relationship because the person doesn't tell you why they are disappearing and reappearing.

A healthy person will keep you in the loop, a game-player will just keep you in the dark so that you are always wondering how they feel about you. It can be mentally exhausting for a sensitive woman to get attached to anyone who isn't being direct. It leaves you trying to piece together all the feelings and emotions, which never quite make sense because you don't have actual answers.

I understand if you are feeling like you just got hit by a bus. The games and manipulative tactics used by some men are dizzying. Luckily, not everyone behaves that way! Remember, this is the "tough love" portion of the book. I am trying to give you the worst-case scenarios so that you can spot the questionable behavior quickly and not take it personally. I was clueless about these games when I was online and I still ended up finding true love. Please don't give up hope. There are genuine people out there. You just need to weed through those who aren't so authentic.

Chapter 6: Watch for Red Flags

Besides the games people play, other more subtle signs can show you that someone is not right for you. You need to be aware of these red flags as well.

As you already know, you must be far more alert online than you would be in real life. Again, there is less ability to read a person's energy, body language, or tone of voice, which makes it very difficult for a sensitive or empathic person to gauge someone using intuition. People are shameless and confident when they are hiding behind a computer or phone. This is clear on social media platforms or in online forums where people say horrible things to those they have never even met.

We're often told not to judge others. Yet, in online dating, you must be in full judgment mode. Scrutinize every interaction, trusting your gut as much as possible. It takes practice at first, but over time, you pick up the signs that show a man is not being 100% genuine.

Following are a few of the more prominent red flags to watch for.

Having an Incomplete Profile

At the bare minimum, any man you interact with online should have a complete profile that includes more than one photo and a basic description of himself. Anyone who has not put in the time and effort to create a meaningful profile is highly unlikely to dedicate time to a relationship. It is not worth your time to respond to a man who fits this description. More than likely, the profile is fake or potentially belongs to a scammer.

Asking for Photos

Sometimes men will ask for photos that are more provocative or sexy than what you have on your profile. This sends a clear message that they are more interested in your physicality than they are in you as a person. Even worse, asking (or demanding) could be a sign that they have ill intentions. It can be a way of testing you to see if you will do what they want. If you conform to their requests, they may perceive you as agreeable and easy to manipulate. This is of course not always why someone asks for photos, but the request, especially early on, should put you on alert.

Please don't ever send someone naked photos, no matter how much you think you like the person. There are many horror stories of women victimized by men who later attempt to blackmail them or vindictively post the photos online when the relationship ends. I would suggest that even women who are in committed relationships never share intimate photos. You just never know where they will end up. A quality, loving man would never ask you to do something that could compromise your reputation or make you feel uncomfortable.

Moving too Quickly

I didn't love the impersonal nature of using the dating app for communications. However, messaging within the app is a safer way to interact at first. If someone is pushing you to give your phone number too soon, trust your instincts and don't be afraid to push back. You can also set up an email or texting account that is only for dating. That enables you to maintain your privacy as much as possible.

Be wary of instant attraction. Romance movies perpetuate the idea of "love at first sight." However, that is rarely an accurate gauge of a strong partnership. True connection takes time.

While it is flattering for someone to seem head-over-heels upon meeting you, speed is a technique that many narcissists use to love bomb you into falling for them. It is important to be on guard if it feels like someone is trying to fast-forward a relationship.

You can't know someone is right for you until you've learned all their ins and outs. Those who rush the process are often trying to prevent you from seeing their true nature. This happened to me several times. Those men told me they were going to take their profiles down because after meeting me they had no interest in dating anyone else. It was flattering, but also confusing because I wasn't sure how I felt about them. In those cases, I ended up committing to relationships that I wasn't sure were the best fit. It turned out that they were not a good fit at all.

Sometimes people are smitten quickly. That happened with my current partnership. Given my history, despite feeling a strong connection right away, I kept my guard up for months until I was sure he was who he seemed to be. That proved to be a much healthier choice for me, since our connection grew deeper, as there was an effort on both of our parts to dedicate the time to our success.

Overtly Sexual and Physically Motivated Right Away

I'll admit that I was a bit of a prude when I first went online. My ex-husband was the only man I had ever been with, and our relationship completely lacked passion and intimacy. He never complimented me and he had very little sex drive, so it was awkward for me to have men messaging me to say I was sexy and that they wanted to "cuddle" me.

"Cuddle" seems to be a code word for sex. I realize that cuddling does not have to be sexual. However, if I have never even met a man and he tells me he wants to "cuddle" or "snuggle" me, something is not quite right. That happened several times with younger men and I cut off contact with them immediately. My rule of thumb became, if you can't say something to me in person, then you should not be saying it to me online.

If you are interested in a purely physical relationship, that is totally your choice. Just be sure that you are very clear about those intentions with yourself and any future partners.

It is very difficult to disentangle emotions from sexual contact for both men and women. As a sensitive woman, you are likely to get your energy attached to anyone you encounter. Being mindful of that dynamic will help you ground and protect yourself from any men you meet.

Anger or a Sense of Entitlement When you Say "No"

This is a biggie! Anger is always a red flag in any type of relationship. It is especially alarming if it happens quickly.

I met a man about a week after starting a new job with a long commute. I also had a new iPhone, which I wasn't even sure how to use yet. I was feeling overwhelmed. However, at that point, I had been online dating for a couple of weeks, yet the only connections I had were with men who just texted and never suggested we meet. It excited me that this man was more assertive and direct, asking if we could get to know each other with a phone call.

As an introvert, I'm not a fan of phone calls. But, the call proved to be more personal than brief texts, and I was happy to have the interaction. We had many laughs and seemed to connect well. I didn't want to be negative, so I hadn't been completely honest about the current stressors of my daily life.

The next day that man started texting me several times a day. I kept my phone on silent, not wanting to give my new co-workers the impression that I was distracted at work. After just a few days of his constant texting, I was feeling drained. After work that day, I sent him a text asking him to slow things down. He sent back an angry text saying, "Why are you online dating then?!"

I was stunned and embarrassed. I had not meant to be disingenuous with him, but I got the job unexpectedly just two weeks after I signed up online. My simple request to slow things down was a minor boundary I was attempting to set. His anger pushing back against it gave me a very clear signal that he already felt entitled to my time.

At that point, my boundary setting was dismal. I immediately felt bad, apologized, and ended up bending my comfort level, allowing him to text whenever he felt like it. That man turned out to be a narcissist who pushed back at my boundaries constantly.

Many relationship experts suggest testing a potential partner with various boundaries — letting them know you aren't available for calls at certain times, rescheduling a date, or asking them if you can try a different restaurant than they chose. If the person reacts in anger to any of those simple requests, it is a sign they can't honor your needs and may be an unhealthy partner for you. Think of how you would respond to such simple requests. You might be disappointed or sad, but it is unlikely you would get angry.

Use your empathic gifts to assess situations based on how you would morally handle them. If your date doesn't respond similarly, then you probably won't be emotionally compatible.

Lack of Steady Engagement

I've already said this several times. One of the most powerful lessons I learned in all my dating experience and research is that a man who wants to be with you will be with you. They will give you their time and attention as much as possible. They will not make excuses or skip dates. They will not disregard your texts or phone calls.

Pay attention to how they respond to you. Do they light up when you enter the room? Do they seem genuinely interested in you? Are they asking you thoughtful questions? Are they willing to adjust their schedule for you? Are they giving you positive feedback? If any of these conditions don't apply, he's just not that into you.

Any man trying to downplay his interests in you, being coy, or "playing hard to get" is not worth your time. If you are drawn to someone and they aren't responding as you had hoped, don't be afraid to confront him on his intentions. Some men hold firm to archaic dating beliefs around not texting or calling too soon and not being too eager. If that's the case, you want to get that cleared up quickly through honest and open communication.

Some men just aren't interested in a relationship. They are bored and just using online dating to pass the time. It is painful to develop feelings for someone who is not emotionally available or ready for a committed relationship. Spare yourself the pain by being very honest with yourself about their behavior.

Blaming Others for Their Life Circumstances

I must admit, I was guilty of this red flag. I spent far too much time on dates talking about what a jerk my ex-husband had been. I had not fully processed all the manipulation and emotional abuse I had been through. I felt vulnerable and thought it best that anyone I dated knew exactly what I was dealing with on an emotional level.

While this is a transparent way to approach a new relationship, it also brings in a lot of negativity. I am self-aware. I typically caught myself in the act, or shortly thereafter, and apologized for having been a Debbie Downer. My dates never seemed to mind, since they all had similar tales of relationship woes.

Once you are over 30, your chances of experiencing heartbreak and emotional manipulation are pretty darn likely. The key is to pay attention to the level of blame the person places on others. In my case, I am painfully aware that I have played a hand in the challenges of my life. I am open about having been through therapy, while also dedicating countless hours studying self-help topics.

In contrast, I dated several men who had been through multiple divorces and still couldn't recognize their role in the demise of those relationships. One man shared stories of the terrible, heartless woman he had dated just before me. Supposedly, she had intended to cheat on him, causing him to move out of her home abruptly. Later, when I realized he was dating someone without telling me, I wondered if he had ever been honest.

It is very common for narcissists to spin their exes as mentally unstable when they are actually responsible for making their former partner seem "crazy." Remember that there are two sides to every story and you are only privy to the side they want you to know. If that side feels imbalanced and biased, it probably is.

Disrespectful Comments

Deciding what is disrespectful is a very personal matter. As a feminist, I don't appreciate overtly sexual comments, especially if they are degrading. I particularly hate the use of the words "bitch" or "cunt." Women typically view those terms as derogatory. A conscientious man would be careful not to use them without fully gauging your acceptance.

I was shocked and hurt when a man I had been seeing for around six weeks called me a "little bitch." We were fooling around, and he said it somewhat playfully, but it hurt me deeply. He was the father of two daughters, which made his insensitivity even more confusing.

The next morning he texted me a playful, teasing comment. I quickly responded with a very passive-aggressive response about how insensitive he was proving to be. He was confused and somewhat apologetic. In retrospect, I wish I had just talked to him about it rather than react like that. It was not my finest moment for sure.

Later in the day, I expressed to him what had really hurt me. He apologized, but then said something like, "Anyone who knows me would know I was just kidding." It didn't feel like a genuine apology. It was more of a dismissal. He implied that I just misunderstood him, rather than acknowledging my feelings. It is not too much of a surprise that he continued to behave in insensitive ways for the rest of our relationship. I kept giving him a pass because he seemed like such a nice man. For this sensitive woman, he was clearly not nice enough.

Another man I dated kept calling me sexual nicknames. He had a silly sense of humor, as do I. At first, I just laughed it off. However, after the third or fourth time, I became uncomfortable with it.

In a phone call, I expressed to him that I found that kind of language to be degrading and disrespectful. He laughed in response. It felt like being punched in the gut. I explained how I had been sexually harassed a great deal in my life, and that was the last thing I wanted from my romantic partner. He seemed to understand what I was saying and apologized at that moment.

However, he continued to speak to me in a degrading, sexual manner throughout our relationship and for almost a year later, as he continued to text me after we broke up. This man proved to be a classic narcissist. His dismissive response to my concerns around respect was one of many red flags that I disregarded. I wish I had honored that terrible feeling in my gut when I tried to explain my desire for respect, and he dismissed me with laughter.

Respect is a very basic need and an essential component of a healthy relationship. Asking someone to treat you respectfully is never asking for too much, even if they try to convince you otherwise. We teach people how to treat us. If you attempt to teach someone how to make you feel supported and safe, and they dismiss or disregard your requests, RUN!

A False Sense of Intimacy

Intimacy is a tricky topic. I have heard it described as "into me you see." It is a feeling of a deep connection with another person. You see each other fully and with acceptance. It is difficult to know what it feels like if you have never communicated candidly with a romantic partner. However, one thing is for sure, it takes time and consistent reciprocity to develop fully.

Before online dating, I only experienced deep, intimate relationships with friends. Although I craved intimacy from my husband, I barely even got a glimmer. He rarely talked about anything deep or truly relayed his feelings. As mentioned, I came to believe that men were incapable of communicating in that way.

Imagine my surprise when the first man I met in person revealed deeply personal information an hour into our lunch date. He claimed that he normally only gave dates an hour time limit, yet he talked at length about his life challenges for over four hours. I felt so special. Then he continued texting me late into the night, expressing that we had a lot in common. I thought I had finally developed a deep connection with a man.

Sadly, in that instance, it wasn't real. Over time, he stopped initiating texts and never asked me out again. The experience left me feeling confused and empty.

To this day, I don't understand that interaction. However, based on things he said, and that he was constantly showing up on the app where we had met, I had to accept that he was very skilled at the dating game. He probably shared those deep secrets to gain my interest and trust. I allowed him to talk freely and that may have been all he wanted.

True intimacy is rare in our current culture. Again, it takes time to develop. If you find yourself drawn in by someone sharing deeply personal information quickly, try to keep it all in perspective. They may just need a friend or a listening ear. They could also have more sinister motives. They may realize that your open heart makes you easy to manipulate.

As sensitive women, we often want to help and fix others. Toxic, manipulative people can sense that intent. Be mindful of whether there is true reciprocity of the emotions and feelings or if you are feeling like their therapist. Even if someone is a kind person, you are not responsible for their emotional health. You do not need to be their therapist or sounding board. That only turns out to be exhausting and unfulfilling.

Emotional Manipulation

I encountered and unfortunately dated quite a few narcissistic men. In most cases, I didn't spot their red flags right away. One man, however, showed himself quickly in the first few weeks of our meeting because my emotions felt like a roller coaster.

To begin with, he kept saying that he wanted to, "finally find a good girl." He talked about how women in his life had hurt him badly. I felt deep pity for him. Even though I wasn't sure I was even attracted to him at first, I found myself driven to show him that good women exist.

He also fixated on unconditional love, challenging me to love him in that way. It made me so uneasy that one night after he pressed me on my willingness to love him unconditionally, I burst into tears. The concept of unconditional love sounds beautiful. However, it can be very harmful when someone requests or demands it. Unconditional love, similar to intimacy, is something that grows with time and trust. When someone wants it quickly, they are really asking for love without regard to their words or actions. It is classic manipulation.

The final straw was that he began telling me how I felt. Since our first date, he had been love bombing me with statements like, "This is such a great relationship. We must be soulmates. You are the most amazing woman I've ever met."

After just a few weeks, we were out for a hike and he kept repeating, "We're having such a great time. You have so much fun with me." Not, "I'm having a great time with you." The shift in the wording was subtle, but it sent chills through my body.

I wasn't having fun at all. He had spent the day mansplaining how to hike the trail I had been on countless times. His deliberate attempts at manipulating my thoughts and feelings were maddening. For the first time in my dating experience, I saw clearly that something was wrong. I knew I needed to end things quickly and amicably, and did so a few days later.

I had hoped to be friends, which is how I felt about all my relationships. I hate conflict and the thought of other people having negative feelings towards me. He laughed at my request to remain friends, saying that was not possible for him. I was a little surprised by that response. I expected he would at least pretend to be my friend. After all, he had been telling me he loved me. Regardless, I was grateful that the break seemed so cordial because narcissists rarely handle breakups well.

But, of course, he didn't just go away nicely. About a week or two later, he texted me, suggesting we have a purely sexual relationship. It disgusted me that someone who would not consider being my friend would have the nerve to think we could have a physical relationship.

When I expressed my feelings of disappointment, he lashed out and said he was going to block me. I appreciated the closure. It confirmed all my suspicions about him and kept me from ever trying to have any connection with him again.

Emotional manipulation can come in many forms. Sensitive women have to be especially on guard for this challenging tactic. Other means of this type of coercion include telling you sob stories about their life, their woes of caring for a sick family member, a difficult work situation, or an illness. Of course, people have challenging things happen to them all the time. The difference is, if someone has signed up for online dating there is an assumption that they are emotionally available for a relationship. Someone who is experiencing a genuine life crisis should not be online trying to date.

If you meet a potential date and they dump a bunch of life drama on you, they are not truly looking to be a partner to you. What they really want is to evoke your pity so you will give them your attention and support, expecting nothing in return. I have met men who had no trouble crying. Such an emotional display made me believe they had deep empathy and possibly even a deep love for me. In reality, they were just excellent actors.

Emotions to watch for include confusion, fear, worry, shame, and self-doubt. If any of these feelings show up for you, give them careful attention. Even if you have been told you are overreacting, please do not disregard negative emotions. They are your body's greatest warning system.

Projection

Projection can come across as a type of emotional manipulation. However, it is often done subconsciously so the person may not even realize what they are doing. In projection, someone assigns characteristics or actions they don't like about themselves to someone else. A classic example is a man accusing you of cheating or of talking to other men when they are doing the cheating.

One man I had been messaging on Match.com seemed to be sending messages to several women at once. Sometimes his responses were odd and didn't quite fit what we had been discussing, implying they may have been meant for someone else. In addition, he never actually asked me out. He just kept sending photos of himself and his kids. It was strange. It felt like he may have been stashing me, waiting to ask me out if his connection with another woman fell through.

He hadn't messaged me for quite some time when I received a text accusing me of being online when my subscription had ended weeks before. It turned out to be an odd glitch with Match.com. However, I found it incredibly strange that he would accuse me of doing something shady when we were not even in a relationship.

I recalled he had complained to me that women were only after money. He said that the last woman he dated stopped seeing him when she realized he lived in an apartment over a garage. I found it interesting that he automatically assumed that was the reason when by my account there were many other reasons a woman might not want to continue dating him. Perhaps, like me, she realized he was distracted and likely texting other women. The bottom line, in this case, is that an insecure man will project blame and criticism on you for his perceived weaknesses, even if you haven't done anything to warrant the attack.

Projection is a perplexing topic because it defies logic. It leaves you feeling confused, and as if you have done something wrong when you have not. As we will discuss further in Chapter 8, narcissists often use projection to disarm and manipulate their targets. Being aware of how projection works helps you shield yourself if someone ever tries to pull it on you. Getting clear on who you are, what you observe, and how you feel prevents you from allowing someone to project their insecurities or inappropriate behavior onto you. Never let anyone accuse you of something you haven't done or talk you out of your truth.

∞∞∞

There are a lot more red flags that could signal someone is not your ideal match. This is where discernment becomes crucial. Again, you must learn to trust your instincts. If something feels off at all, it probably is. Of course, there are green flags too! We'll go over the skills that can sharpen your discernment and discuss the traits of a healthy, balanced relationship in Phase 3.

Please don't get so caught up in trying to spot red flags that you forget to have fun. Meeting new people is fun! It shouldn't feel like work or as if you have to be on edge waiting for people to do something that feels off. When we fixate on a negative energetic state like that, we can attract the very energy we are trying to avoid. Be cautious, but optimistic.

Chapter 7: Get to Know the Players

Now that you know the games and the red flags, let's cover the men you might encounter on the playing field that is online dating. You've already gotten a taste of these types as I've explained aspects of the different personalities already. Here we're going to do a deeper dive.

This list is admittedly very judgmental. Of course, every person is unique, but humans do possess the same psychological patterns and traits. It is amazing how often the same behaviors emerge.

It is as if some men are following a script. With all the dating videos and books available, they may be doing just that, following some awful dating advice designed to manipulate you.

It is wise to recognize some of the worst (and best) of what you might encounter so that you can handle them effectively. Most men fall into multiple categories from the following.

The Classic Player

You've heard of the "Player." He is the man who approaches getting women as a game. This term started before online dating was even a thing. It is synonymous with a "Ladies' Man" or a "Casanova."

Given how the online world has made dating even more of a game, the "Player" is probably the most common type of man you will encounter. Most men online are players to some degree. They can present themselves any way they want, so naturally, most will pretend to be cool and charming.

The classic "Player" type appears sarcastic, cocky, and even aloof. They act as though they are too cool for online dating. Yet, they seem to have far too much experience. Most of the players that I met had been in online dating for a year or even longer. They didn't seem to want a solid relationship, but rather were looking for hook-ups and flirtations. They knew all the games of online dating and were happy to play them.

The lines they sent were generic and unoriginal. Chances are good that they were the same message they had been sending to countless other women. Lines like, "You're beautiful," or "I like your profile," could apply to anyone online. When there is no personalization, it strongly implies that the man is just fishing for attention through the quickest, easiest route.

Often, after chatting back-and-forth with someone who seemed to be a "Player," it would become obvious they hadn't even read my profile. This was an immediate red flag and a total turn-off for me. If someone had not even bothered to do the bare minimum to get to know me, there was no chance that he was truly interested in me as a person.

I met men who were pretending to be players when they were quite nerdy. It was so odd. They sent cool and coy texts, but when I met them, they were noticeably awkward and shy.

One man had texted me these amazing, deep messages for over a week. Yet, once we met for coffee, he was quiet and could barely make eye contact. I felt bad for how uncomfortable he seemed. When we parted, I gave him a quick hug. Minutes later as I was driving away, he sent a text that said, "Your hug sent me to the moon and back." I found that incredibly disingenuous. An honest, confident man won't hide behind a digital device. He will say things to your face.

I gave that man some time though, respecting that he might be shy. I continued texting with him and we ended up meeting for a hike. We had a good time. Again, as soon as I drove away, he texted about how amazing he thought I was. The next day he sent me a text meant for another woman. I was offended. The guy had no game, yet he was still trying to play several women at once. That was not for me.

Most men do message with multiple women at the same time. That is very common and considered acceptable. However, I tried to focus most of my attention on one person at a time, especially if we had met in person. Once we had met, I would ask if the man was seeing other women. It is an important topic to broach right away. Even if a man seems completely into you, he, especially if he is a "Player" type, will probably keep a connection with other women just in case things don't work out (i.e., stashing/cushioning).

The Professional Dater

Similar to the "Classic Player" the "Professional Dater" is on every app and seems to be online all the time. The apps often have an indicator telling you who is online. Some men show up constantly. Those types were always a bit of a red flag for me.

To be fair, the apps sometimes lie and people may not actually be online when the app says. We will discuss this further in Chapter 13. However, having a presence on all the apps and being active all the time implies someone who isn't serious about finding a long-term relationship.

As I mentioned, there is a somewhat addictive nature to online dating. It feels good getting attention from new people. Men who are just looking for an ego boost or a physical connection are more likely to be on the apps for a long time, never actually committing to a relationship.

Of course, some people don't meet their ideal match quickly, so they end up in the online dating world longer than they would like. They may just be unlucky in love. Those men are far more genuine than the "Professional Dater." They won't leave you wondering about their intentions.

The "Professional Dater" is likely to speak of the many terrible women they have been on dates with. They will share stories of how most women don't look like their pictures, and all the times they ended dates early for that reason. They will have more horror stories than seem possible for one person. Given that they are the only commonality in all of those dates, they are clearly part of the problem. More than likely, they are expecting more from their dates than they will give of themselves.

The "Professional Dater" can offer helpful advice on how to navigate online dating because they have learned all the tips and tricks. I enjoyed interacting with these men via text or messages. I could pick their brains and ask them for advice, knowing that they were not likely to ask me out. No harm, no foul. Be aware of this type though. If you assume you could be the one to change their ways and make them retire from their pro dating status, you are bound to be disappointed.

The Misogynist

Misogyny is rampant online. Misogynistic men see women as less than themselves and seem to feel entitled to a woman's attention. These types catcall you via messages. I received things like, "Hey baby, you're sexy," or "I can show you a good time." Some men even told me how good they are in bed. It is like being in a bar, but worse, the men verbally assault you in your own home.

Sometimes their misogynistic tendencies are apparent in their profile. They might have sexual content or shirtless pictures. One man on Plenty of Fish, who claimed to be a law student, had written out a word puzzle that spelled out "F*ck Me." I saw the pattern right away and messaged him with a puzzle of my own that spelled, "F*ck Off." He was thrilled by my response saying, "Wow, you're awesome." He elaborated on how stupid most women had been, contacting him to ask what the puzzle meant. I informed him it was too bad that he thought taunting women online was funny because I am in fact "awesome." He actually responded with an apology. I rarely engaged with misogynists, but in that case, I felt he needed to be put in his place.

If their profile doesn't reveal their misogyny, they typically let it slip once you communicate. A noticeably out-of-shape man in his 50s contacted me on OkCupid saying that I had a great body. He added that I should explain to other women what it means to be in shape. He was referring to the fact that women (and men) classify their body type in the app. I often heard from men that most women did not answer that question accurately. *Guess what?* Neither do most men! That man disgusted me with his blatant hypocrisy. In his case, I realized there was no tactful way to respond, so I just ignored his messages.

This is common though. Men who are out-of-shape and un-kempt have no problem approaching women who are far more conscientious about their appearance. It is a frustrating double standard of the online dating world.

As an offshoot of misogyny, quite a few men I met mans-plained, the maddening art of talking down to women. I have discussed this phenomenon with other women in online for-ums. The pattern seems to be on the rise. Not all men who mansplain are true misogynists that have a disdain for and dis-respect of women. Some of these men are just insecure and try-ing desperately to sound intelligent.

Regardless, this type of man is rarely a healthy partner. He will probably treat you as an object or act as though his opin-ions are more important than yours are. Sometimes, men like this will change once they are aware of how condescending and hurtful their words come across. However, I don't suggest you waste your sensitive, kind heart on someone like that. A quality man will treat you with respect, as an equal, right from the start.

On another note, it is a good idea when connecting with a man to get a sense of how he treats his mother, sisters, or any other female friends. Even though I am deeply sensitive, I have a morbid fascination with how serial killers think. Through re-search and documentaries, I have learned that one of their core traits is a disordered, negative relationship with their mother. They essentially grow up despising and distrusting women. Be on the lookout for any signs that a man dislikes the women in his life, as it will indicate how he might ultimately treat you.

The Victim / Energy Vampire

As a sensitive woman, you are likely already attracting victim types and energy vampires into your life. These people vent and complain, dumping all their problems on you.

Your positive, compassionate energy attracts their dark neediness. It is amazing that even online, with very few cues to work from, these types of men will find you.

I couldn't believe the sob stories that I heard from men, often in the very first few messages with them. One younger, attractive man told me he was a "cuckold." I had never even heard that term. Apparently, his wife had started a sexual affair with another man and relinquished him to the basement while she lived with her new lover in the main house. It sounded so unbelievable. I certainly felt bad for his hurt. However, I didn't want to get involved in a situation like that. I told him I was sorry he was going through such a rough period, and then I ran.

Honestly, what is someone like that doing in online dating other than trying to find a woman to take pity on him? It scared me to think that some kindhearted woman might want to save him.

There are very few scenarios where it ever makes sense for a man to be online dating if he is already in a relationship (no matter how dysfunctional it is), or if he doesn't have a home, car, or job. I mean, *really*? How can they date someone if they don't even have the means to support themselves?

I'm not trying to be cruel, but this is reality. Men have almost 20% more earning power than women. Men who show up online acting as though life has been unfair to them have no business complaining to a woman. We all have our challenges in life!

You are looking for a partner, not a project. Men who come across as victims are often just trying to prey on kind, sensitive women. Please be very aware of this type and remember that you are not responsible for helping or healing anyone you meet. You are online to find a partner who can enhance your life, not drain your energy, time, or financial resources.

On this note, many dating experts say that if a man asks a woman on a date, he should pay for that date. If there are reasons he does not want to do so, he should be honest about that so you can decide if you are comfortable with that arrangement.

I believe in equality and fairness. I never expected anyone to treat me to a meal. I generally offered and often ending up paying. However, depending on how the date was initiated and the man's financial status, there were times when I let the man pay.

My partner is old school and believes that the man should pay for dates. He told me that in all the years he dated, I was the first woman who tried to pay for my meals. Do what feels best for you. Whatever you choose, never let anyone guilt you into having sexual contact because they paid for dinner. That is an archaic and ridiculous expectation.

The Emotionally Unavailable or Scared Man

I have to admit, I don't think I was emotionally available when I first started online dating. I wanted the fun and companionship of dating. However, after such a long, draining marriage, I wasn't sure I could open myself up fully to another person. It is not surprising that I attracted men who were similarly afraid of genuine connection.

Being emotionally available means that you are fully ready to establish an intimate, committed relationship with another person. You welcome them fully into your life, getting to know all about them. Likewise, you openly share your time and emotions with them.

Someone who is emotionally unavailable, or scared of connection, is prone to get into an endless texting scenario. It is as if they enjoy the illusion of connection implied through digital interactions, yet they are not ready to commit to an in-person relationship.

What I found with this type of man is that they would text me daily, even sending pictures of themselves and their kids, but that was it. They never progressed to asking me out on a date. It felt weird. I suppose it relieved me on some level though since I could just tell we had nothing more than a surface connection.

If a man keeps texting you, yet never asks you out within the first two weeks, he is not likely to be your ideal match. The man I mentioned several times before (who ghosted and zombied me), texted me almost daily for a month before finally asking me out. I was just about to give up hope on him when he asked me to meet up for a drink that night. I jumped at the chance to meet him. In hindsight, I wish I hadn't. In the end, he caused me a lot more heartache than he was worth because he was not emotionally available.

The Bored Man

There are far too many bored people hanging out in online dating. It is just too easy. Anyone who has a little free time can set up a profile and be online in minutes. This is a major reason why the free online sites and apps are bad news. There is no investment on anyone's part. As such, the free sites attract bored and unavailable men (and women) in droves.

The "Bored Man" is very similar to the "Emotionally Unavailable Man." This is someone who is not truly available or fully invested in starting a relationship. These could be men who are already in a relationship, either a marriage or a dating scenario, where they aren't totally happy. Perhaps they just want to test the waters of dating without going all in. They send lots of messages and texts with very little substance and never ask you out.

These men are seemingly harmless, but they can waste your time! After encountering a slew of bored men while trying Plenty of Fish and OkCupid, I got frustrated and took a break from dating altogether for several months. After that reset, I vowed not to give my energy to anyone who wasn't serious and willing to meet within a week. You might want to approach your dating experience with this mentality right away so you don't get burned out by the mindless back-and-forth messages.

The Busy Family Man

I met several men who seemed like great matches. Each of these men had a solid career, owned a home, and had loving families they adored. Every time I met this type of man, I was incredibly excited about their potential. I thought my sensitive heart had won the lottery. Finally, I would enjoy the love and attention of a dedicated, sweet man. There was just one big problem — none of these men had time for me.

One man was working 60+ hours per week in a construction job so that he could pay off his daughter's college tuition. I found his dedication to her to be incredibly endearing. However, after having him fall asleep during a phone call one night, then having him blow off our second date because he got home late, I quickly accepted that he had nothing left to give to a relationship.

Another man bristled at the idea of sharing a plate of chicken wings because his budget was so tight. He told me that with alimony and child support, it was hard to go out to dinner regularly. As I previously mentioned, I didn't mind the idea of sharing the costs of dates. However, as someone who lives on a tight budget myself, I realized that a man with that kind of financial strain would not be a healthy partner for me. Again, a man really shouldn't be online dating if he can't afford to date. The same is true for a woman. Healthy relationships require reciprocity in all aspects — financially, emotionally, and in terms of time.

It is certainly possible to have a family and a busy job while still balancing a new relationship. However, it requires a committed effort and some very open communication about availability. If you are juggling family and other commitments, you might be the ideal match for this type of man. You will certainly be able to empathize with one another and your needs are likely similar.

Since I had been in a marriage where I never really felt as though I was a priority, I needed a man who put me first. While my heart often craved the "Busy Family Man," my head knew that he could never be my long-term match.

The Spiritual Man

Many sensitive, empathic women have a strong spiritual connection. That is certainly the case for me. I didn't flaunt my spirituality in my profile. However, I was clear to share that I believed in God and faith. On several occasions, this drew in men who claimed to be spiritual as well.

While they probably were spiritual to some extent, they also had narcissistic traits and appeared to use their focus on spirituality to look more appealing. One man seemed to compete with me. Every time I shared something I had done in terms of spiritual work, he tried to one-up me. It felt incredibly uncomfortable. Our spiritual experiences and connections are unique and individual. They are not something to use as competition.

Another man, who I ended up dating, drew me in with his belief in the Law of Attraction. I thought he agreed that putting out positive energy and doing the right things were a means of being a better person, but his focus was simply on manifesting more money and a better car.

There are healthy spiritual men. I just caution you to be on alert around men who use spirituality as a persona online. Spiritual women are compassionate, forgiving, and openhearted. These are all traits that a manipulative person would love to abuse by claiming to be spiritual.

If your spirituality is important to you, please feel comfortable sharing that with a potential partner. Keep in mind, your view of spirituality could differ from his. The best partnership is between two individuals who accept and support each other's faith and practices without a need to compare or compete.

The Great on Paper Man

This man is one of the most heartbreaking of all. He looks amazing on his profile. Maybe he has an excellent job, fascinating hobbies, and a seemingly perfect life. Perhaps you even had great initial messages causing you to be excited about his potential. Then, when you meet him, he is not at all who you thought he was. There is no chemistry, no spark, and communication is even difficult.

This speaks of course to taking things slowly and not getting too attached to someone's perceived potential. It is very easy to get ahead of yourself when someone looks like the perfect match.

I met a "Great on Paper Man" in the last week of my first three-month Match.com subscription. I had already met some nice men, and I was continuing to talk to some of them. However, no one had wowed me.

Then this man showed up in my matches. I thought my luck had changed. He was just slightly outside of my ideal geographical range. After messaging me, he quickly assured me he didn't mind driving to meet me and that he knew we could make it work. He was an engineer at a well-known company. He lived in a wealthy town, had a pool, a boat, and a motorcycle. In addition, although he was divorced, he supposedly had an amicable relationship with his ex-wife.

His pictures didn't knock my socks off, but I wasn't as interested in physical appearance as I was in meeting a stable, kind person. Moreover, his messages were intelligent and engaging. Additionally, given that the clock was ticking on my subscription, I think I was emotionally invested in him before ever meeting.

The irony with this man is that he ended up being one of the worst dates I had, as I will detail in Chapter 20. He wasn't at all the person portrayed in his profile. As we interacted during our date, I wondered if someone else had written his messages for him. Very little of the real-life version of this man matched his online persona.

The key to avoiding the disappointment of the "Great on Paper Man" is to take a wait-and-see approach. Don't assume someone is your ideal match based on what is in their profile or even what they write in their messages. You can only experience true chemistry and connection by physically meeting someone.

The Hero / Man in Uniform

You will notice the "Man in Uniform" right away from his profile. He's the most obvious to spot. Just like the name says, he's in a uniform. This is the firefighter, police officer, military man, or doctor, who has pictures of himself on the job. I was a sucker for these "hero" types. I have great compassion and appreciation for the dedication these men seem to have for their careers.

There are a couple of problems with thinking this way. First off, I am not alone. Many women are attracted to these types of men. They get a lot of attention. Why else would they feature their career so prominently in their profile? They know women love a man in uniform.

The second problem with assuming these men are heroes and a great catch is many times that is not true. One firefighter I met shared that some of his colleagues were arrogant jerks. He also told me that many of the police officers he knew were egotistical, controlling, and prone to cheating. You can't assume anything about someone based on their job choice alone.

I fell into this trap more times than I'd like to admit. I often reached out to these types of men, and only received a few responses. Every time, the messages weren't especially engaging. It didn't feel like they wanted to get to know me. It seemed as if they only responded because I had said something nice to them. I think they just enjoyed the attention.

I still have great admiration and gratitude for anyone who puts their life on the line. However, I recognize that not everyone does those things for altruistic reasons. Additionally, as sensitive women, we have to shield ourselves from people who have a lot of drama in their lives. A man who is out fighting crime or battling fires is not likely the best match for a sensitive woman who could end up sick worrying about his safety.

The Committed Man

I saved the best for last! I only experienced one example of the "Committed Man." Once I met him, I knew I may never need online dating again. If you are looking for a long-term partner, the "Committed Man" is the one you want to meet.

What stood out about him right away is that he was 100% focused on making a relationship work. He had been divorced. Afterward, he spent years working on healing himself. He knew what he wanted and was willing to do the work required to have a healthy partnership.

From day one, he communicated openly with me about his values, spiritual beliefs, and ultimately what was important to him in a relationship. He requested that, if I ever had any misgivings or disappointment in anything he did or said, I would talk to him about it. This established a safe space for discussing anything and everything.

I had never really felt comfortable telling a man everything I was feeling or thinking because I had been so steadily shamed for being too sensitive. This "Committed Man" didn't invalidate my feelings and welcomed all of my sensitivities, accepting that they were part of who I am. His stance was, if I didn't feel good about something, he wanted to know so that he could correct it. I certainly felt the same. It was a refreshingly honest approach.

Just as important was his propensity to listen to me and pay attention to my needs. As I mentioned, just before meeting him, I became frustrated with the mindless messages. I changed my profile by making a more direct request.

He honored my requests. He has since said that I am so easy to please that he can't imagine not doing so.

Most of us are very simple. We expect little more than respect, mutual support, and appreciation. The "Committed Man" that honors these basic needs and wants is a treasure.

There are, of course, other types of men. I share this information not to make you overly jaded or judgmental, but rather to prepare you. Every type of man has the potential to be the right match for you depending on what you are looking for in the relationship and how much work both of you can dedicate. Some men are going to be a "no" right away. Allow yourself the freedom to eliminate these options, so you can make space for the man who is right for you.

Chapter 8: Be on Alert for Manipulators

I have mentioned narcissists several times already. It won't come as a surprise that I want you to be on high alert for these types of disordered manipulators. These men are so dangerous that they deserve their own chapter. Heck, there are loads of books, websites, and YouTube channels on this very topic. I will include several in the "Resources" section of the book. You can dig deeper if you have had the misfortune of encountering a narcissist.

Chances are good that you have encountered disordered people throughout your life. It is possible you never even realized it. Empaths and sensitive women (often called "lightworkers") attract energy vampires who are seeking their light. These dark individuals typically display signs of a personality disorder such as narcissism, sociopathy, or psychopathy.

When I look back on my online dating objectively, I would guess that a good 75% of the interactions I had were with disordered individuals. That is a scary statistic for sure. I recognized many of these men quickly, sometimes within the first few messages with them, or just by reading their boastful profiles.

However, as I previously shared, I dated one man for months before recognizing that he had all the classic signs of an overt narcissist. Additionally, it took a few weeks of dating a covert narcissist before I uncovered his signs too. Even though I thought I knew the signs well after having been married to a covert narcissist, I was still somewhat in denial about how confusing and charming those types can be.

My reality is even more depressing. Energy vampires and narcissistic individuals have surrounded me my entire life. There has been an endless parade of friends, family members, colleagues, managers, and love interests draining my energy and abusing my kindness. At the end of 2019, I did a life review assessing all the individuals who fit the patterns that I now recognize are common for energy vampires. I could easily list at least 25 people in my life who displayed signs of manipulation, victim mentality, controlling behavior, and flat-out emotional abuse. I do not think some of these people had any awareness of how they hurt me. However, that does not excuse their behavior. Luckily, now that I am aware of these types, they no longer directly influence my life. I will not let them!

For a time, though, I thought I was destined to be a narcissist magnet. I have met other sensitive women in online forums who feel the same. I have since realized through supportive experts on the topic that sensitive or empathic women are not the only ones who interact with these types. These negative people are everywhere. The problem is that our desire to fix, love, support, please, and heal others prevents us from putting up the appropriate boundaries around these disordered types. Simply put, people who have healthy, firm boundaries and a clear understanding of their worth do not put up with energy vampires or manipulators. They don't show them kindness or attention, so the energy vampires leave them in search of a more viable source of love and light.

The best way to avoid a disordered individual is to be very clear about your value and needs. You deserve kindness and respect always. You do not have to give away your time, energy, or compassion to anyone. You can be a good person without assuming responsibility for anyone else's happiness.

The best defense from someone else's manipulation is not getting attached to them at all. Their thoughts, feelings, needs, and wants are all their own. Focus on your needs and wants first, without worrying about them. This is much harder than it sounds of course. We will cover this topic more thoroughly as the book progresses.

Narcissists - The Master Manipulators

For now, let's take a closer look at a sensitive woman's worst nightmare, the narcissist. We've already discussed some of the negative aspects of narcissists when we talked about red flags. Since these types of people can damage a sensitive woman's psyche in devastating ways, this topic is worthy of further exploration.

Before we go there, I want to note that there has been a backlash against labeling people with any type of personality disorder. Professional psychologists stress that it is quite rare to diagnose individuals with true Narcissistic Personality Disorder (NPD). I have no desire to diagnose anyone nor to determine exactly what kind of personality disorder they have. I have wasted far too many hours trying to figure out hurtful people. If someone hurts you, lies to you, steals from you, or otherwise harms you, they are not someone you should have in your life. Their actual diagnosis is irrelevant.

That being said, even if someone isn't a full-blown narcissist, they may exhibit a specific set of narcissistic traits. It is uncanny how often these types seem to follow the same playbook. For the sake of simplification, throughout this book, I refer to anyone high in narcissistic traits as a "narcissist."

The hallmark traits of a narcissist include selfishness, self-importance, a sense of entitlement, a lack of true empathy, and a need for constant attention and validation, which is referred to as "supply." They will text and message a lot at first to see if you will fulfill their need for attention and praise.

If you are an empath or a codependent accustomed to people-pleasing, providing supply as validation, support, and attention is very easy for you. It is how you naturally operate. When someone is first interacting with us regularly, it feels great. We love to feel needed and valued. However, over time, these interactions can become draining when you realize the connection is one-sided. The conversation typically centers on them with very little concern for you.

Don't feel obligated to respond immediately, or even at all, to anyone. You can start putting up boundaries right away, explaining that you aren't able to text freely during work hours, or that you don't always keep your phone on you.

It might feel like you are pushing someone great away by establishing these strong boundaries. However, trust me. What you are actually doing is protecting yourself from emotional abuse. Narcissists are incredibly unhealthy mentally. They lack the capacity to love another person. They fear true intimacy and honest connection. Their partner is just an object to fulfill their needs and make them feel less empty.

Regardless of their true shortcomings, narcissists come across as incredibly confident and charming. They seem amazing, like everything you've been looking for in a partner. They use your kindness against you in unfathomable ways. They build you up, only to tear you down.

The Progression of a Relationship with a Narcissist

Narcissists use a set of methodical tactics to draw you in. You must be able to spot the signs of a narcissistic relationship objectively so you don't fall into the insidious trap.

In what is called the "idealize or idolize phase," they put on a strong effort to wow you and win you over. That phase can last months or even years, however long it takes to lock you into a committed relationship.

Once they believe they have you, their true colors come out as they begin the "devalue phase." At that point, they lose interest, dismissing and disregarding you in hurtful ways.

When they have grown tired of you, or if they find it difficult to continue manipulating you, they progress to the "discard phase." This is when they actively seek to replace and/or leave you.

These three phases can cycle endlessly as the narcissist plays with your head and heart. The pain and confusion are devastating. A narcissist may use any (or all) of the following strategies depending on how the relationship is progressing.

Testing Your Boundaries - They want to see exactly what they can get away with. They may ask for pictures or bombard you with texts to see how quickly you respond. They may tell you terrible things they have done to see if you are OK with it (i.e., cheating or being disrespectful to others). They might ask for money or for your help with something. They are trying to determine if you are a giver who they can manipulate. If you say "no" to their requests, or put up a boundary, they may get angry or will shame you to gain control.

Learning Your Vulnerabilities - They will ask you in-depth questions about yourself and all the details of your life. It may feel amazing to have someone give you so much attention. However, they are only doing it so that they can extract information that they can later use against you. They will want to know about your previous relationships and any family situations that they can exploit. Be very careful to not share private or intimate details of your life with anyone before really getting a sense of who they are first.

Love Bombing - We've talked about this before. Love bombing is when someone praises you constantly, telling you the most wonderful compliments you've ever heard, or lavishing you with gifts. It feels great and prevents you from seeing who and how they really are as a person.

Mirroring - You like yoga, go figure, so does he! You love concerts. Suddenly you're being swept off to your dream concert. When someone mirrors you, they reflect back what you are saying, pretending that they share the same beliefs and like the same things. Give limited information about your likes and hobbies. Then question the person further if they say that they like those things too. Try to ask open-ended questions that require an explanation. If they keep agreeing with what you say without further elaborating, that is a strong sign that they are not being honest.

Fast-Tracking - They will speed up the pace of the relationship, trying to "lock you down," pushing you towards committing to them before you even really know them. This could mean introducing you to their friends and family quickly or announcing your relationship on social media. They seem all-in before you even have time to observe their behavior.

Enmeshing Your Lives - They will actively tie you to them through a financial or emotional commitment or even in trying to live with you. Never give anyone you meet money and avoid living together for at least a year. Always be sure you have an out, so that you do not have to rely on someone who hasn't proven that they are trustworthy. If you are sensitive and concerned about the needs of others, things like pets, children, large purchases, and living arrangements can all tie you to someone. Be mindful of always maintaining your independence in all relationships.

Over 20 years ago, before I knew anything about narcissistic abuse, my now ex-husband fast-tracked and enmeshed our relationship. Just a little over two months after we started dating, I met his entire family at his grandmother's funeral. A little while after, I broke up with him because he had been insensitive. He begged for my forgiveness. After I reluctantly took him back, he bought me my first cell phone and put me on his plan. This was a little less than four months after we had met. It was a subtle thing, but it tied me to him in a way that felt difficult to leave. We also ended up living together after just nine months. The more strongly I got connected to him and his family, the harder it became to walk away. I fell in love with his nieces and nephews. That connection made it incredibly painful for me to leave.

Evoking Your Pity - Emotional manipulation is a major tactic for narcissists, especially the covert type who play the victim. They will use your compassion against you by giving you a sob story or by crying when you try to leave. You must understand that these emotional games are all an act. Narcissists don't feel sadness, remorse, guilt, or shame the way you do. However, many of them know how to mirror your emotional state or call up emotions on cue.

Shaming or Guilting You - A narcissist will imply that you are a terrible person if you have the nerve to express your wants or needs. They may directly say that you are a mean, selfish, or nasty person, which is a trigger for anyone who cares about being kind. They will use any information they gleaned from you to pick at your core vulnerabilities and sensitivities. In addition, they will call you "too sensitive," which causes most sensitive women to feel shame and self-consciousness. Shame and guilt are two of the most toxic emotional states. Healthy, empathic people would never try to shame or guilt another person because they know how much it hurts. Narcissists use these negative emotions as weapons to weaken and punish you.

Competing With You - Oddly, the man who had been vying for your attention is suddenly competing with you. They will make you feel as if you have to prove yourself and your worth. If you experience success or something that you are excited about, they will belittle it and overshadow it with something that they have done. A healthy partner wants you to shine. A narcissist is jealous and threatened by your successes. They may give you a backhanded compliment if you get a job promotion, like, "Oh, that's great that no one else wanted the job." They are technically congratulating you, yet in the most hurtful way possible.

Belittling Others - Narcissists seem to have many friends. Over time, you realize they don't have a genuine connection with any of those people. They will talk badly about everyone, even their family who they supposedly love. According to them, everyone is stupid or awful. One narcissist I knew had a friend who was always extremely kind to him, making him his favorite snacks and inviting him to all her parties. It was odd to witness him being kind to her face, then hearing him put her down for being "fat and pathetic" as soon as she turned her back. The sad thing about this dynamic is that it feels oddly comforting that the narcissist chooses you when they are so critical and dismissive of everyone else. The problem is they will eventually be cruel and dismissive of you too.

Exhibiting No Accountability or Responsibility - A narcissist is never wrong. Even when they are blatantly wrong, they will have some excuse that prevents them from being accountable. A narcissist I knew was livid when their bank refused to cash a check. He ranted about how stupid the bank had been. When I asked for clarification, it turned out that he had written the check out for a different amount from what he entered in the numeric field. By basic banking standards, both fields on a check must match for the bank to cash it! Not according to this man, who was adamant that the bank should have known what he meant. It is scary the lengths a narcissist will go to prove that they are right, especially when they are not. We all make mistakes. That is part of being human. If someone believes they do not make mistakes, they are not mentally healthy. Furthermore, narcissists will insist you are always wrong. That is the terrible tradeoff of being with one. You end up having to be accountable for their mistakes, while also taking full responsibility for all the challenges in your relationship.

Showing a Lack of Genuine Empathy - As a sensitive woman, you know exactly what empathy is. You feel other people's emotions. You can easily put yourself in their shoes and understand what they experience. Chances are you feel sad, mad, or glad in response to other people's experiences all the time. A narcissist can only fake empathy. They wonder why you are so sad when a friend has hurt you. They may even say you're overreacting or being silly. They just can't get it. The same is true when they hurt you. They don't care. They can go about their day as if nothing ever happened, even if you are a crying mess. It is as if they don't even see you.

Healthy people can't watch another person suffer without wanting to help. A narcissist can do so easily. They don't feel inclined to help others, donate money to charity, or support anyone who is going through a rough time. They focus solely on their needs. They only pretend to care about others if it offers them a reward or praise. One man I dated was ice cold when I was crying over a pet that had to be put to sleep. He stared at me blankly and said, "It's probably for the best."

Dropping the Mask - Narcissists will be incredibly charming, doting on you and supporting your needs, until one day they can't keep up the charade. That is when they "drop the mask." The man I just mentioned, who was cruel when my cat had to be put to sleep, had been love bombing me steadily for several months.

At that point, against my better judgment, I proclaimed my love for him. As I was saying, "I love you," I saw his eyes change. It was almost like a flash went off and a creepy sneer came over his face. Without missing a beat, he said, "Awwww, I love you too, baby. What's not to love?" His energy seemed to shift from that moment on. He stopped being a supportive partner. There were no more flowers, very few compliments, and he no longer included me in weekend plans. It was like we had hit a wall.

As time stretched on, I felt less and less connected to him. It was as if his energy was receding now that the chase was over and he settled into the notion that he had me. Two months later, he showed up at my townhouse unexpectedly at 6:30 in the morning. I was confused and angry. His stance was that he should be able to come over whenever he wanted. He was wrong. We broke up that very day.

Later he accused me of wanting to date other men, which was crazy. He was projecting and gaslighting me. I foolishly maintained a friendship with him. A year later, I learned he was dating someone less than a week after our break-up, yet he continued to text and call me professing his love the entire time.

Projecting & Gaslighting - As we have discussed, projecting is when someone accuses you of something that they are doing. Narcissists often use this tactic to claim that their targets/partners are cheating or lying. It is incredibly confusing because you know you would never do what they are saying. This makes you doubt your reality and feel crazy, a situation known as gaslighting. When someone gaslights you, they will consistently lie to you, even about insignificant things.

At the end of my marriage, I realized my husband kept telling me everything I said was wrong. It was demoralizing. I tested him by making very simple, easily provable statements to see what he would do. Consistently, his first response was to say, "No it isn't."

One cloudy winter morning, I commented that it looked like it might snow. Sure enough, he shot back quickly with, "No it doesn't." I laughed and said, "How do you know that?" He got flustered and angry. A few minutes later, it started to snow. I knew it wasn't even worth the energy to say, "I told you so."

No matter what I said or did at that point, he would never validate my experiences. Such is the case with most narcissists. After spending time with them, it is hard to know what is real. You are so used to being challenged and belittled that you have very little energy left to defend yourself.

Devaluing You - Nothing you do is ever good enough for a narcissist. They will find fault with virtually anything. I was excited when I bought my husband what I thought was the perfect wedding gift, a ride-along in a racecar. He was a big fan of NASCAR, so I thought he would be thrilled. His response, as was the case for everything I did, was lukewarm. All of his friends were excited for him, but he acted as if I was sending him to have a root canal. I kept assuring him we could cancel the trip if he didn't like it. He did actually like it. He simply refused to acknowledge my efforts or show me the most basic form of appreciation.

I witnessed the same behavior nonstop from my Mother-in-

Chapter 9: Establish a Support System

When you are in the craziness of the online dating world, it is hard to recognize just how crazy it is! Your friends and family can serve as grounding and guiding forces reminding you of your inherent worth here in the real world.

I've never liked keeping secrets, and it felt like being online was a dirty little secret. I started telling everyone I knew I was online dating, possibly as a cry for help.

Most people who had any experience with online dating were empathetic. However, those who had never experienced the odd behaviors were baffled by what I shared. Even though they couldn't offer tools or tips, they gave me perspective around the value of real-world connections.

My perception became cloudy quickly as I was bombarded with a combination of "likes" and empty messages about my physical appearance, teamed with messages that weren't returned. It felt like being pushed and pulled in every direction. Not to mention, the focus that so many men placed on my photos was objectifying. It made me feel uncomfortable. As my self-esteem started to slip, I realized I needed support.

Set Your Compass

I turned to my best friend and my mom for regular guidance. Once I realized I was in over my head, I later turned to a therapist who offered additional helpful support.

My best friend, Chelle, was my "compass," the person who always gave me clarity. Likewise, when I needed a reminder that I was worthy of love, I knew I could count on her. She has known me longer than any other friend. She is also a sensitive woman who understands my heart. Although she has never experienced online dating, she works with teens and is aware of the online culture. In addition, she has a strong marriage, so she can recognize the core components of a healthy partnership. When I shared details of some of the crazy-making behavior that I was experiencing, she offered validation and reassurance that I was not losing my mind. I can't emphasize enough how important it is to have at least one totally supportive person there for you during your dating journey.

My mom was also a constant source of support. She would listen to the stories of my dating escapades with amusement. Naturally, after being married to my dad for 45 years, she did not know what I was experiencing. Still, she could remind me I deserved to be happy. Sometimes that was all I needed.

The therapist I began seeing a few months after starting online dating was all about tough love. Her best and most consistent advice was, "He's not for you." She would listen to me justifying someone's odd behavior, shake her head, and remind me I deserved better.

When I questioned if the man who had been treating me so wonderfully might be a narcissist, she calmly explained that she couldn't be sure from what I had said. However, given my history, it was pretty likely. I tucked that information away because I wasn't ready to accept it.

Another man I met had been telling me I was looking for a romantic "movie guy" who didn't exist. I proclaimed to my therapist that maybe I was just expecting too much. I wondered if my goals were unrealistic. She gasped and reminded me that many women want romantic love, and any man denying that genuinely romantic, loving men exist was clearly just unwilling to step up to be that kind of partner. Even though I stopped seeing her after moving to a new home, I valued the solid, firm advice she had provided. While getting support from a friend or family member is helpful, your friends don't want to hurt you. It can be much more effective to get the truth from an unbiased professional.

Find Support Online

When I first started my dating journey, I found solace in the information that I uncovered online. There is a great deal of dating support available via Facebook Groups or through videos and blogs shared by dating and relationship experts.

I must admit, however, I disagreed with some of what I read and watched. I had been in online dating on-and-off for over a year when I was watching a video where a dating expert said that sensitive, empathic women should avoid online dating because there were far too many men poised to take advantage of us. I thought, "Uh oh! Too late."

I knew what he said had strong merit. I also knew that as an introvert who worked with all women, online dating was one of the few chances I had to meet a variety of eligible men. There had to be a happy medium. I believe that the knowledge I am sharing here through this book is part of the solution. You can date effectively online, as long as you are always mindful of protecting yourself and your precious energy.

Maintain a Daily Grounding Practice

Protecting your energy requires a daily grounding practice. This will help you stay in touch with who you are so that no one can manipulate you. A daily grounding practice is healthy for everyone. It is especially important for sensitive women facing the challenges of online dating. You will be exposed to a great deal of new energy. In addition, you will be forced to question your worth. You must have tools that remind you how amazing you are.

When our energy gets too high or scattered, it can lift out of our body, leading to dizziness or anxiety. Physically grounding your body by filling it with light energy and connecting to the earth is a powerful remedy. One of the classic forms of grounding includes a quick visualization focusing on drawing light in from above your crown, down through your body, out your feet, and into the earth. Start by placing your feet firmly on the ground. Sometimes even doing that simple act with intention is enough to pull your energy solidly back into your body. If you can, having your feet directly on the earth (i.e., barefoot on the grass, a practice called "earthing") is even better.

My daily journal was an incredibly valuable tool during the dating process. I shared my deepest feelings in my digital journal, as well as in several printed versions. The writing process helps you make sense of what is often nonsensical behavior. Seeing the details written out in black and white provides clarity and perspective.

Daily affirmations are also helpful. When I found my self-esteem declining, I knew I needed to reframe my point of view. Every morning when I first woke up, I sat down in my cozy meditation area and wrote "I am" declarations in my Wonder Woman journal. I would write things like, "I am loving. I am compassionate. I am beautiful. I am radiant. I am fun. I am positive. I am happy. I am grateful. I am a great friend. I am a dedicated employee." I wrote until I felt good. You possess so many amazing qualities. You must recognize them, especially when in a situation that could cause you to question yourself.

I also keep a gratitude folder. It includes loving cards, photos, and other mementos, like drawings that my nieces and nephews made for me when they were little. Looking through these items made me feel loved and appreciated. They warmed my heart and reminded me how much love I already had in my life.

Release Negative Energy Quickly

While online, it is common to experience manipulations and even cruel comments. It can knock you off your feet. Be prepared to release that negative energy quickly.

I messaged one man in the first few weeks after I joined Match.com because his profile said he enjoyed visiting Rhode Island. Since I grew up there, I thought that was something fun that we had in common. We chatted for several days and things seemed to be going well. Easter passed during that time. The following Monday, he mentioned that it was his first Easter spent alone after his divorce. The same had been true for me, so I wrote, "It's too bad we didn't know we were alone. Maybe we could have met for a coffee?" He responded quickly, saying, "I would not have met you. I only meet people who are special." I was stunned. I wasn't super into him by any means. Still, I couldn't believe anyone would say something so hurtful, especially when I was just trying to be kind. I couldn't even respond. The next day he sent a message that said something like, "So you're not going to talk to me anymore?" I assured him that, yes, that was most definitely the case.

What I realize now, that I wish I recognized then, is when someone hits you with such a negative energetic punch, it can lodge in your body. You must focus on quickly releasing any of the negative thoughts, emotions, and feelings that arise when interacting with someone with dark or negative energy.

Smudging yourself with the smoke of sacred wood like Palo Santo or dried plants like sage or sweet grass can easily dissipate negative energy. As a sensitive woman, you can benefit from smudging your energy field every time you interact with others, especially if the interaction leaves you feeling drained.

To do so, use a large shell or fireproof bowl to collect any embers or ash. Then, light the end of the smudge stick. Wave it gently to blow out the active flame, while still allowing the smoke to continue. Move the stick over the front, back, and sides of your body, allowing the smoke to waft over you. For added impact, state or think an intention. I like to ask the Universe to, "Fill me with your love and light." Pick a phrase that feels comfortable for you. You can also move the smoke across your computer or digital device to clear any negativity further.

After a negative online interaction, you can also do a quick cutting of the energetic cords that developed between you. There are meditations on YouTube, or available for purchase online, that help with this practice. It is done by envisioning the cords of energy that form between you and others and dissolving those cords so that the energy is released with love back to where it belongs.

Fire ceremonies are also helpful in releasing someone's negative attachments to you. Put the person's name on a slip of paper and then burn it in a small fireproof container. Set your intention to release that person with love.

Sensitivity refers to our emotions and our physical energy. You must know your susceptibility to take on others' negative energy. If you continue to feel sad or out of sorts after an interaction with someone, you might need to clear your energy field more fully. There are a variety of techniques to work on this including doing an energy-aligning meditation, taking a detoxifying bath with Epsom salts and lavender oil, using a selenite crystal wand to clear your energy field, or booking a reiki session with an energy healer. We will go deeper into energy clearing practices in Phase 3.

Request Support and Guidance from Spirit

As you know, I am a very spiritual person. However, I realize not everyone will be comfortable working with Spirit. Please take what resonates with you and leave the rest. I am not trying to proselytize here. I just want to help by sharing the spiritual tools that worked for me.

I started working with my spirituality in my 30s. I have studied Christian mysticism and shamanism. I feel very drawn to animal messengers and number signs in particular.

I met a wonderful fellow empath while completing a master's degree in Integrative Health & Healing. She told me she accessed spiritual guidance through "Medicine Cards." These are like tarot cards but they include animals that offer a message related to the animals' inherent properties. In 2012, I started using these divining tools daily. They have enriched my life greatly. I have since added several other oracle decks to pull from. On most days, I ask the Universe, "What do I need to know today?" Then, I pick a card, noting the message it conveys. I regularly find myself moved to tears by how pertinent the message is at that moment.

In retrospect, I realize that when I started dating the first man who turned out to be a narcissist, I kept picking the dragonfly card. That card represents "Illusion." I thought for sure that the card was warning me about another man who had also been contacting me at the same time. I can now see that I was given a clear sign that "things are never completely as they seem," which is a perfect description of what a narcissist's behavior is like!

Another time, while I was messaging with a man who claimed to be spiritual, a crow flew directly at my bedroom window. At first, I thought that was a good sign, because it was 11/11, a spiritual day. I knew crows represent "Law" which can be difficult to interpret. However, the sense I got was one of fear and distrust. I didn't want that to be true, so I reinterpreted it to be a positive sign of our spiritual connection. It took just a few weeks to realize that the man was yet another manipulative narcissist. Spirit was trying to warn me, but I was too stubborn to see!

It is crucial when asking Spirit for help that you not fight the intuitive response that you get right away. This is a hard lesson that I continue to learn. It requires getting very good at discerning the signs you get in your body. Many of us receive our intuitive knowing through our solar plexus, which is located just above the navel. When something is negative, it may feel restricted, as if someone has punched you in the stomach. When something is positive, it will feel light and open. Practice getting to know these feelings. They will be very helpful guides.

Maintain Objectivity

It is incredibly important that you see your interactions with new men objectively, not getting overly attached to outcome or potential. Focus on always being honest with yourself. Believe what people tell you, especially if it is negative. If someone says they aren't interested in dating, believe them. If they say they are too busy to see you on your schedule, accept that.

Most manipulation is done in the affirmative, as in "You are my soulmate," or "You're the best woman I've ever met." Since statements like that feel so good you want to believe them and disregard how odd they are in the context of having just met.

Sensitive women want to see the good in others or in a situation. We hold on to the hope of a positive outcome. Hope is a beautiful quality to maintain, but don't let it cloud your judgment or it could lead you to situations that harm you.

You are by far your greatest source of support, especially when you learn to read and honor the clues that arise naturally within your body, mind, and spirit. However, we all need the support of others. Don't forget to reach out to the people you trust when you need comfort, validation, and compassion. When you feel supported, it is easier to avoid and disregard negative interactions online.

Chapter 10: Practice Safety First

You must put yourself and your safety first. This means dropping the need to be polite. You are going to have to be firm, sometimes even rude, throughout the dating process. Get clear on this from the start. Your emotional and physical well-being must be your number one priority. There are many ways to protect yourself online. Please take the following suggestions seriously.

Guard Your Energy

We've already discussed releasing negative energy if it comes your way. It is much better, however, to prevent it from ever attaching to your spirit. As a sensitive woman, you must always prevent people from tapping into your energy.

Everything is energy. Every look, every "like," every text, every time someone interacts with you or your profile they are transferring energy. That may sound weird, but it is true.

To protect your energy, you must set a conscious intention to do so. Often, all you need to do is make a declaration. Saying a simple statement aloud such as, "I reclaim and protect my energy with love," can help shield you from energy vampires.

As mentioned, smudging yourself and your digital devices daily can also help release negative energy. I love the smell of Palo Santo, so I use that for smudging first thing in the morning and before I go to bed at night. Sage also works well.

Wearing protective crystals, or carrying them in your purse, can also guard your energy field. Many healers suggest black tourmaline, fluorite, quartz, obsidian, and hematite to help block negative energy.

Essential oils of frankincense and rose can also help to raise your vibration so that you are more receptive to love and positivity. You can wear these oils on a lava rock bracelet or directly on your pulse points.

Even though I knew the benefits of energy medicine and natural healing after studying those fields for many years, I didn't honor their power the way I should have while dating online. I didn't fully accept that even remotely people can attach to you. Now I use these tools daily. They help immensely in protecting my sensitive energy field.

I had quite a few experiences where men were looking at my profile daily. That made me uneasy. Match.com gives you this type of information, which is a bit odd. You might even sense when it is happening just through your intuition. If someone gives you a creepy vibe, you can block his profile. I only did this a few times, but the option exists for a reason. Creeps are out there and you don't need to endure their icky energy.

Give Limited Information

One good rule when first connecting with someone is; a little mystery is good, sharing your life story is not. I laugh when saying this because I was really awful about this. I tend to overshare.

Empaths, who are commonly misunderstood, feel the need to establish a personal connection with others. We sometimes do this by blurting out personal and vulnerable information. If the person is similarly kind and empathic, that tactic works well in creating a bond. For individuals who are toxic or disordered, the information is fuel for manipulation. It is much better at the beginning of a relationship to stick to neutral topics, keeping the interaction playful and light.

I often shared pretty early on that I had been married to a narcissist. I thought this was important information for someone to understand about me as we approached a potential relationship. While that may technically be true and the most honest approach, it gave the narcissistic men a window into my vulnerabilities. It told them I was primed for their tricks. Several of the narcissists that I encountered immediately had stories of their narcissistic exes. It made me feel relief, that, "They can't be a narcissist if they have been with one." Unfortunately, that is not true. Many narcissists are quite clever. They know they aren't able to maintain a healthy relationship, so they make up stories about their exes being unhealthy and manipulative.

Give minimal details at first. Don't worry, you can reveal all of your juicy secrets in time. There is no need to rush.

Never give away personal data like your banking information, social security number, or credit card information. Also, don't share log-in information for online platforms like Netflix or Amazon until you are sure this person is trustworthy. Keep your address private, always meeting at public locations until you feel safe.

Furthermore, be very careful about sharing photos of any kind through your phone. If you decide to do so, turn the location services off under the privacy settings. Several men texted me photos they took at their homes. When the pictures came through on my iPhone, their home address was included as part of the properties of the photo.

Do Your Research

Thank goodness for the internet! Seriously, you can find a lot of information with good old Google. As soon as someone gave me their phone number, I was putting those digits into the search engines to learn as much as I could.

I have read articles that said not to "stalk" people you are planning to date. I think that is terrible advice. You're about to immerse yourself into this person's world. At the bare minimum, you should know what their digital footprint looks like.

By searching for someone's phone number, you can learn where they live, their full name, and their marital status. I'm embarrassed to admit I didn't know one man's last name until we had been on several dates. I knew where he lived and worked, as well as his kid's names, but I didn't know his last name. It felt so awkward. After that experience, I always asked a man for his full name before ever meeting.

With someone's full name you can check out his social media accounts and any other online information. This is an important step. It can provide insight on the person's political opinions, how they present themselves publicly, and can verify any details he has been sharing with you already. For instance, one man I met had told me he was a teacher in a particular district. I could verify that information easily by visiting his school's website. It is crucial to be sure that people are who they say. There are far too many stories of men swindling women by pretending to be someone else.

I never conducted a formal background check on anyone. Some experts suggest you do so for anyone you are planning to date seriously. This is an especially good idea if you have children or if the person is raising any red flags for you. There are online services that allow you to do that for a small fee.

Use the Apps for as Long as Needed

Using the apps for messaging can be a little clunky because many people don't access them during work hours. Regardless, message within the app for as long as you need. Remember that moving too quickly is a red flag. Take your time.

If you are enjoying communicating and it feels like there is a potential connection, it is common to exchange phone numbers so you can begin texting. Again, there is no need to move to this phase of communication quickly. I often did because I didn't like the apps and I wasn't particularly worried about someone having my phone number. Just remember moving to that step allows them to know more about you, as we discussed.

If you feel uncomfortable giving out your phone number to new people, you could set up an alternate number just for dating. You can do that through Google Voice.

Have a Phone Call or Video Chat

Before meeting, most people recommend having a phone call or video chat. I really don't enjoy phone calls, and I absolutely hate being on video, so I rarely took this advice. I knew I could never fully assess chemistry with someone unless I met him in person.

However, the few times I had phone calls first, those men turned into serious relationships. I think the takeaway here is that if you feel a connection with someone over the phone, you are much more likely to feel connected with him when you meet in person.

I am writing this during the pandemic, so phone and video chatting have become a common part of the dating world. Always do what feels the safest and most comfortable for you when first getting to know someone.

Give a Friend the Details

Once you decide to meet, share all the details you uncovered about this new man with a close friend or family member. I mentioned earlier that my best friend is my compass, guiding me with helpful advice and support. She was also my record keeper during the dating process.

Every time I planned a date, I texted her the man's name, occupation, the town he lived in, his phone number, and any additional identifying information. I would also tell her where and when the date was taking place, texting her as soon as I was home.

This may seem paranoid, but I don't think you can be too safe. If something ever happens to you, you want the police to know as much about the situation as possible.

Meet in Public

Every first meeting should be in a public place where you know other people will be around. My favorite meeting spot was Panera Bread. You can buy your drink or coffee before the man even arrives, then set up in one of the cozier couch areas away from the crowd. It offers a laid-back atmosphere while also being very safe.

If you are planning an outdoor date, make sure you choose a well-populated, open area, like a public park or the beach. Don't go anywhere that you wouldn't normally feel comfortable going by yourself.

Have an out, such as a time limit or plans later in the day. This will make it easier to leave if you aren't having a good time. Several men did this to me, stating at the beginning of the date that they had to be somewhere later. At first, I was a little hurt over what seemed like being double-booked. However, it became obvious that they were just giving themselves an out because they extended our date well beyond when they said they had to leave.

In retrospect, I realize it is a wise tactic to give dates a time limit. It makes it easier for you to end the date without feeling awkward. As I mentioned, my dates sometimes lasted up to five hours. I love getting to know new people, and I found myself enthralled by my dates' life stories. They always seemed to enjoy talking to me too. However, long dates like that sped up our connection. It probably would have been better to cut the dates shorter to keep some enthusiasm and mystery for the second date.

Trust Your Instincts

First impressions matter, especially when it comes to safety. Pay close attention to how you feel when you first meet your date. Your body doesn't lie. It is your best indicator of how you feel about someone at your core.

You are likely to be nervous at first regardless of who the person is. Dating can definitely be nerve-wracking. The nerves you will feel are more like butterflies or even a bit of nervous tension. That is normal. What isn't normal is a feeling of discomfort or fear when you first meet someone. Furthermore, if your nerves don't seem to let up the more you spend time with them, that is a strong sign that they aren't your person.

The covert narcissist that I dated briefly made me very uneasy when we first met. When I pulled up to the public park where we were meeting, I felt so uncomfortable that I didn't want to get out of the car. He had a stern, almost angry look on his face, and his body language seemed closed off. I blocked out that instinct because I knew it would be incredibly rude to leave. It took probably an hour of walking around the beautiful park with him before I felt more at ease. As I reflect on this now, I can't believe how badly I disregarded the signs, opting instead to give him chance after chance. I hope you will do as I say here, and not what I did.

Some men will be overtly sexual right away. If they make you feel uncomfortable at all, make it clear to them you are looking for a friendship first. If they don't take the hint, simply tell them you aren't feeling like they are a good match and leave.

Pay attention to any lingering concerns you feel towards someone. If you repeatedly question what someone says, or the intent of something they do, chances are good that they aren't your ideal partner.

Plan for Healthy Boundaries

It is important to plan for healthy boundaries because once you are in a relationship it gets much harder. Sensitive, kind women often struggle with boundaries in all areas of our lives. Romantic relationships are especially challenging because our hearts get so deeply intertwined. We are far too willing to put the other person's needs before our own and endure behaviors that hurt us.

Setting clear deal-breakers right up front is a great way to protect yourself and keep your dating efforts focused on people who are healthy for you. Certain habits like smoking, excess drinking, doing drugs, cheating, or gambling are obvious and easy things to screen out. Life circumstances like having kids (or not) or being in an established career may also be important to you. Get clear on what you want and don't want in a partner to save yourself time and anguish. It is helpful to write out your deal-breakers in advance. What we commit to in writing is often easier to honor.

There are obvious characteristics that all healthy relationships exhibit. You want someone who is at the bare minimum kind, honest, respectful, considerate, trustworthy, and polite.

If someone disregards those basic tenets, or otherwise feels threatening or uncomfortable, be prepared to confront them and/or block them immediately. Consider this, if you set a boundary or push back at a healthy person they will not find that strange at all. Only unhealthy people react negatively when you set a boundary. Remember, you do not need to be nice or polite with men who are aggressive, rude, or sexually inappropriate. They have lost the privilege of your kindness.

It is wise at the beginning of a relationship to test a new partner's ability to respect your boundaries. I mentioned this before. Small boundary checks will help you gauge a man's empathy and respect for you. If you ask to change the time of a date, how does he react? A healthy person would just take that in stride. A manipulative or controlling person would get angry. If you say that you are cold when riding in his car or at a restaurant, does he shrug it off or does he attempt to support your needs? Someone with empathy would always want you to feel comfortable and safe.

You must always choose yourself and honor your own needs first. Be willing to disappoint other people in favor of protecting yourself. It is very difficult to do if you have always put others first. It will be very uncomfortable when you first start asserting yourself. Don't let that deter you. It is a process. A loving partner will be open to working on it with you.

A new relationship is the perfect place to test out new, stronger boundaries. You don't have anything invested yet. Instead, you have the potential of finally having your needs met by someone who hasn't gotten used to treating you like a doormat.

Slowing down the progression of the relationship is a natural boundary that can protect you from harm. Once you have shared intimate details with someone or had a sexual connection, chemical bonds form that are hard to break. The initial intoxication of a passionate relationship can be blinding.

Having healthy boundaries with someone leads to a feeling of security and ease. You know you can trust the person and there is an inherent feeling of safety around them. If you feel anxious, nervous, or afraid around someone, it is an indicator that they aren't honoring your boundaries, or simply that they aren't a good energetic match for you.

Your physical, mental, and emotional safety must be your top priority when dating. Never let your desire to be kind cloud your judgment. Remember that you don't owe anyone anything. You are free to cut off connections at any time. If someone ever harasses or threatens you online contact the app administrator immediately to have them blocked or removed. You can never be too safe.

Chapter 11: Know Yourself

One of the greatest gifts of online dating was getting to know myself well. As someone who is a self-help addict, always focused on growth, it surprised me how many layers of myself I had buried throughout my life.

It was enlightening and inspiring to dive deeply into the aspects of myself that make me unique and complex. Of course, knowing who I was and what I enjoyed was an important step in finding a compatible partner.

The act of dating helped me discover aspects of myself that I didn't even know were there. Most of the men I met were very different from me, which ultimately proved to be positive. They often encouraged new hobbies and traits that I never explored before.

We are all such complex individuals. It is difficult to uncover every little nuance of what makes you tick. Following are some topics to guide you in uncovering your true self, so that you are prepared to share your gifts with someone else.

Are You a Highly Sensitive Person (HSP)?

When I refer to sensitivity throughout this book, I am thinking in a broader sense of someone who is sensitive to energy in all its forms, including the feelings of others. If your sensitivities are especially intense, you may be what Elaine Aron, Ph.D. calls a "Highly Sensitive Person" or HSP.

People who fall into this classification have a highly attuned neurological system. This can create challenges when exposed to excess sound, light, smells, data, emotions, or even certain foods and medications. Pretty much everything in our environment can cause us to struggle if it reaches a threshold level.

One example I have of this in my own life is my sensitivity to medications. When I was in the ER for an emergency appendectomy, the nurse was prepping me for surgery. She naturally wanted me to be free from pain in the interim. She took out a syringe of morphine. As she injected me, I immediately felt a burning sensation and started to go numb quickly. I begged her to stop at half the dose. She assured me I would need more. I knew I wouldn't, especially since I would be under anesthesia soon. The morphine she injected was more than enough to put me in a very numbed state.

How did I know it would be like that? I have always been very sensitive to medication. My doctors know to give me a minimal dose of any medication. In recovery from my surgery, I only used the prescribed pain meds at half the dose for two days, not the recommended week. I never had pain, and I was shocked at how quickly I experienced detox symptoms of sweating, chills, and nausea. My body was not happy to have that foreign substance present and wanted it out as quickly as possible.

As we have discussed throughout this book, when you are sensitive, you must be more mindful of your environment. That is especially true in terms of who you let into your life. When seeking a partner, you must have someone who can support, not challenge, your sensitivities.

Are You an Empath?

I know you are a sensitive woman since you are reading this book. Could you be an empath too? An empath feels and senses other people's emotions and needs as if they were their own. They are not just mindful of people on an emotional level; they are attuned to them physically as well. One of the trickiest aspects of being an empath is that most likely you have had that trait your entire life. Therefore, you don't realize that other people don't operate in the same manner. Many empaths do not know how much other people's energy influences them.

For years, healers and teachers I encountered told me I was an empath. I always just shook my head in agreement thinking,

"Oh yes, I am very empathetic." I didn't realize that what they were saying went beyond just my ability to put myself in another person's situation and understand their issues. It was deeper and included my body's ability to sense the sadness, fear, and anxiety of other people, so much that I often mistook those emotions as my own. Looking back, my earliest memory of being an empath was when I was four years old. However, I didn't accept and understand what it meant to be an empath until I was in my late 30s.

Empaths must take extra precautions when dating online. We are sponges for the negative energy and drama that exist in that medium. If you are interested in learning more about tools for supporting your empath traits, please refer to the "Resources" section at the end of the book. The energy medicine and protective practices shared throughout the book will also be especially helpful for you. I know they have been life-changing for me.

Are You Codependent?

Learning that I was codependent was painful. For one, the person who suggested it to me did so in a very cruel, judgmental way. I was approaching my 40th birthday, and I had met this woman in a group focused on personal growth. She had been asking me for help and support because her life was in turmoil. I felt responsible for helping her fix her problems and bent over backward trying to make her feel better about herself. Meanwhile, she seemed almost delighted in telling me she thought I was codependent. It seemed to make her feel superior to me. While I'm grateful for having finally learned the truth, it is quite ironic that this lesson came from someone who had been benefiting from my codependent, people-pleasing ways.

I had no idea what codependency even was, so I set out to the internet and bought "Codependent No More," the definitive work on codependency from Melody Beattie. It stunned me how well my life fit the patterns described.

Codependents put the needs of others before their own. They want to make others feel good and validate or support them as much as possible, even when the person doesn't reciprocate that kindness. I believed I HAD to put others' needs before my own. I honestly didn't think I had a choice. I watched women being assertive and firm and wondered how they had the brazen confidence to do so.

Shortly after getting married, I was talking with the wife of my husband's friend. I was explaining how much I hated the cracked, faded linoleum in our kitchen, but my husband refused to do anything about it. The woman looked at me as if I was crazy and said, "Why don't you just call a flooring contractor and get it fixed?" Her suggestion surprised me, even though it made perfect sense.

Going against my husband seemed so defiant and disrespectful. I knew he would be angry if I spent money without his approval. I always gave him a say in every decision, even when doing so made little sense. We had more than enough money to fix the floor. While I thought deferring to him was the polite and correct thing to do, I now realize that it was my codependency in action. I was more concerned about his wishes than my own.

When you are codependent, your inner programming is not like everyone else's. Whereas the average person believes they can assert themselves and get what they want, codependents think we are not allowed the same privilege.

Over time, codependents grow resentful and exhausted. We realize we are endlessly giving away our time and energy to people who don't return the favor. Because we are so willing to give of ourselves freely, we attract energy vampires who gladly take our energy, time, and love without acknowledging or reciprocating the efforts.

If you realize you are codependent, you must take extra precautions when dating. Be aware of your tendency to over-give in relationships. Also, recognize that you may look for validation outside of yourself to prove your worth and soothe your need to feel good enough. If you are seeking external validation from a potential partner, you are likely to end up with a toxic person who uses that need to love bomb and manipulate you.

Codependents sometimes look to relationships as a form of rescue. We buy into the idea of happily ever after and the knight in shining armor rescuing us from all the challenges of life. You must burst the fairy tale bubble and recognize that someone else will not complete you. You are already complete and more than good enough on your own.

The antidotes for codependency are learning to love, self-soothe, and validate yourself. Work on giving yourself the love, time, and attention that you so easily give away to everyone else. Focus on finding balance in your relationships, learning to both give and receive. Refer to the "Resources" section for more information and support on dealing with codependency.

What Are Your Love Languages?

I learned about the five love languages while watching Oprah interview Gary Chapman on "Super Soul Sunday." I had been struggling in my marriage and thought that understanding the love languages could be the solution. I immediately sought the online quiz to determine mine.

Our love languages are essentially the things that another person does that make us feel loved. They are based on what we experienced in childhood.

The five languages, which people prefer in different degrees, include:
* Words of Affirmation (Compliments)
* Quality Time (Undivided Attention)
* Receiving Gifts
* Acts of Service (e.g., cleaning, cooking meals)
* Physical Touch (e.g., holding hands, massage, not necessarily sex)

My dad always gave my mother flowers and thoughtful gifts. He also praised her cooking and regularly acknowledged what a great mother she was. As such, I grew to associate "words of affirmation" and "receiving gifts" as signs that someone loved me. That is exactly what my quiz results showed.

I was so impressed with the accuracy of the information that

I ordered the book, "The 5 Love Languages." I thought if my husband and I could just honor each other's love languages that we would have a more harmonious connection. The trouble in my case was that my husband didn't care how I received love. After learning that information, he told me during marriage counseling that he didn't need to buy me flowers or compliment me.

I didn't realize at the time that he was a narcissist. His response to the information was classic though. Narcissists have no interest in working on themselves or their relationships. It is probably why the marriage therapist looked at me with empathy after three sessions and declared, "I don't think I can help you."

Even though it wasn't able to save my irreparable marriage, understanding the love languages provided excellent insight into my personal needs, as well as general recognition around how people want to be shown love. This is useful information in creating loving interpersonal relationships of all types, from romantic partnerships to positive connections with coworkers.

Once you understand the different love languages, you can often determine what someone's language is just by observing them. For example, if you have a coworker who lights up every time you compliment them, it is likely that "words of affirmation" are one of their love languages. My partner loves to hold hands and cuddle. I recognized before he even took the quiz that one of his primary love languages was "physical touch."

Determining your love language will help you approach your dating experience knowing exactly what you need to feel supported by a new partner. If you meet someone who tells you they hate giving gifts or they can't stand to hold hands, when you know that those are aspects of your love languages, you won't be a good match.

The best way to determine for sure what your love language preferences are is to take the quiz. You can do that online or by ordering the book. See the "Resources" section for more information.

What Is Your Attachment Style?

Attachment theory has become a hot topic in the past decade. According to many relationship experts, our attachment style dictates how we connect with others, particularly in terms of our most intimate relationships.

Theoretically, our attachment style developed as soon as we were born in response to how we interacted with our primary caregiver. For most of us, this would be our birth mother. How we bonded with her supposedly carries through to our adult lives.

Different theories have subtly different names for these attachments. Some theorists only include the first three styles because the fourth is just a combination of two of the primary types. The attachment styles (also called attachment strategies) include:

Secure - The optimal situation, where the individual was raised receiving the love, comfort, and support they needed to feel safe. They are confident in their relationships. They trust that their needs will be met and are comfortable giving their partner independence. They can give and receive love and support easily.

Anxious - The individual does not feel secure in relationships. They are afraid of abandonment and tend to exhibit clingy or needy behavior. They need constant validation and often worry about the relationship.

Avoidant - Again, the individual doesn't feel comfortable in relationships. They tend to push people away. They get suffocated when given too much attention and fear intimacy. They tend to prefer independence and don't enjoy getting too close to others.

Fearful-Avoidant - A combination of the anxious and avoidant types, this person is especially conflicted in relationships. There is a push-pull effect where they are afraid of being in a close relationship, yet they also desperately want to be loved and close to others.

We all have these strategies playing out in different degrees in our relationships. Our dominant style can depend on our life experiences and how aware we are of our behaviors. For instance, someone who has a secure attachment style can grow more anxious or avoidant if they have encountered manipulative people. Furthermore, they can regain their secure attachment style by learning how to self-soothe and establish firmer boundaries.

One of the greatest benefits of understanding attachment styles is that it gives us a framework for understanding why we are exhibiting unhealthy patterns, such as being too clingy or pushing potential partners away. Seeing our patterns clearly can help us correct them so that our relationships are healthier and more balanced.

If you are behaving in anxious ways, you might need to give yourself more comfort and loving support. In contrast, if you are avoidant, wanting to push someone away, you might need to work on being more grounded and receptive.

When we meet someone who has an attachment style that conflicts with ours, their behavior is often very confusing and uncomfortable. Understanding that each of us has slightly different ingrained patterns of interaction is helpful for acceptance and compassion. For example, not every man who is pushing you away is playing games; some may have an avoidant attachment style. While this offers insight, it doesn't warrant seeking a relationship with such a man if you possess an incompatible anxious attachment style. Ideally, we choose a partner who supports our attachment style with ease.

There are online tests for assessing your attachment style. See the "Resources" section for more information.

What Is Your Personality Type?

Learning my personality type completely changed my life. Looking back over past tests from the early years of my career, I used to test as an extrovert, which was definitely not accurate. I previously answered the Myers-Briggs Type Indicator® (MBTI) according to how I thought my employer wanted me to answer.

Sadly, for many years I was trying to be someone I was not.

When I rediscovered personality theory in my late 30s, I was astounded and relieved by how accurately the INFJ personality type explained my behaviors. Supposedly, INFJs are the rarest type. This explained why I have always felt so incredibly different from everyone else. It also provided a greater understanding as to why I am an empath, a trait that is commonly associated with the INFJ type.

Reading through the description provided by 16Personalities.com, I felt a sense of peace come over me. Finally, I could stop fighting my natural inclination for deep introspection and the desire to serve and help others. I could simply surrender to the reality that my traits were an obvious outcome of my inner design. Once I was aware of my inherent strengths and weaknesses, I could work with them to be the best version of myself.

In addition, knowing how I think, feel, and interact with others alerted me to the personality types that work best with mine. Interestingly, my ex-husband possessed the personality type that clashes with my sensitive type the most. It made the end of our marriage that much more understandable.

I used to think that I needed to get along with everyone. However, now that I understand personality theory better, I accept that some types simply can't coexist in harmony. There are aggressive extroverted individuals and even argumentative introverted types who conflict with my desire for kindness and collaboration. I allow myself to maintain a distance from these types for my mental health.

I highly recommend that you take the 16Personalities.com test online to learn your type. It can offer valuable input regarding what you need to thrive in terms of relationships and all areas of life.

What Is Your Astrological Sign?

Astrology has intrigued me since I was a teenager. At that time, I started reading my horoscope in the weekly paper. That was the only access I remember having to information on astrology. I knew I was a Leo, but that didn't mean much until the rise of the internet when information became more readily available.

In my 20s, I started seeking more information on my astrology by ordering reports and delving into my natal chart. What I learned was that as a Leo I am a natural leader who loves to be the center of attention. That assessment initially embarrassed me because I considered those attributes to be arrogant. I don't want to be vain or bossy. Plus, as an introvert, I am much happier working behind the scenes.

I have to accept that despite this fact, I often end up in leadership positions and I do tend to be in the spotlight. I possess some Leo qualities including a strong desire to create and express myself (hence this book)! My Leo traits have also roared in my dating practices. I learned that Leos like when men chase us. I must admit, most men that I dated actively pursued me, even when I resisted their attention at first. I always preferred a more assertive man to one who was timid or noncommittal.

I have read that our sun sign represents how our ego operates in the world, while our rising sign reflects what our soul is trying to achieve. This offers interesting clarity to me because I relate far more to my rising sign of Cancer than I do to my sun sign. Cancers are known to be emotional, sensitive, nurturing, and dedicated to family, which are all traits that I feel I possess and value. I have three planets in Cancer (a stellium), which indicates being empathetic and intuitive.

Your natal chart is the map of where all the planets were at the time of your birth. Although we focus on the sun sign when assessing someone's traits, the placements of all the planets in your chart give a more comprehensive view of who you are. I grow more fascinated the more deeply I dig into my chart. It explains so many elements of my sensitive, yet determined nature.

We will talk about astrology again concerning compatibility. If you are intrigued, I also share my favorite astrologers and astrology sites in the "Resources" section.

What Are Your Relationship Patterns?

Your sensitivities, personal inclinations, and inherent sense of comfort, safety, and love all shape how you interact with others. It is powerful information, particularly in terms of how you experience romantic relationships.

Most of us operate on autopilot, moving through life without fully seeing what is going on around us. This means dysfunction and harmful behaviors escape our radar because they are so normal and familiar. We repeatedly experience unhealthy relationship patterns because we don't even realize they exist.

I had only been with one long-term romantic partner. However, I certainly had many failed friendships and work relationships that pointed out my tendency to over-give, not receive, and then get resentful and exhausted. While I could easily see that I had consistently become enmeshed with narcissists, I wasn't sure why, or how I could break that painful cycle.

I had to take a hard look at what was making me so easy to manipulate and how my innate qualities were playing into the dysfunction I was experiencing. Stepping outside of your own viewpoint to witness your life objectively is challenging and even painful. It is hard to accept accountability for your role when you only ever wanted to be good and do well. However, seeing both sides of the situation is crucial for living a fully empowered life.

Being a sensitive INFJ and an empath with codependent tendencies shapes how I function in the world. I am an overachiever. I have a hard time establishing boundaries. I try desperately to be liked by pretty much everyone I meet, even individuals I don't like. This is a recipe for attracting manipulative people. It took seeing all the pieces to finally reclaim my power and start nurturing healthier, more mutually beneficial relationships. I hope that recognizing and accepting your inherent tendencies and relationship patterns will help you do the same.

Get to the Heart of Who You Are

We delved into some hard questions in Chapter 1 about whether you are ready for online dating. Now we are going even deeper to be sure that you fully know the true "you" that you are bringing to your dating experiences. Please take some time to consider all the core pieces of your personality, upbringing, sensitivities, and insecurities. Then, find a quiet, cozy spot in your home; light a candle; play your favorite, soothing music; settle in with a cup of tea; and journal on the following questions:

How do my sensitivities currently affect my relationships?

How can I use my unique traits to maximize my joy and love in relationships?

What do I need to heal emotionally before getting into a new relationship?

Where might I have blind spots in new relationships (e.g., giving people the benefit of the doubt too often, or not holding boundaries)?

What do I love most about myself?

What traits do I lack that a balanced partnership might provide?

You are amazing! Your upbringing, personality, and even the stars have all aligned to create this one beautiful human. You are loved and lovable exactly as you are. I hope realizing that gives you great clarity, support, and encouragement. Everyone on this planet is here for a reason. The world needs all types of people, especially sensitive types like you. I know sensitivity often feels like a curse. I hope you can now reflect on this attribute as a valuable part of who you are. Your ideal partner will honor and support your unique nature so that together you can fulfill your life purpose.

Chapter 12: Determine What You Want

There are many reasons for being in online dating that run the gamut from simply finding someone to go out to dinner with, to establishing a loving, long-term partnership. Your initial reason for dating might change depending on the people you meet or what is happening in your life. That is all fine. You are always in control.

Regardless, it is always good to get clear with yourself on what you want. Your intentions always shape your efforts and support your outcomes, so please take some time to consider why you (and the men you meet online) are putting yourselves out there.

In my experience, the core reasons for utilizing online dating include the following.

Connection

At the most basic level, everyone online is looking for some form of connection. Arguably, that's what all humans crave. We all just want to be seen and heard. There is nothing wrong with initially using online dating to meet new people, chat, and feel things out. Not everyone is looking for love or even a partner. Some people just want someone to talk to or a distraction from the mundane aspects of life.

I mentioned with disgust that there are many bored men online who will waste your time with texting and no actual dates. That was a jaded statement on my part. I wanted to have more than just connection. My profile clearly stated that which is why I found those types of men to be so frustrating.

If you decide you are only ready for connection at first, and you are not sure you want to be all in, that is perfectly normal. Just be clear with your intentions when you interact with men. Let them know you are just testing things out.

Be warned, some men will be angry at this. They will see your presence online as disingenuous. This is where you have to be clear in your profile that you aren't looking for anything serious. If a man is mad because he didn't read your profile, that's on him.

Most apps have the option to denote that you are just looking for friends. Another warning here; men rarely honor that request. I went through a period right after being ghosted where I wasn't ready to date again, but I went online seeking connection. I said in my profile, and again when men messaged me, that I was just looking for friends. In every case that a man started chatting with me in a friendly manner, he always ended up saying something sexual like, "I really wish I could cuddle you right now," or "I am a really good kisser. I might change your mind."

This happened at least four times before I deactivated my profile and realized I was better off connecting with friends and family. I love being friends with men. However, I have had to accept that very few men can handle a strictly platonic relationship with women. It is possible, of course, just not likely.

Entertainment (Casual Dating)

Similar to simple connection, many people are not looking for anything deep. They are just looking to have fun. We usually refer to this as "casual dating." When I first started online dating, I was more focused on entertainment than love or companionship. I wanted to try new restaurants, go to concerts, and hike trails in my new town. My heart still felt bruised. The idea of finding true love seemed like a distant possibility. Having fun was a much easier goal.

The first two men I started messaging with online did not seem fun at all! They were parents to teenagers, and they complained about all the nonstop responsibilities in their lives. I offered them compassion, but after a few weeks of messaging, I felt drained. I wished them well and told them we didn't seem to be on the same life path.

Then, I met the narcissist that I ultimately dated for five months. He was fun personified. He was silly and outgoing, the perfect fit for me at the time. On our first date, we laughed non-stop. He said to the server, "We're on a first date and I'm killing it!" Typical narcissist, but a funny and entertaining one, I must admit.

I initially had reservations about him, and even let him know, requesting that we just be friends to start. He agreed. However, a month later he invited me to my dream concert. It was a bucket list event. He picked me up at my office with a basket filled with gluten-free treats and wine. At the concert, he danced with me on the grass singing a love song in my ear. *How could I resist?*

Even though I look back at that relationship with dismay, because I never saw all the very blatant narcissistic patterns, I can't say I regret it. We had lots of fun and that helped me greatly on my healing path.

Seeking a partner for entertainment is a healthy goal if you are new to the dating scene. It is far less pressure. The worst thing that can happen is that you don't have as much fun as you'd like. In that case, just keep looking.

Sex (Hook-Ups)

As mentioned, I was a bit of a prude when I joined online dating. Shortly after getting married my husband lost interest in sex. Over time, I did too. You can't miss what you never really had. I didn't even know what genuine passion felt like. I had become his mother, cleaning up after him and managing all the household tasks. There was nothing sexy about our relationship. As such, I grew to underestimate the male libido.

I was shocked and somewhat disgusted to learn how brazenly sexual most men are online. I know this sounds naïve. I did still live in the real world where movies and TV are highly sexually charged. I just didn't believe that men (and women) were so sexually driven in real life.

If you are like me, this might be a shock for you too. A large majority of men in online dating are primarily looking for sex or hook-ups. Some will be honest about it through explicit profiles and suggestive photos, but many will seem sweet and innocent until they have made their way into your phone.

I never received a "dick pic." I consider that a success. I can't imagine why a man would think that is a good idea, yet many do. I've heard lots of stories of women in their 20s and 30s regularly receiving naked photos from men. The consensus is that if this happens it warrants promptly blocking that person. You could explain to them that you find that kind of behavior to be inappropriate. However, I suspect anyone doing that has lost a grasp of what is appropriate and nothing you say is going to change that. Try not to get hurt or disgusted, rather see the absurdity of it all. At least the man showed you what kind of person he was.

Of course, these warnings are the prude in me talking. If you want a purely sexual relationship, that is your business. I hope you know by now that I am 100% on your team. I only want the best for you.

As long as it is safe and consensual, I see nothing wrong with using online dating apps to fulfill your sexual needs. We are all human and we have the same biological needs (to varying degrees). Just please be aware of your sexual health and use protection. My OB-GYN warned me when I first got divorced that many women just out of long-term relationships are lax and unaware of the rampant nature of diseases like HPV.

As I've said before, the key to being ethical online is to express your intentions clearly and honestly. Seeking a solely sexual relationship is only acceptable if both parties agree and no one's emotions are going to get hurt.

However, please recognize that as a sensitive woman it is exceptionally difficult for you to remove your emotions and feelings from a physical connection. This is true for everyone, but certainly more so for an empath or HSP. When we establish a physical connection with another person, our energies intertwine. This energetic connection is especially difficult to break. So be mindful that you are combining your energies with every intimate connection.

If sex is the last thing you are looking for, you want to be clear about that too. Be very direct in your profile that you are not looking for just a physical connection. This is often enough to weed out the sexually focused men. Yet again, some men will take that as a challenge and try to convince you otherwise. This is why it is important not to get attached to anyone until you are sure they are totally on the same page as you.

Companionship

Those who are looking for companionship want the full package of connection, entertainment, and sex, minus true love. They are committed to finding a partner, but they aren't necessarily seeking romantic, life-changing love.

I would guess that most people who want a committed relationship are looking for companionship. Having a companion makes life easier. It means you have someone to face life's joys and challenges with. A healthy companion makes everything better. It is a wonderful and attainable goal to strive for when starting online dating.

True Love

As little girls, we are encouraged to crave a true love connection. It is the stuff of fairy tales and Disney movies. However, by the time we reach our 30s, many of us have given up on that goal. Either we haven't found it or we thought we found it and it turned out to not be what we expected.

I thought my marriage was a true love connection. I clung to that hope throughout the 17 years we were together. Once it was over, I felt numb over the reality that my husband never truly loved me. At best, he enjoyed the outward pieces of me that made him look good. That was heartbreaking to accept. For the first several months after we agreed to divorce, I felt an actual ache in my heart that cycled through pain and numbness.

Despite this pain, I had a thread of hope in my heart that I could find true love. I think it was always on my mind from the moment I started online dating. However, I set my sights much lower at first, which was probably a wise goal.

When you are first setting out in online dating, it is much easier to seek companionship or entertainment. This will allow you to test the waters a bit or "kiss a few frogs," as my mom would say.

After cycling on and off the dating apps (because I was in actual relationships or taking a much-needed break), I found that love was like a muscle. The more I exercised giving and receiving love, the better I was at recognizing and nurturing it.

Just to be clear, the love depicted in the movies, the "love at first sight," or the cheesy romantic lines, are not at all indicative of genuine love. In fact, "love at first sight" is most likely a toxic attraction. It seems to be the natural inclination of an empath when they meet a narcissist. It is as if the narcissist's darkness draws in the empath's light. This is what I experienced when I first met my husband. It is also how I felt after one of my first dates. It is eerie how powerful the energetic feelings can be even though the attraction is unhealthy.

Because genuine love takes time to build, seeking that kind of deep connection right away can lead to trouble. While I think it is important to honor your own needs and I firmly believe that everyone needs and deserves love, I caution you to pace yourself in that quest. Mind intention is powerful. If you set out looking for true love, you will find it.

Be sure that you are truly ready for that deep of a connection. Many women believe they want to find their true love connection, but aren't willing to put in the effort to nurture such an important relationship. Take heart, most people aren't ready right away, and will grow into that state over time and with effort. We will go into this further in Phase 3.

How Do You Want to Date?

Now that you've thought about what you want to achieve in your online dating experience, it is important to get clear on how you want to approach the dating process. There are no right or wrong answers here. You just want to stay true to who you are and what you prefer. As an introvert, I found it hard to message with too many men at once. Once I went out on a date with someone and determined I liked him, that was it for me. I didn't date multiple people at the same time. That was just my preference.

Many experts suggest dating several men at once so you know you aren't settling. That is wise advice. I just couldn't follow it because it made me feel very uncomfortable. You always have to do what feels best for you.

The following questions will help you assess how you want to date online:

* *Will you date multiple men at once?*

* *Will you talk with multiple men at once?*

* *How do you prefer to communicate (e.g., text, phone, video chat)?*

* *How long do you want to text with someone before meeting him?*

* *Do you feel comfortable asking a man out, or do you want him to make the first move?*

* *How do you want to feel when interacting with a new man?*

Identifying how you want to feel is a great way to shift your energy and set an intention. Do you want passion, comfort, or humor?

Once you are clear on how you want to date and feel, you must stay true to yourself. You can always change your mind. Just don't let anyone change it for you. To prevent this, try to express your dating preferences right away or at least once you feel ready to give a man your phone number. At the very least, let him know how you prefer to communicate. I appreciated at least a daily check-in text once I felt we were starting a relationship. If a man went a day or two and didn't text, I felt that was a sign that he wasn't into me. There are certainly men who just don't like to text, so get clear on that to avoid hurt feelings.

Dating should never make you feel confused or dejected. The right man will honor your needs and meet you right where you are. Asking for regular texts, or even asking for space, is not crazy or odd if it is what you prefer. Again, just be sure to express it clearly. Men can't read our minds. When we hold that expectation, things often go awry.

Consider Love Role Models

As you are thinking about what you want from, and how you will experience, online dating, consider the loving relationships you would like to emulate. There is power in being able to recognize what you are looking for in true living color.

I am very grateful for the loving partnerships I observed in my life. My parents had a great partnership. I have siblings who also have strong marriages. The odd thing is that when I was ready to settle down, I didn't strive for the same type of connections that I observed. I settled for a less than ideal partnership, thinking that what I was experiencing was the supposed magic of opposites attracting. I also believed what he told me, that I was just too sensitive and the romantic love I craved wasn't realistic.

While I was still married, I completed my master's degree and later became a coordinator for the college. Throughout that time, I met a group of very caring, empathetic men. They displayed total love and devotion for their significant others. It warmed my heart to observe men speaking highly of their partners. It made me cringe, however, when I realized my husband never spoke of me or treated me in such a loving manner. As I mentioned before, I had thought that men just didn't have the emotional depth that I needed. The men I met at the college changed my opinion. Suddenly, accepting less became harder. That was a powerful and important shift for me.

At first, I used the information I was observing to nurture a more loving connection with my husband. This included the help of a marriage counselor. When that did nothing to improve our situation, I had to accept that I would be much better off on my own, rather than feeling the constant anguish of knowing I wasn't loved and supported in the manner I deserved.

At the beginning of my online dating journey, I worked with a young woman who was completing her master's degree. She was totally in love with her fiancé. When she talked about him, her entire being lit up. One evening before we were heading out for the day, I overheard her talking to him on the phone. He had offered to pick up dinner. Flustered from all of her work and school obligations, she let out a sigh and said, "Yes. That will make my life easier." I couldn't help but smile. The thought of finding someone who would make my life easier gave me so much hope.

I'm not suggesting you covet someone else's husband or even seek to claim what someone else has. That, of course, is not a healthy or ethical mindset. Instead, you want to recognize what appeals to you, so that you can set your intention on the type of partnership you want to attract.

You made it! You finished the hardest part of this book, accepting the harsh reality of what is waiting for you online. Now we get into the more positive, fun aspect of actually getting out there armed with the tools for successfully creating the relationship you desire.

So, I'll ask you one more time before we proceed to Phase 2 — are you ready to put yourself first and demand that your needs are met throughout the dating process? If you aren't there yet, please take some time to get clearer on setting your boundaries, recognizing your self-worth, and committing to yourself fully. You are always in control. Let that be your mantra as you move forward.

Phase 2: Put Yourself Out There

Yahoo! You are ready to get on out there. I know what I've shared so far had a negative edge to it. I wanted to warn you so that you would prepare for the worst. As I said, I encountered practically every dating pitfall out there. Some of that is probably par for the course. It is a bit of a learning curve.

Armed with what you now know, you won't have such a steep learning curve. You are prepared for the red flags, the games, the players, and all the odd behavior that is unfathomable to your compassionate heart. By accepting and honoring the truth around the bad, you can more easily recognize and nurture the good when it arrives.

Chapter 13: Review the Dating Sites

The dating apps are constantly changing. Understanding their technical aspects is far less important than understanding what you are likely to encounter from the men using them. You can easily do some research on the details of an app before ever setting up a profile. So, I will leave that part up to you.

What I am sharing here is just my experience using the various apps. I tried some of the most popular choices and had somewhat different results on each. I share them below in order of my preference. Try as many as you like. They are just tools for finding your partner. They are not as important to your success as how you show up when using them.

Match.com

In my experience, Match.com was the most effective dating app. It led to the most dates and provided the most consistent interactions. When I was a subscriber, I was meeting new people every week. There were far more men on Match.com than any of the other apps/sites I tried.

The free version is useless, which is an advantage over the other apps. It means that anyone active on Match.com has made a monetary investment. Like so many things in life, people don't value, or even take seriously, the things they can have for free. The modest cost of a monthly subscription is a small price to pay if it means you can weed out time-wasting scammers.

I preferred using websites to apps. I tried the Match.com app for a short period, but I found I repeatedly "liked" profiles by mistake. In addition, the constant alerts every time someone liked or messaged me were overwhelming. It felt so intrusive. Therefore, I used the website exclusively, at set times, usually at night after work or on the weekend. Most men are online during those times as well.

One major caveat for Match.com is that you can't always trust the information they share, particularly in terms of who is online and active. At the end of my first three-month subscription, I met a man who seemed nice. I told him that my subscription was expiring, and I was going to be taking a break for a while, but if he was interested in communicating, we could do so by phone. We started texting and continued to do so for a few weeks.

He was one of the many men who did a lot of texting, sending me photos of himself and his kids, but never asking me out. One night he texted me and said, "How's it going being off Match? LOL" I was confused and asked him why he asked. He sent me back a screenshot he'd just taken showing my profile with a green active dot over it, which meant that I was supposedly online at that moment. I was shocked. I hadn't been online in weeks and thought I had paused my account. I went into the account right away, deleted all of my pictures, and put a note in my profile saying I was no longer a subscriber. I didn't want anyone to think they were contacting me and I was just ignoring them.

Learning that gave me a great deal of perspective. How many times had I contacted men, and they didn't answer because they weren't actually on the site anymore? While I was assuming they weren't interested, which was dejecting, I could reframe the story to believe that they never got my message. I hope you will benefit from this knowledge. Never completely trust the information a site shares. Furthermore, if you want your account offline, take down as many pictures and details from your profile as possible.

OkCupid

I found OkCupid to be the most fun and informative dating site. I never used the app, just the website on my computer.

I joined the free version of OkCupid shortly after moving into a new home. I wasn't sure I wanted to pay the money for a dating subscription, but I was longing for connection.

The site asks a wide variety of interesting and entertaining questions which are used to assess your compatibility with the men on the site. You can then sort your matches by those who have the highest compatibility. Theoretically, that weeded out some of the work of trying to determine if someone had common interests. However, as with anything, it isn't foolproof. Some men answer the questions the way they think women want them to.

Regardless, I love to learn about people, so I enjoyed reading the answers men gave. I met two of the men I dated seriously using OkCupid. One was a busy parent who never really had time for me. The other was a covert narcissist, who ultimately made me very uncomfortable. That man approached me twice. The first time I felt very overwhelmed and even uncomfortable about his energy. He messaged me saying something dramatic like, "Are you ready to actually be loved?" I told him that while that sounded lovely, I wasn't on the same page. It wasn't that I didn't want to be loved as he suggested, it is just that by then I knew that anyone using such a bold line was not likely to be genuine. I kick myself for not trusting that first instinct, giving him another chance when he contacted me again several months later.

I met several men through OkCupid who were younger than me. I didn't feel like we had much in common. Still, we messaged for a while through the app as friends. There was an option for just looking for friends. Some men there did honor that intention.

Plenty of Fish

I was very leery about setting up a profile on Plenty of Fish. As I mentioned previously, the first time I did I was bombarded with spam messages before I even had any pictures or details posted. I realized spamming was more common there than through the paid apps.

However, I met a woman who had met her husband on the site, so I decided it was worth a shot. There were many men on the app, so it was worth trying once I learned to delete the messages that had no substance.

I only met one man with whom I communicated seriously on Plenty of Fish. We messaged for about a week before setting up a meeting at a Panera Bread. I felt very comfortable with him and we chatted like we'd known each other for years. I thought we were really connecting. However, it quickly became clear that he didn't have time to date. During our first date, he candidly shared that his marriage had ended because he hadn't paid enough attention to his wife. This was one of those cases where he told me everything I needed to know about him right away. When he missed our second date because of working late, I accepted he was a workaholic who hadn't learned that partnership takes effort.

I met another man through the app who seemed great, but he turned into one of the worst dates I ever had. We met up at a casino for a free concert. He showed up drunk, talked through the show, and kept telling me I was too thin.

I can't blame Plenty of Fish for the quality of men that I encountered. Nevertheless, I believe that since it has a lot of free features, it doesn't attract men who are fully vested in the idea of meeting someone for a long-term connection.

Bumble

The supposed appeal of Bumble is that women get to make the first move. While that seems great in theory, I found it to be oddly challenging. There is only an app, which meant that I couldn't hide behind my computer the way I preferred. In addition, there is only a small space to write about yourself and your hobbies. So, while it is supposed to be empowering for women, I found it frustrating. How can you possibly assess if someone is a good match if all you have are a few pictures and a one-sentence description? I only lasted on the app for about two weeks before I gave up.

In that time, I swiped through many profiles, not finding any I could truly connect with on looks alone. I ultimately matched and messaged with three men based on what they had shared in their brief bio. One was someone who was on a business trip! He showed up in my feed simply because the app uses your physical location to find eligible men.

If you don't respond quickly to messages (I believe it was within 24 hours) the messages disappear. That felt like far too much pressure for me. Plus, it meant that two of the men quickly asked for my phone number so that our messages wouldn't disappear. I ended up giving that information even though I wasn't sure how I felt about them.

Both men turned out to be poor matches. I spoke with one on the phone for over an hour. He was polite in every way and spoke to me as though we were strictly platonic friends, never implying he was even attracted to me. The next day he texted saying he wished he could cuddle with me. His total change in tone was disappointing. I developed very little tolerance for men who weren't honest with their intentions. Hiding behind flirty or sexual texts felt so cowardly. I let him know I only wanted to communicate with people who could be open with their intentions. He apologized, and I felt bad about how it played out. Still, I held my boundary. I'm glad I did. When I met my current partner, I never had to question his intentions. He was always clear and direct about being attracted to me and wanting to pursue a relationship.

MeetMindful

I had almost forgotten that I tried MeetMindful.com because there was so little interaction on it. I'm throwing it in as an honorable mention.

The premise of the site is that it connects individuals who live a mindful-based lifestyle. This somewhat broad term could mean people who are spiritual, into meditation, or otherwise focused on a more connection-based view of dating. True connection and mindful dating were exactly what I wanted. I was thrilled by this app's potential. Yet, after a few weeks of no interactions, I had to accept that there were very few men actively on the site.

It doesn't hurt to sign up for a free profile and hope for the best, which is what I did. I had one nice, quiet man reach out to me unexpectedly several months after I signed up. We went on two dates. He was probably a great catch for someone, yet he didn't have enough time for me and there wasn't a spark. If you live in an urban area, there might be a bigger pool of men. However, I would not get your hopes up for this app.

eharmony

I was excited about eharmony. I bought into all the ads about how they match people based on compatibility, so it was the first dating site I tried. As someone very interested in personality theory, I thought it was the perfect way to find a connection. What a complete and total disappointment!

I let my enthusiasm and naiveté cloud my judgment, signing up for a six-month membership. It was expensive but far more economical than paying month-to-month. I rationalized I was getting a good deal. What I hadn't considered was the fact that there were not enough men willing to pay the high subscription rate, which meant there was a small pool of viable candidates.

I was disappointed to find that at any given time there were only around a dozen or so men in my geographical area who were compatible. What was even worse is that most of those men never responded to my messages. It was incredibly disheartening. I felt like I was destined to be alone. When I joined Match.com a few weeks later, I was surprised by how much attention I was receiving from the many men there. At that point, I realized that even if eharmony had a great matching formula, they were not a good choice for anyone outside of a heavily populated area. It also seemed that some profiles were fake or inactive because they would show up and disappear within days.

The one man I met from the site had found a loophole to the expensive subscription. He jumped on during one of the free weekends, messaged me, and immediately gave me his Gmail account. On our first date, he admitted he couldn't afford the subscription, or dinner for that matter.

When I contacted customer service to complain about my lack of matches, they forced my account to look at a wider geographical area. This meant that I started getting messages from men who lived in other states and were much too far for me to consider. I wanted a partner who I could see easily, not someone who was just a long-distance pen pal. I again contacted customer service to no avail. They kept repeating their no refund policy, completely unconcerned by how dissatisfied I was. As such, I would not suggest you use their service.

Tinder

I never tried Tinder despite its popularity. It has such a negative reputation for being a hook-up site, that I couldn't even bring myself to sign up. From what I understand, the platform is like Bumble in that there isn't much room for discussing yourself and your hobbies. You can only post photos and a simple statement about yourself. I have a friend who identifies as a lesbian. She has met many people through the app, including some that she dated seriously. It works for some people. Just recognize that you are likely to encounter people who are only looking for a sexual connection.

Remember that the apps and sites are just tools you are using to find the right person. Use those that feel most comfortable to you in the manner that gives you the most control. Try not to get consumed in checking your messages or "likes" all day long. Set a designated time when you can focus your attention on your dating efforts. This will create a helpful and healthy boundary between you and the online world.

Chapter 14: Set Up a Successful Profile

My profile evolved dramatically over time. In the beginning, I sounded sickeningly sweet and innocent. I had a long list of the things that I love, including animals, sunsets, children, gluten-free pizza, and Sauvignon Blanc. I threw in that I loved to laugh and smile. One jerk messaged me just to say that everyone loved to laugh. While I didn't appreciate his comment, I had to recognize it was mostly true. As time went on, I got better at representing myself in an authentic, yet not overly sweet manner. I realized that coming across as too nice was a sure-fire way to attract manipulators.

You can, and should, come across as friendly. However, it is even more important to be clear on what you are looking for in a potential partner. Your profile should aim to attract your ideal partner while repelling the jerks. Remember that while it is tempting to cast a wide net, you are better off appealing only to the men that are the most likely to be your best fit.

Check out the Competition

It is wise to check out what the competition is doing. This is a recommendation I received from one of my first dates, who had been online for years. We were talking candidly about how strange the dating process was. I asked him whether my pictures were appropriate or too sexy. He laughed and said that many women had cleavage shots and my pictures were very modest. He suggested I set up a fake profile so that I could see what other women were posting. I was intrigued. I knew it would help my confidence a bit if I had a perspective on what other women were doing.

Using a Gmail account, I created a basic free account as a woman looking for men. I didn't include any photos and left as much information blank as possible. The last thing I wanted to do was draw attention from an unsuspecting man. I only used this fake account once for my research purposes. It was very eye-opening.

As my date had said, women had far more revealing photos than I expected. Many had very close-up selfies taken at an interesting angle. They were often in low-cut or tight clothing. Many had what one man who messaged me called the "duck face," which was a seemingly sexy, kissy face. As that man said, it looked more comical than attractive.

That man messaged me to say he liked how genuine my profile seemed. It was strong validation of what I am sharing here. Men looking for a connection, and not just sex, appreciate honest profiles of genuine women.

Another thing I noticed is that some women looked like airbrushed models. That had me a little on edge. How could I ever compete? It took me a while to realize that their stunning appearance resulted from using filters on their photos. I didn't know that was even possible until my best friend showed me a filter on Snapchat. I was shocked at how it softened my features and gave me the look I had seen in those other dating profiles. Suddenly it made sense why so many men had stated in their profiles, "Please don't use filters on your photos."

It also made it clear why almost every man that I met in person seemed relieved when we met for our first date. They all told me horror stories of women who looked nothing like their profiles. That seemed so odd to me. Why try to lie about something like that? You are only going to irritate and anger the man once you meet. Trust me on that. These men were all very angry about being tricked. The last thing you want is to start a relationship based on a lie.

The profiles that I found appealing were all happy, smiling women doing something active. They didn't share too much information but kept it light and fun. I am not a traveler, but that was a very common focus. Many women had pictures of themselves on vacation, out hiking, or with a pet. These all seemed like effective ways to show that you are fun and adventurous.

My photos at that time were static, posed shots of me dressed up for special occasions. After seeing how great other women's more real-life shots were, I added a few selfies that were more reflective of what I look like on a daily basis.

Do a Life Inventory

Your profile is similar to a resumé and cover letter. Instead of trying to get a job interview, you are trying for a first date. You have very little space to highlight all your best qualities, so you have to get clear about what you want someone to know about you.

Taking a "life inventory" is a good first step in deciding what to include in your profile. Write out a list of all the traits that make you unique. Get detailed and creative. You won't use all these elements. However, by being thorough you are giving yourself a wide range of material to choose from. This list can also be helpful when you are preparing to talk about yourself on your first date and beyond. Following are some items that are helpful to include:

* Your career and personal passions
* Your favorite things: types of music, TV shows, movies, books, activities, food, and restaurants
* Your hobbies and pets
* Your children and family
* Any personality traits that feel important to share (i.e., Are you shy and introverted, or extroverted and talkative?)
* Your spiritual & political beliefs (Some apps ask for these, but you can choose to avoid these topics completely if they make you uncomfortable.)

Think Like a Man

Your profile should highlight your most interesting qualities, as well as what you are looking for in a relationship. It must also stand out from the sea of other women. As such, it is important to put yourself in the shoes of the type of man you are trying to attract.

Men are not necessarily interested in every little detail of your life. They want to envision what it might be like to spend time with you, or how well you will fit into their world. They want to know if you are fun and willing to try new things.

If they have children, they want to know that you will welcome their children into your life. If they enjoy adventurous activities like riding a motorcycle, they want to know that you might be willing to hop on the back of a bike. Men are more playful and activity-driven than women tend to be. We must appeal to their playful spirit as much as possible.

That of course doesn't mean lying about your interests. It means thinking about how the activities you enjoy could mesh with a man. For example, if you don't enjoy watching football, but you do love cooking up appetizers for the game, share that. Most men love to be nurtured in that way. I don't love to cook, but I had quite a few men ask me if I did. Cooking and baking are appealing qualities you should highlight if you enjoy them.

Men love the girl next door, the authentic woman who isn't afraid to be herself. Try to be as relatable and down-to-earth as possible. Share your silly side.

After you have written a draft of your profile, ask a male friend or friend's husband to offer their honest opinion. My partner did this with his profile, asking a friend's wife for insight. She softened his language, so it was more welcoming. That change obviously worked, because the warmth of his words drew me in.

Men think differently than women. You need to remember that when trying to appeal to the opposite sex.

Create a Powerful Profile

Most of the apps include suggestions for setting up your profile. Since each app includes room for slightly different information, check out the app's "Help" page before creating your profile. You can also Google "sample dating profiles." There is a lot of information available on the topic.

You can set up a draft of your profile text as a Word document from which you can copy and paste when you are ready to launch your actual profile. Using your "life inventory," pick the key pieces of information that you are most excited about sharing.

Don't be too concerned with getting your profile perfect. It will inevitably change over time as you recognize what is working and what isn't (i.e., if you are attracting the wrong type of man). Changing your profile regularly is a good practice. It alerts the app/site that you are an active user, which means it will serve your profile in men's feeds more frequently.

On that note, when you first join an app you are treated like the new woman in town. The app will typically feature your profile prominently for the first few days leading to a great deal of attention. Prepare for this initial onslaught by only posting during a period when you know you will have time to answer messages (i.e., over the weekend). Since this is the time you are making your first impression with the largest number of men, it is also best to have all the information in your profile complete.

Following are some simple tips for creating a profile that will help you succeed on all the apps:

Plan for Privacy - If you are concerned about sharing your personal information, you must put some privacy measures in place as you prepare your profile. For instance, if you are opting to use a special phone number or email address specifically for dating, be sure to set that up in advance. When you sign up, you will also need to choose a screen name. Don't use your actual name if possible. A clever or intriguing name that relates to your life works best. You can also select a neighboring town as your location to make it more difficult to locate you, while still keeping your matches geographically appropriate.

Exude Confidence - Everything is energy! Your vibration attracts men to you. This doesn't just mean being positive, it means being strong and confident. You want to draw in confident, positive men, so hold that intention every time you interact online. Before you even start working on your profile, listen to some empowering music and think about all the great qualities you possess. I have a Spotify playlist you might enjoy. You can find the link in the "Resources" section. It may feel weird at first, but saying positive "I am" statements can help (e.g., I am strong. I am smart. I am brave. I am kind. I am beautiful. I am lovable. I am AMAZING!)

Be Unique - Once you have checked out what other women are doing, choose to be different. Include a meaningful quote or reference a line from a favorite song. Talk about a favorite vacation or a local restaurant that you enjoy. One of my favorite profiles was from a man who said he was looking for a relationship like Doug and Carrie on "King of Queens." I love that show and felt his goal was sweet and relatable.

After tiring of the mindless texting, I included a meme with my profile pictures that said something like, "I hate small talk. I want to talk about atoms, magic, the meaning of life, music, memories, what keeps you up at night...I like people with depth who speak with emotion. I don't want to just know what's up." That drew in more interesting, introspective men who also craved deep conversations.

Be Funny - Everyone loves to laugh, as a snarky man once reminded me. Capitalize on that connecting force by including humor in your profile. On OkCupid, there was a question about a favorite classic movie. I wrote, "The Wizard of Oz was one of my favorites, even though the flying monkeys FREAKED ME OUT!" A man messaged me saying that those monkeys freaked him out too. That's all it took for us to connect. We ultimately ended up dating for several months.

As I mentioned, my profile started out far too sickeningly

sweet. Over time, I changed it to reflect how I might speak to someone on a date. I included an "old school list of turn-ons and turn-offs" that shared some of my values written playfully.

Be Authentic - People can sense authenticity. If you are being your honest self, you are far more likely to attract the person who will like you just as you are. This means trying not to filter yourself.

Keep refining what you are looking for in a man based on what you are learning from your online interactions. For instance, as I realized that indecisive, noncommittal men were not for me, I stated that I wanted "a man who knew what he wanted and wasn't afraid to go for it." This immediately changed the type of man that messaged me to those who were more confident and assertive.

Include A Mix of Your Best Photos - If you don't have photos that you like, ask a friend to help you set up a photo shoot. Pick out your favorite outfits and do your hair and makeup. Then take as many pictures as necessary to get at least three to five that make you feel great. It might even be worth seeking the help of a local photographer.

Try to include a mix of posed photos, casual selfies, and at least one picture of you doing something you enjoy (e.g., hiking, visiting an art gallery, baking cookies). After I moved into my house, I took a selfie just after painting my bedroom. My hair was tucked up into a baseball cap and I had paint on my face. It was not very flattering. Still, several men commented that they loved that I was into DIY. It is great to have honest photos that show who you genuinely are.

Please be mindful of your background when taking selfies. So many men had awful selfies taken in the bathroom of their gym or in their messy bedroom. Not only does it look bad, but it can give away personal information about what locations you frequent.

Keep your photos current and make sure they look like you.

Finally, don't wear sunglasses so that men can see your eyes. The eyes are the feature that connects us with others most deeply.

Be Clear and Direct - As I mentioned several times, once I had enough of all the endless texting, I put in a note at the end of my profile stating that anyone interested in me should read my full profile and be prepared to ask me out. You might want to say something more neutral like, "Please be prepared to talk on the phone to see if there is a connection." Men who are not interested in playing games respond well to clear direction. They will appreciate knowing exactly where you stand and what you are looking for. I always included a statement about looking for more than a physical connection, so that was abundantly clear.

Get Feedback - I asked every man I met in person what they thought of my profile and my pictures. I appreciated the constructive feedback. I constantly changed my profile as I realized what was working. As I mentioned, when I first started online I had several posed pictures where I was dressed up for special events. While men often commented on how beautiful I looked, a few men I met told me those pictures intimidated them because they thought I was someone who dressed up all the time. Keep in mind that most people are very literal. They will think that how you present yourself in your profile is how you are most of the time.

General Profile Tips

There is always new information popping up on the internet about what works for attracting the opposite sex. Two somewhat funny points to consider are: 1. Men seem to like women dressed in red, and 2. Liking guacamole is a positive for most people. I used both tips, and they garnered attention. I had a list of my favorite foods and when I added guacamole, which I do love, several men commented on it right away! My most popular photo was also one of me in a tunic with red leggings. I'm squinting from laughing, which made me think it wasn't my best shot. However, most men I asked said they liked that one the best. To this day, my partner keeps that photo on his phone as my contact picture. When I asked him why he liked that one so much, he said it was because I looked so happy.

Again, make sure your profile is clear about what you want in a partner. Your profile is where you can share if you are looking for someone to go to concerts with or if you want a long-term relationship. You should also be clear about what kind of man you prefer. If you work in a professional job and prefer someone similar, state that clearly. Because I had been married to a white-collar professional who hadn't been a good fit, I was open to all types of men, including those with blue-collar jobs. If that won't work for you, it is better to state that so that you don't waste anyone's time.

Like the apps, your profile is just the tool used to establish an initial connection. Don't get too consumed with making it perfect or including every detail of your life. Consider what details would attract you and make you want to learn more about someone. Focus on sharing that type of information. Remember, you can change it as often as you like. Feel free to get creative and experiment.

Chapter 15: Consider Compatibility

In Phase 1, we delved deeply into aspects of who you are and what you want in a relationship. As you put yourself out into the dating world, this information is crucial for assessing your potential compatibility with the men you meet.

I didn't think very much about compatibility when I first started online dating. I had the sense that after a failed marriage and very little dating experience, I was going to need to meet many men to determine exactly what kind of man was a healthy match. While that is true, and it ultimately worked out for me, I believe you can save yourself some time and heartache by considering compatibility.

Compatibility is both an art and a science. It is a complex mix of logic and practicality, teamed with chemistry and intrigue. There is no perfect formula for compatibility. There are ways, however, to maximize your chances of recognizing a compatible relationship.

Sometimes the connection is obvious, as in the instance of my sister and her husband. They are both marine biologists who live for the ocean. When they first met, the physical attraction, combined with their values and shared life's passion, made their compatibility clear. Other times the best matches are not necessarily "good on paper," they just work.

You must give in a little to the mystery of compatibility. Often, genuine compatibility is just something you feel because it brings a sense of peace and ease. You feel at home in the person's presence. Healthy compatibility encompasses the full range of your emotional, spiritual, and physical needs. Following are some of the basics of genuine compatibility.

Healthy Compatibility is Rare

The first man I met in person after starting online dating gave me some wise advice. He said, "Not everyone is for everyone." This is crucial to remember, as you will meet a wide variety of new people, most of whom will not be right for you. True compatibility is rare and worth waiting for.

My codependent tendencies caused me to want to be liked by every man I met, even the ones I knew weren't right for me. Given this strong subconscious drive, I felt dejected when men didn't respond to my messages or ghosted me after communicating.

Since then I have realized that rejection is not a reflection of my worth. You can be the most delicious, refreshing cup of tea, yet you will still not be the "cup of tea" for a man who only drinks coffee.

I wish I had known then how easy, comfortable, and uplifting a healthy relationship is. Now that I have that kind of effortless connection with my current partner, I am grateful that so many incompatible men rejected me. Even though it felt like heartache, my heart was actually being spared the pain of fighting for a relationship that wasn't meant to be.

Your Relationship Successes Offer Insight

Look to your current and past positive relationships for clues on the types of people you get along with best. For example, do you gravitate to friends who are talkative and outgoing or to those who are quiet and reserved? Perhaps you recognize that your best friend is exactly like you and you appreciate that connection because it is so easy to relate to one another.

This is helpful information to consider when seeking a compatible romantic relationship. It speaks to what is familiar and comfortable for you. What kind of people do you enjoy being with? Which of your friends brings out the best in you? Try to get clear on the traits that your healthy partnerships possess.

I enjoy being with friends who are good listeners and positive cheerleaders. I endured friendships and romantic relationships that didn't possess those qualities and they never worked. I now won't accept anything less from the people I let into my inner world.

Understanding Introversion and Extroversion is Key

Most of the time people do better with a partner who shares the same primary way of interacting with the world. Introverts typically need more quiet, alone time, while extroverts prefer being out with others.

This isn't an absolute rule, however. Some introvert/extrovert matches work well. My partner is an ENFP, the most introverted of the extroverts. He is outgoing yet also appreciates his independence. As a bonus, his extroversion means he has no problem making calls for dinner reservations or handling the logistics on things that make me uncomfortable, which is a great relief for me. He also enjoys quiet nights staying in and long drives filled with deep conversation, which I love. Our connection is a wonderful balance where our personality traits meld well.

In contrast, my ex-husband was extroverted and never wanted to do the quiet activities that I enjoy. When we first got together, I tried to bypass my natural, introverted nature. I grew up with extroverted parents who told me I was too shy and that I needed to come out of my shell. I always felt that my introversion was a flaw, so I pushed myself to be more social. Over time, I became exhausted trying to be more extroverted.

It took me until my late 30s to accept that I could not keep pushing myself to be someone I wasn't at my core. It became painfully obvious that I was not compatible with someone who wanted to be going out most of the time.

Your Family Dynamics Play a Role

Oddly, despite recognizing my tendency to prefer more introverted, quiet activities, throughout my dating experiences I sought extroverted men. I think this was simply because that is how my father was. We often seek a partner who is like one of our parents.

I adored my dad, but as I mentioned, he was very critical of how shy and quiet I was. I often felt like I was not good enough in his eyes.

I grew to associate being outgoing as a sign of success. It isn't surprising that I looked for that quality in a partner. I needed to recognize and accept both the positive and negative aspects of my parents. In doing so, I realized the behaviors that were not acceptable to me and rewired what felt like compatibility. Instead of seeking someone who criticized my natural tendencies, I focused on finding someone who accepted me just as I am. What an amazing shift!

It is very common to be drawn to that which is familiar, even if it isn't necessarily healthy. When I first met my husband, I was very excited that he had three siblings, as I did. We had a similar upbringing, which gave me a sense of ease. Our families turned out to be incredibly different, though, and I didn't fully recognize that until after we were married.

It is helpful to review your relationships with your immediate family members, especially your parents. What predominant traits do they possess? Do you find yourself drawn to their traits? Are those traits healthy for you? Have you dated people like your parents before?

After my divorce, I took time to delve into my family dynamics so that I could break any negative patterns. My dad's death was a major catalyst in my decision to end my marriage. Once he was in the Spirit world, my connection to him grew even stronger and more compassionate. One day while I was meditating, he appeared and apologized for being so hard on me. I felt deeply loved. He continues to send me signs, letting me know he is still guiding me. As mentioned, I had a strong sense that he was going to send me a loving partner.

When I met my partner, it amazed me how unbelievably similar he was to my dad. They look alike, have the same deep laugh, and my partner even uses phrases that I only ever heard Dad say. The best part; he possesses all of my dad's best traits and none of his negative aspects.

Your Deal-Breakers Are Always in Play

If you haven't had many healthy relationships, it can be very challenging to recognize when a relationship exhibits genuine compatibility. As a result, it is often easier to eliminate men based on characteristics you do not want.

We talked about establishing your deal-breakers in Chapter 10. Re-evaluate the list you wrote, focusing on the specific personal characteristics you included.

Think again about your past. What types of men have not historically worked well for you? What character traits do you find annoying or frustrating? For me, I had been in so many narcissistic relationships that I was on particularly high alert for men who were arrogant or insensitive.

Be sure that your deal-breakers don't become a blind spot though. In trying to avoid narcissistic men, I fixated on finding men I perceived as nice. At times, I focused so heavily on that one trait that I disregarded other important characteristics like intelligence, positivity, and shared interests.

Opposites Do Not Necessarily Attract

We often hear the term "opposites attract" as partnership advice. While it is true that people are drawn to traits they do not possess, that is not always an element of healthy compatibility.

This was certainly true with my desire to be with extroverted men. It often meant that I ended up with a man who ultimately exhausted me and who found my introverted nature to be boring over time.

When I first met my husband, I clung to the "opposites attract" theory as justification for staying together. There were so many aspects of our relationship that were challenging, everything from vastly different eating habits to different music preferences, and most definitely a difference in empathy for others. I told myself that I would get used to all the differences because love would make it work. What an unhealthy thought!

Of course, some differences are healthy. This is potentially why the opposites attract theory developed. For example, as I mentioned about my current partnership, he uses his extroverted nature to support me. Because he loves going out, he is always offering to do the errands that I don't enjoy. Likewise, he tells me that my introspective nature grounds him and makes him feel understood. Our differences are not challenges, but rather supportive complements to our growth both as a couple and as individuals.

You deserve to be in an easy, joyful relationship, not one based on navigating constant differences. Please don't fall into the trap of believing our challenging differences are worth overcoming for the sake of love.

Shared Values Create a Strong Foundation

Values are the foundation for everything we do. Naturally, having the same values is part of a healthy, strong relationship.

My husband and I had strong shared values. It was probably the best aspect of our connection and the reason we lasted so long, even when so many other aspects were off. We have the same basic political beliefs, are concerned about the environment, love nature and animals, and are frugal with our money. He also possessed the core basics of what I felt made a good person, being respectful, considerate, trustworthy, and polite.

As I mentioned, however, he lacked genuine empathy for others. He often said hurtful things just to get a laugh. He had done things to tease our nieces and nephews that left those sensitive children sad and confused. I could not tolerate his lack of self-awareness and compassion.

We talked about values a bit before in Chapter 1. Think again about what your core values are and how they may fit or clash with a potential partner.

Common Interests Bring Joy

Meeting someone who has the same or similar likes or dislikes as you can feel like winning the lottery. We are all such unique individuals. It is difficult to find people who enjoy the same things. This is worth holding out for though because it makes your connection so much happier and more meaningful.

The following attributes/characteristics can make or break a relationship depending on how strongly one of you feels about these aspects:

* Educational background
* Spiritual, political, and astrological beliefs
* Hobbies
* Musical preferences
* Interest in sports
* Food preferences
* Favorite TV shows
* Movie preferences
* Artistic interests
* Outdoor activities
* Vacation desires (active or restful)
* Travel interests (avid traveler or homebody)
* Physical fitness/health goals
* Alcohol or substance use
* Sex drive
* Lifestyle (luxurious/wealthy or simple)
* Wants kids / doesn't want kids

While it is important to have outside interests and to support each other's independence, there should be some overlap of activities or interests. Even something as simple as spiritual beliefs can insurmountably challenge a relationship. My stance is that you do not have to believe what I do, but I expect you to support my right to believe what I wish.

As I previously mentioned, I am very spiritual. I often get signs from Spirit that bring me great joy. When I shared them with my husband, he would scold me and tell me he thought my beliefs were silly or wrong. He is an Atheist and our beliefs became incompatible over time. One of my favorite things about my current partner is that he supports all of my spiritual and astrological beliefs. He has seen signs from my dad, which is a wonderful validation of our connection.

Astrology is a Piece of the Puzzle

I already shared how much I love astrology in Chapter 11. While many people are skeptical of astrology, I have found that it offers excellent insight into why I behave the way I do. Understanding my full natal chart (the map of what was happening in the sky at the time of my birth), offers input into how well I get along with other types of people, including potential love matches.

Most of the dating apps included a person's sun sign. However, it is difficult to assess compatibility based on sun sign alone. A person's entire natal chart dictates overall compatibility.

To get a truly accurate reading of compatibility between two people, which is known as synastry, you must know birth date, birth time, and the location of birth of both people. Obviously, if you are just swiping through profiles, you won't have this type of information, so you must generalize.

Basic astrological compatibility relates to the elements the signs represent. Following are the elements of the sun signs and their ideal matches:

Fire = Aries, Leo, Sagittarius
Fire signs are most compatible with other fire signs, as well as air signs. Aries, Leo, Sagittarius, Gemini, Libra, Aquarius

Earth = Taurus, Virgo, Capricorn
Earth signs are most compatible with other earth signs, as well as water signs. Taurus, Virgo, Capricorn, Cancer, Scorpio, Pisces

Air = Gemini, Libra, Aquarius
Air signs are most compatible with air signs, as well as fire signs. Gemini, Libra, Aquarius, Aries, Leo, Sagittarius

Water = Cancer, Scorpio, Pisces
Water signs are most compatible with water signs, as well as earth signs. Cancer, Scorpio, Pisces, Taurus, Virgo, Capricorn

As soon as I got serious with a man, I would ask him for his birth information so I could run a synastry report online. You can do this easily through various websites, which are included in the "Resources" section. When I shared what I uncovered, the men always agreed with the assessments. Interestingly, of the four men I dated for at least a month or more, only one was astrologically incompatible. He was the most manipulative and turned out to be a covert narcissist. I had a bad feeling about him from the start. His natal chart proved what I already sensed, that he was not a good match.

Of course, astrology is only one piece of the puzzle. Every couple has the potential to overcome their natural inclinations if they are willing to put in the work. However, if you are on the fence about someone and their chart indicates you are incompatible, it is worth considering.

Personality Theory Offers Insight

Again, I shared my feelings on personality theory in Chapter 11. It not only gives you deep insight into what makes you tick, but it also informs how you interact in relationships. Similar to the signs in astrology, certain personality types are more compatible than others are.

Personality theory is becoming more popular, so occasionally men indicated their type in their profile. However, it is rare for you to have this information. As a result, once I knew I was interested in a man, I would ask him if he knew his type. If he didn't know it, I would ask him to take the free online test through 16Personalities.com.

I have heard of men taking the test repeatedly to get a result that was favorable to the woman they were interested in. In addition, sometimes people answer questions the way they think they should, not how they actually feel. Be aware that it is not a perfect system.

You will often sense someone's personal characteristics just by interacting with them. Once you are clear on your own mode of operation, you won't need to know the other person's type, you will just sense whether you work together.

Since there are sixteen personalities, the actual compatibility between types can get a bit complicated, so I won't expand upon it here. You can search for the different types online to find articles on whether a type might work with yours.

The two men that I had the most fun with, including my current partner, were both ENFP, which is considered to be an INFJ's best match. Likewise, they were Aquarians, which is also an ideal match astrologically. I honestly didn't set out to date them based on their sun sign, and I did not know what their personality type was until we had been dating for some time. Clearly, sometimes we are just drawn to our best match without even having intellectual information. Therefore, I would not stress too much about these elements. They are more valuable at confirming a potential match once you have met, versus eliminating someone before getting to know them.

If you are interested in understanding more about how your personality type interacts with others, please see the "Resources" section for my favorite websites on the subject.

Chemistry Is Crucial

Shortly after starting online dating, I came across a local Facebook group for singles. Several times men posted in the group asking what it meant to have chemistry. I knew what it felt like, but wasn't sure how it developed or even how to explain it to someone else. Members of the group described it as a strong physical connection or a "spark."

After giving it some careful thought, I believe that chemistry is when the physical, chemical, and emotional energies between two people interact in a positive, magnetizing way. While we tend to focus on the physical attraction aspects of chemistry, true chemistry goes beyond appearance.

Pheromones, or the scent that someone gives off, can create chemistry. How someone moves, the tone of their voice, or their personal style can all evoke a positive reaction in another person.

Physical intimacy, especially how someone kisses and touches, can also make or break the chemistry between two people.

As I keep saying, everything is energy. How our energies interplay determines the chemistry we have with other people. When you have chemistry with a man, you feel happy and even giddy in his presence. Often, you feel drawn to him, wanting to be close enough to touch. Just thinking of the person will bring you joy and may even make your heart and breathing rates speed up.

Consistent chemistry is better than an explosive first connection that peters out. I was particularly attracted to one man I dated. He had stunning blue eyes, smelled fantastic, and I loved how he dressed. As our first date progressed, his sweet, gentle presence seemed to magnetize me to him. As we left the restaurant, I noticed he was leaning toward me as we walked. We both seemed to stall our goodbyes. When he hugged me before parting, I felt like my heart was going to burst out of my chest. We later affirmed to each other that the attraction was mutual, as neither of us had wanted to leave.

Those initial chemical feelings drove our connection for several months before it became clear that we weren't heading in the same direction. We didn't have many common interests, and he didn't seem to have time for me. The chemistry wasn't enough to keep us together long-term, which is often the case. Chemistry is exciting and will often fuel an initial connection. However, there needs to be the full package of compatibility for a relationship to last.

In addition, chemistry is not always healthy. As I previously mentioned, the electric, instant interaction when an empath meets a narcissist always ends in misery for the empath.

Sensitive women are prone to disregard the importance of chemistry in favor of finding someone who is kind and treats us well. Prior to experiencing true chemistry, I would have suggested that chemistry and passion were not necessary for a strong relationship. However, now that I have a relationship with a man who treats me incredibly well and has crazy chemistry with me, I know there is no comparison. That inexplicable spark keeps us longing for each other. He says that in the past the initial spark always wore off and he became bored. Over two years later, our connection is still burning bright.

You can't manufacture genuine chemistry. It happens naturally and you will typically feel it quickly upon meeting someone. If you don't feel that passion after a few weeks of dating, it is unlikely to develop.

Likewise, if a man tells you he doesn't have an attraction to you, move on. Men are far more primal than we are. If they don't feel the spark, even if they like your personality, they are likely to have a wandering eye or to leave eventually.

Similar to the broader topic of compatibility, the short answer on chemistry is that you like who you like. It is essential to accept the importance of chemistry when seeking a relationship that lasts.

Fetishes Exist

I knew people had fetishes, but I never met anyone who openly admitted to having one. As a result, I didn't realize how prevalent they are.

There were men on the dating apps who openly shared in their profiles that they had a fetish. The honesty was refreshing, yet still a bit confusing for me.

A fetish is when sexual desire is linked to an object, an activity, or a body part that is not typically considered sexy. Foot fetishes are probably the most common. Men who have foot fetishes may find it pleasurable to massage a woman's feet or paint her toes.

I bring this up simply so you realize you might encounter men who have fetishes or other very specific sexual preferences. If that makes you uncomfortable, you will probably not be compatible with that type of man. However, you never really know what you like until you experience it, so keep an open mind here.

Porn May Be a Problem

I mentioned how some men send women naked photos. That is probably the most obvious sign that a man is hypersexual and primarily fixated on the physical aspects of a relationship. However, it is important to recognize there is a whole undercurrent of men who regularly watch porn without ever sharing that detail with their partner. On the surface, this doesn't seem like a big deal, and it doesn't have to be

The problems result however when a man develops an unhealthy attachment or addiction to watching porn. For one, the sexual contact depicted in pornographic videos is often fast, hard, and overtly aggressive. There is no romance, foreplay, or personal connection displayed before sexual acts take place. Most women do not find that kind of rough, impersonal sex to be enjoyable or even tolerable. Unfortunately, men who consistently watch porn believe that women like those kinds of sexual interactions. They think that the women who are acting in those videos represent most women when that is not true.

Furthermore, men who regularly watch pornographic imagery grow to depend on that medium to become aroused. As such, a real, in the flesh woman does not turn them on the way their trusty porn can. Erectile dysfunction is a common outcome for men who are addicted to watching porn.

I dated a man whose behavior in the bedroom felt a little strange. He almost seemed to need to watch what we were doing. In addition, he had difficulty achieving and maintaining an erection. It was very confusing and demoralizing to me. I felt inadequate and unattractive, even though he tried to assure me it wasn't my fault. In a moment of frustration, he blurted out that he "must be watching too much porn." That notion had never even crossed my mind. It was oddly comforting to put a cause to the uncomfortable outcome.

Over time, the intimacy with that man improved as trust built between us. I wish, however, that I had questioned him more directly about what was going on for him. It is especially difficult to speak up in the bedroom, but it is essential to do so if you encounter someone who is behaving in ways that are not sexually compatible with you.

The physical aspects of a relationship help couples to bond.

You must be aware when sexual challenges are present and how to address them. For more information on the challenges of porn, please see the "Resources" section.

Feelings Matter

Your body can tell you how you feel about someone, often from the moment you read their profile. As a sensitive woman, you are far more attuned to the energy exuded by others than you may realize. At first, it might be butterflies in your stomach and sweaty palms, indicating that you have a nervous excitement. Over time, that will progress to a sense of ease in your body. Set yourself up for success by carefully considering how feelings of compatibility might show up for you.

Beyond the spark of physical chemistry, there needs to be a desire to get to know the person. You should be both excited and intrigued when first meeting someone.

We often disregard our initial feelings in order to be nice or to give someone a chance. That rarely works well for a sensitive woman. Your intuition is strong. You know at your core how you feel about someone. Please don't disregard those feelings, especially if they are telling you something is off.

The Eyes Have It

I found it very difficult to assess a man based on his profile pictures. However, there is something to be said about paying attention to their eyes. They really are the "windows to the soul." If you are scrolling through pictures online, pay close attention to the man's eyes. They will often give you an indication of whether you feel a deeper sense of connection.

Compatibility is serious business. It is the glue that keeps a relationship together. Take the time when first meeting someone to consider all the elements of compatibility. They don't all have to apply

to have a healthy relationship. However, the more compatibility factors that exist, the easier and more enjoyable the relationship will be.

Chapter 16: Be Open-Minded

Throughout this book, I harp on honoring your needs and wants when seeking a partner. While I firmly believe you should stay true to your desires, I want to share a bit of contradictory advice. To increase your odds of finding a connection, it is important to give every man you meet a chance.

Sometimes we don't know what will truly make us happy because we haven't found it yet. Therefore, staying open to potential partners is crucial for your personal growth and relationship success.

I don't want you to disregard a strong gut reaction telling you that someone is not right for you. However, I believe that if you are ever on the fence, you should take the risk. Here is why.

Your History Is a Poor Indicator

Unfortunately, if you are single, chances are good that your past relationships have been unsuccessful. What you have been doing has not worked. There is no shame in this. All of us struggle with maintaining successful relationships. The key is recognizing where you are going wrong.

Many of us have a physical type. For example, you may be attracted to tall, dark, and handsome men. However, every time you get into a relationship with this type of man, he turns out to be arrogant, self-absorbed, and not at all a healthy match. Basing a relationship on looks alone is a recipe for disaster. Still, it is common because the chemistry is so strong.

There are many other relationship patterns that you are likely to play out continually, even if they haven't worked for you. In my case, my negative pattern was attracting narcissists. It was maddening. Despite what I thought was my awareness of the issue, I had not broken the spell.

I was holding on to the same unhealthy beliefs. I thought I needed to be nice and give away my power in favor of what the man wanted. I wasn't clear and direct about what I wanted.

Luckily, I finally got fed up and focused more attention on healing the codependent tendencies that were fueling the problem. This meant working on my subconscious mind. I did this through a variety of modalities including EMDR with a therapist, EFT (Tapping), listening to meditations affirming my self-worth, and doing writing exercises to increase my self-love. [We will cover these activities in Phase 3].

Once I recognized my worth and shifted my focus to my own needs, I attracted a healthy partner who was not like anyone I had met before. Because I had vowed to be open-minded, I gave him a chance even though he was not at all my typical "type."

We all carry negative thought patterns in our subconscious minds that keep us from making healthy choices. We can't rely on what we have done in the past, because that never worked. We have to focus on trying something new, giving different types of men a chance.

Competition Is Fierce Online

Competition is always a factor in dating. However, in real life, it is less pronounced. When faced with the ease of scrolling through photos online, filtering out people based on looks alone becomes a reflexive behavior. This goes both ways. You might end up doing it to your matches, and they will do it to you too.

Over time, you realize that eliminating men based on looks alone leaves you with very few matches. Similarly, if you only contact very attractive men, you are not likely to get much of a response.

In my experience, the few men I contacted who had model good looks didn't respond, or worse, they responded and were noticeably cocky. Men who are physically fit and attractive receive a great deal of attention from women online. They get caught up in the addictive nature of the attention. They aren't motivated to work on a relationship when they can just move on to another woman as soon as things get challenging.

The message here is that you need to broaden your perspective on what you find attractive. This was very easy for me since I was always more attracted to how someone treated me than what he looked like. Of course, that had its challenges because I ended up with narcissists who faked kind behavior at first. Regardless, being able to look past physical traits will always give you more options for finding someone who matches with you in the ways that matter most - emotionally, intellectually, and spiritually.

Practice Brings Ease and Clarity

I never really dated in high school or college. The way boys and young men used women for sex disgusted me. I had no interest in being anyone's one-night stand or someone they bragged about to their friends in the locker room. The genuinely kind and sensitive boys I knew ended up in the friend zone. They felt more like brothers than romantic partners. My husband was one of the first men I dated seriously, which didn't happen until I was 24. As a result, after my divorce, at 42 I was very much a newbie to the dating scene.

Given this reality, I accepted that I was probably going to need to meet and date many men before I found my ideal match. This proved to be true. I am glad I embraced the notion because it contributed to my success.

Even though I didn't always feel this way, I am now grateful for all the men I interacted with online. They helped me to hone my communication skills, gain confidence, and recognize what characteristics I was looking for in a partner. I would not have been ready for the mature, honest relationship I have now if I hadn't consistently put myself out there.

There were certainly times when I worried that it would never happen for me. That's normal. I hear it all the time from frustrated women who are ready to give up dating online or already have. Please don't lose hope. Every man you meet is a lesson or a blessing. He will either teach you what you don't want, or he will be exactly what you need. It is worth the effort to keep trying.

No One Is Perfect

There is no such thing as a perfect person. Just like you, anyone you meet is going to have flaws and emotional baggage. The key is finding someone whose imperfections work with yours.

Also, anyone who seems too good to be true is likely hiding something. All four of the men that I had serious relationships with had messy homes. However, only two of those men were brave enough to invite me over to their places. I am a bit of a neat freak. I like everything to have its place. I could have looked at a man with a messy home as a deal-breaker, but I know that a tendency toward neatness is not common in single men. I realized that I needed to prioritize the traits that were most important to me. I was much more concerned with how a man treated me than any surface issues like appearance, possessions, or neatness.

One of my greatest weaknesses, in my opinion, is chronic fatigue. It causes me to have to cancel plans and limit activity at times. When I first started dating, I was worried about sharing this information with men. I was pleasantly surprised that none of the men minded.

When we first started dating, my current partner insisted on spending time with me when I was very sick with a cold. He said that he wanted to see me at my worst. He felt that if we could still want to spend time together under difficult circumstances, then we were more likely to weather the storms that life inevitably brings. After experiencing a marriage where I was always criticized for being sick, it has been incredibly refreshing to have someone accept me as I am. An interesting outcome is that I am rarely sick anymore.

To have a partner who accepts and supports you unconditionally, you must do the same for them. When meeting new men online, cut them some slack. I have heard of women having long lists of qualities that they don't want in men. Not only is that focusing your attention on the negative, which is likely to bring that to you, it is also severely limiting your chances of finding someone great.

Stick to your deal-breakers when they come to protecting your mental and emotional health. However, try to be more accepting of surface attributes like looks, financial situation, or job. All of those things can change. In addition, they don't speak to a person's character or their ability to treat you with love and respect.

Sex Is Healthy

I had a great deal of shame and guilt around sex. I grew up wanting to be a "good girl" and held tightly to that ideal. Circumstances in my marriage amplified my discomfort around sex, leaving me feeling inadequate and uneasy in the bedroom. I share this very personal information with you in case you have ever struggled in feeling confident or empowered in your sex life.

In 2010, I began studying Emei Qigong. The instructor taught us about the concept of Jing, which is our sexual energy. She explained that Jing is a powerful force that is vital for optimal health. At that time, my sex life was dismal, as was my health. I was dejected, thinking that I may never have vibrant health if I stayed in my marriage.

When things ultimately ended, I felt hopeful. I knew that being single allowed me to break the years of shame and guilt I had around sex and cultivate a healthier, happier relationship with my sexual side.

The remedy turned out to be easy. I just needed a compassionate partner who was aware of my history and mindful of my apprehension. The first man I dated seriously was very willing to offer support. He helped me through my fears by encouraging open communication and by consistently giving me positive feedback. My current partner has been even more supportive and attentive. I still feel uncomfortable talking about sex, but that has gotten easier with practice.

Women receive many mixed messages about their sexuality. We are told not to be too sexy, while also being told we should always please our man. There are also loads of double standards whereby men can have as many sexual partners as they wish, yet if a woman does the same, she is called a "slut." I hope you will break through those negative messages and stay open-minded about your sex life. The joy and freedom are worth it.

The bottom line with being open-minded is that we are all creatures of habit. We keep doing the same things, hoping they will lead to different outcomes. Or, we focus on our wants instead of our needs, which can lead to situations that aren't healthy. When you stay open to possibilities, you have a lot more opportunities to uncover what is right for you.

Chapter 17: Maintain Healthy Self-Esteem

Online dating can be hard on your emotional state. We have already discussed the rejection that happens daily on both sides. While you might accept that not everyone is going to be into you, rejection is never easy. If you aren't proactive, it can lead to emotional wounds that lower your self-esteem.

Before going online, I felt good about myself and believed I could meet someone great. I'm a positive person, a good listener, and an open communicator with a great sense of humor. People told me I was attractive, and I had received a lot of attention from men throughout my life. Even though my husband stopped complimenting me and seemed to lose all physical attraction for me shortly after we were married, I thought I was confident and secure.

However, once I was in the online world of men who seemed singularly focused on my physical appearance, my insecurities raged. Objectification has a strange impact. Even when men are making comments that are supposed to be compliments about your looks, it can leave you feeling empty and gross.

I knew that there were many other women online, and suddenly, I felt like I was not attractive enough to compete. A few men I interacted with early on seemed to confirm that fear when they told me I wasn't their type or avoided my messages entirely.

What I didn't know then was how common those types of interactions are. Many women (and men) don't get responses at all. My expectations had been unreasonable and my assumptions were silly. You never know why someone avoids you or ghosts you. Oftentimes, it has nothing to do with you.

Please don't make the mistakes I did by reading into every little thing. It will make you crazy. Sometimes people are jerks, other times they are just super busy. Regardless, both realities aren't personal.

I can see now that I was my worst enemy by not focusing on protecting myself and building my confidence daily. People can be childish and petty when hiding behind a device. You must not take the things they say or do to heart. That is easy for me to say, but I know it requires a lot of hard work to build strong self-esteem. Following are some tips for building your confidence and self-esteem before and during your online dating experience.

Acknowledge Your Past

If you have been in a toxic relationship, it is incredibly important that you acknowledge that situation fully. Right after my divorce, I was still in a bit of denial over how much my husband had harmed my self-esteem. It took me four years of research, time, and space to recognize how much damage his subtle, dismissive tactics had caused. In the meantime, I had been online dating, not even realizing how emotionally fragile I was.

It was only after meeting my current supportive partner two years ago that I understood what a healthy relationship looks and feels like. He has taught me I have a right to have my needs met, and that I can ask for what I want without feeling shame or guilt.

As I uncovered the truth about covert narcissists, I learned that they hide behind a persona that seems nice, especially to the outside world. They don't yell or hit. Rather, they use more subtle methods of control like mocking, criticizing, withholding affection, and gaslighting. They put all the burdens of the relationship on their partner. My husband had constantly told me all the problems in our relationship were because of me. According to him, he didn't have any problems. I believed that lie right up until I finally snapped out of my trance the day we decided to split.

Once you have experienced trauma or any form of emotional abuse in a relationship, you must be extra vigilant about building and guarding your self-esteem. Let go of the shame and guilt of your painful past. It is not your fault!

Most of the sensitive women I have met have had some form of trauma or abuse. Unhealthy individuals readily manipulate our kindness. That does not make us weak. It makes us stronger, braver, and more powerful. We have lived our life in the light, rather than becoming consumed by the darkness around us.

Address Your Fears

We all have fears. In fact, many sensitive women struggle with anxiety. I developed severe panic attacks around 2010 shortly after realizing my dad was struggling with Alzheimer's disease. At that time, I had a job that I hated in a company that was always in financial distress. When I raised my concerns with my husband, he told me I couldn't quit because we didn't have enough money. That was a blatant lie that he frequently held over my head. I felt very out of control in my life. That, teamed with getting too much thyroid medication, and undiagnosed Celiac disease, put my body into a constant state of agitation.

It took me several years of working with meditation, energy healing, Qigong, and other relaxation techniques to get on top of my anxious feelings. Ultimately, leaving my husband and moving into a townhouse alone with just my sweet loving cat reduced the negative energy dramatically. It was highly likely that since I am an empath, I had been absorbing my husband's negative emotions all along. Much of the anxiety I experienced was not even my own.

Despite feeling more in control of my anxiety, when I first started online dating I worried that the nervousness of meeting new people would put me over the edge. I was experiencing a lot of change all at once, including a stressful new job working with a variety of new people. It felt like I might be pushing myself a bit too hard.

Throughout my struggles, I learned that the remedy for all

unwanted thoughts, feelings, and energies is to recognize and address them. It is interesting how just being aware of the negativity can allow it to pass. I focused on recognizing my fears, writing them down in my journal, and then combatting the negativity by giving myself love and compassion. I would remind myself of how much I had already been through and how every challenge propelled me to something better.

I also practiced working through worst-case scenarios. What would I do if I had a panic attack on a date? That was easy. I would just excuse myself and go home. There was no situation that I couldn't remove myself from. The same is true for you. If online dating ever gets too scary, you can easily bow out.

I was honest and open about my anxiety with any man I was considering dating seriously. It amazes me how being honest often provides the support you need. Any compassionate person is going to help you if they know you are struggling. Besides, these days most people have either experienced anxiety themselves, or they know someone who has.

I told the first man I dated that I sometimes had anxious feelings, and he understood completely because he did too. What a relief. Occasionally, I could feel his anxious feelings. I would ask him what he needed from me to support him, and we would work through a solution together that put us both at ease.

Perhaps you aren't necessarily anxious, but you have other fears around finances, job, family, or health. Take some time to write these out, so you can take away their power. Fear is the opposite of love. Being able to minimize fear in your life will open up space for love to grow. We will cover additional tools and remedies for combatting anxiety in Chapter 19.

Push Yourself

Confidence comes by conquering the things you think you can't. Set goals for your life and start working toward them. Every success helps you to see your value more clearly.

After my first stint in online dating and a five-month relationship, I took time to myself to buy a house and move on my own.

That process was all new and very scary. Some days I worried that I wouldn't have the energy to get everything done. Yet, I persevered, ending up in a cozy home I love.

When I rejoined online dating after settling into my home, I felt like an entirely different person. I had much more confidence in my abilities and great pride in the life I had rebuilt for myself.

If you have been through, or are going through, divorce, I already know you are a warrior. That process is difficult and emotionally draining, yet so empowering. If you reframe the experience as a tremendous learning process that makes you stronger and more resilient to life's changes, you will be those things at the end of your journey. Divorce is the ultimate form of reclaiming your freedom. Even if you feel battered at the end, you are free.

I tend to shy away from challenges. However, every time I face something difficult head-on, I see myself come alive. I recognize my inner power and strength, which no one can take from me.

It is very brave to put yourself out there in online dating. Congratulate yourself for showing up and even considering something so uncomfortable. The easiest choice would be to give up and settle into a life of solitude. That kind of life could be more comfortable for a sensitive woman, but it wouldn't offer much room for growth or the potential for more love.

Work Your Body

Our bodies carry great power. Your physical strength supports your mental, emotional, and spiritual strength. When I was married, I had very little strength and stamina. I could only do short, slow yoga practices, and I barely had the energy to take walks.

My doctors had always told me that pushing myself harder physically would help me build stamina. However, I had so little energy to work with. Their advice felt frustrating and impossible. Once I was on my own with no one actively draining my reserves, my doctors' recommendation actually worked.

I lived right off of the main street in a quiet little town in Western Connecticut. The wide sidewalks offered a safe place to walk. I would put on my favorite uplifting playlist and walk at least four times per week. Every time I would push myself to go a little farther, eventually working up to completing four miles in an hour.

It was so empowering to see my energy return. Those long, brisk walks gave me so much joy and peace. Moving my body helped me release any pent-up emotions that had been lingering since my divorce. Likewise, the endorphins produced made me feel great.

If brisk walking isn't your thing, consider other forms of cardiovascular exercise. I also enjoy dancing or power yoga sessions to get my heart pumping. Cardiovascular exercise will not only make your body stronger and leaner, but those endorphins I mentioned provide a powerful antidote to depression and low self-worth.

At that same time, I also started diligently working on my core. I had read about the plank challenge, a call to hold plank pose for one minute every day. After having done core-based yoga for many years, I suspected I could hold it for much longer. At first, I pushed myself to hold it for two minutes. Then one day I decided not to watch the timer at all and just held it as long as I could. I was surprised and excited when I realized I could hold it for five minutes. That experiment taught me two things: 1. I could do far more when I didn't limit myself, and 2. I was much stronger than I thought.

The core is where our solar plexus chakra is located, just above the belly button. It is considered to be our source of power and will. Many empaths, including me, receive energy and emotions in that area. It is what I mean when I say trust your gut. There is often an energetic feeling in the center of my belly that tells me if something is off. I found that strengthening that area physically made me feel more empowered emotionally and spiritually. Furthermore, I love how I look and feel when my core is tight and toned. It improves my posture, which also makes me look taller and more confident.

Improving your posture leads to multiple positive outcomes. Exercises like Pilates and yoga are especially effective at this goal. I am a huge fan of both styles of exercise as they lengthen the muscles and strengthen the back, giving you a leaner appearance. You can try these forms of exercise for free via apps and through YouTube. Of course, check with your doctor to be sure this is appropriate for you. If you get the green light, incorporate at least 15 minutes of these types of exercise three to five times per week.

In addition, practice good posture daily by aligning your head over your neck, keeping your shoulders back, and stretching your spine long and tall. You can even practice doing this when you are waiting in line at the grocery store. Every little effort helps.

Confidence is a challenge for many sensitive women. We often feel overwhelmed by the energies around us. Working on our physical bodies gives us a surprising strength that supports us in all areas of our lives.

Fake It Till You Become It

You've probably heard "fake it till you make it" many times. I must admit, as someone who wants to live an authentic life, I find this advice a little annoying. However, when you consider that our subconscious mind is often keeping us trapped with negative thoughts that aren't true, it makes sense that we need to fight fire with fire. By practicing who we want to be, we train our minds to see ourselves in that way. This positive feedback loop leads us to be more confident. Social psychologist Amy Cuddy refers to this as "faking it till you become it."

The actions we take shape our beliefs around our potential and vice versa. If you want to be successful at dating, you must believe you can be a successful dater.

Take some time to think about your ideal date. Visualize your most confident self showing up for that date. Play it out in your mind. Then, write about it using very specific details in your journal as though it is happening. How do you feel (e.g., happy, calm, excited, energetic, hopeful)? What do you look like? What are you wearing? What topics are you discussing? What is your date like? (Is he funny, handsome, charming, kind?) Try to put as much detail into this experience as possible.

Be Kind to Yourself

The world of online dating can be unkind. You must be your own best friend and ally always. This means focusing on speaking positively to and about yourself, and refocusing negative thoughts about yourself as soon as they arise.

Treat yourself the way you would a loved one. If a friend or family member came to you and said that someone had insulted them online, you would probably have their back, telling them that the person was an insensitive jerk. You must do that for yourself too as soon as someone throws a dig your way. Don't give it one ounce of merit.

I think about the man who told me I looked 10 years older than I was. The man had been actively pursuing me for several days. How could I possibly think he meant what he said? Would a man try to date someone that he thought looked too old? That doesn't even make sense, yet I am embarrassed to admit I allowed his negativity in. Cut any negativity off immediately knowing that even if the insult is true, it doesn't matter. Insults only prove that the man delivering them is not your match, a fact that you likely already know!

In Chapter 1, we talked about creating a "love list" of all the things you like about yourself and your life. Revisit that list and add as many of your positive qualities as possible. Dig deep to get to every aspect of the amazing woman you are. Consider all the things that others say they like about you, along with those that you value most. When someone hurts your feelings, pull out that list and remind yourself of your greatness.

In addition, don't forget the positive daily affirmations practice I mentioned in Chapter 9. Every morning, and definitely before a big date, write in your journal all of your positive qualities using "I am" statements, like "I am beautiful. I am kind. I am funny. I am interesting. I am thoughtful. I am smart." Write continuously until you feel good about yourself.

Honor Your Physical Beauty

While I wish physical beauty wasn't important, we all know that it is. Therefore, it is important to acknowledge the parts that contribute to your beauty. Focusing on those strengths will support your outward confidence.

Every woman has something about her that is beautiful. We already talked about the elusive nature of chemistry. Interestingly, the qualities we don't like in ourselves are often the very things that someone else finds attractive. Although we tend to believe that most men are looking for a model-type who is tall and thin with a small waist and a large chest, men are attracted to women of all shapes and sizes.

While some men said my body was perfect, others told me I was too thin. It was confusing and disheartening at times. Nevertheless, it reminded me that beauty is highly subjective. Remember what I said about a cup of tea. You can be the most delicious cup of tea, yet if someone doesn't like tea, they aren't going to appreciate you.

I have always had people tell me they liked my smile. That became a common comment from men online. However, it surprised me to learn that some men found my long nails appealing and other men liked the sound of my voice. In addition, while I have always found my sharp, angular features to be unappealing, my partner is Greek, and he feels my facial features make me look exotic and European.

When adding to your "love list," consider every little aspect of your physical appearance. Focus on your best qualities, while minimizing those that make you self-conscious.

Celebrate Yourself

Knowing you are complete and magnificent on your own is an important element of confidence. You don't need a partner to live a fulfilling and happy life. When we focus too much effort on needing a partner, it diminishes our inherent self-worth. You must be able to find joy in your autonomy.

Being single means you don't have to compromise. That is an amazing relief if you have been with a manipulative or disordered person who never honored your needs. Of course, you may have to adjust to the needs of other family members. However, for the most part, without a romantic partner, you have far more control over your life. You are solely responsible for decisions about when you eat or sleep, what music you listen to, and what shows you watch. You have more "me time" than if you gave that away to a partner.

When you live a fulfilling, fun life as a single person, your bar for relationships gets higher. Any new partner must compete with your current life, which is already wonderful. This is the ideal scenario for attracting someone great. You won't just accept anyone with a pulse. A new partner, or even a new friend, must compliment your lifestyle and add to it in a positive manner.

Having purpose in your life also helps you recognize how valuable you are to this world. Everyone is on this earth for a reason. When you recognize what that reason is, it helps you to feel more comfortable in your autonomy. You aren't just here to meet people and have new experiences. You are here to use your unique talents and gifts. Your ideal partner must be able to support your life purpose, as it is such a powerful force in living a healthy, fulfilling life.

Keeping your self-esteem healthy and strong is crucial to preventing yourself from accepting a partner who is less than you deserve. It also serves as foundational support to your happiness and success. Please consistently check in with yourself to be sure that your mental health isn't declining. If you start to feel depressed or unworthy, take

some time away from dating to work on those challenging thoughts and emotions. Seek help from a trusted therapist or supportive friend when you feel your self-worth slipping.

Chapter 18: Connect With Ease

Your first contact will come through the app, so there isn't much room to over-share information. This is a good thing. Those initial messages should be light and fun. However, they should still be meaningful on some level, since you need to be sure that the person is worth your time.

As a sensitive woman, everyone you interact with has the potential to either raise or lower your energy. Pay close attention to how you feel when interacting with a new person. First impressions matter, even those made online.

Here are some tips for keeping things moving forward while ensuring you are on the same page with a new connection.

Don't Over-Share or Move too Quickly

Don't tell a new contact deeply personal details, especially any of the past hurts you've had. An unscrupulous man will use this information against you. If you tell him you have stayed with someone after they cheated, he will probably assume that you will allow cheating. If you reveal fears about not wanting to be alone, he might latch on to you and play the role of savior, knowing that is what you want. If you tell him you had a narcissistic husband, he may believe that you are easy to manipulate. Don't forget about how many game-players are out there. They are using those initial messages to gauge how easy you are to play.

In the online arena, connections seem to move more quickly. There is a sense that you know one another when that isn't really the case. An odd comfort develops when we are behind a screen. Remember that everyone you encounter is a stranger.

The longer you are online dating, the easier it becomes to drop your guard. I'm not suggesting you be paranoid or uptight. I just want you to be aware.

You can't be sure about someone's character until you have observed their consistent behavior for several months. Don't fall into the trap of thinking that you know someone simply because you have messaged or texted daily.

I pride myself on being an open book. I don't have much of a filter and tend to tell people all my vulnerabilities as a means of seeking understanding and deeper connection. The unfortunate outcome is that I ended up interacting with many manipulative men. I shared far too much about my insecurities when I should have saved those details for my closest friends.

Manage Expectations

You can allude to your expectations in your profile by saying what kind of relationship you are looking for. It is common for people to say they are just looking for something casual, or to emphasize that they are not just interested in a physical relationship. Be warned though, sometimes men skim right past your profile, barely reading it at all. Some apps don't even give you much room for stating your intentions. As such, it is important to express your expectations early on when messaging someone.

If they contact you, with a "Hi, How are you?" You could respond with something light around how your day went, like "Work was crazy busy today, but I was so glad to have some time outdoors. How was your day?" Presumably, they will reply. Within the next several messages you could ask, "What are you looking for from online dating?" That will get the ball rolling so that you can pin down if they are on the same path.

This is difficult to bring up because it feels a bit pushy and stuffy. I don't think I ever addressed it in the first few messages. Although, I wish I did. Uncovering what someone is looking for in a relationship is foundational to whether you will work as a couple.

Even though it can be awkward to be direct, it is important to do so as soon as possible. Once you establish a mode of passively communicating with men, allowing them to take the lead, it becomes very difficult to assert yourself. In addition, the longer you wait to address something, the more awkward it gets. I can't help but think of the man who I dated for two weeks before asking him his last name. I felt like such a fool.

It is easier to ask tough questions early on before you get too attached to the person. When you first meet someone, you have nothing to lose. So, I encourage you to be brave and ask some hard questions right away.

In terms of dating expectations, you will want to consider things like:

Are they just looking for something casual or do they want a long-term relationship?

How often do they like to see a partner (e.g., only on the weekend or every day)?

What is their schedule like?

How do they like to communicate (e.g., daily texts, phone calls, video chats)?

Are they currently dating anyone?

Are they messaging with other people? (The answer is likely to be "yes" but it doesn't hurt to ask just to get their perspective.)

Of course, you won't always get honest answers. However, even if they lie, you are more likely to get a sense of that versus had you not addressed the issue at all.

I encountered several men who believed it wasn't a lie if they withheld information. One man, who prided himself on being honest, actually started dating someone else while trying to maintain a connection with me. When I found out about it a year later, he claimed he was not under any obligation to tell me that information because they hadn't been sleeping together. Clearly, some people have a different perspective on honesty.

Stay Positive

Negativity is draining. Try your best to stay upbeat in your messages, even if you're having a bad day. You don't want to appear negative in your first interactions with someone. Also, try to avoid self-deprecating humor as much as possible. This is something that women often fall back on because we are so used to putting ourselves down. Saying something like, "I look terrible in my pictures," can come across as if you are fishing for compliments or that you simply have low self-esteem. Confident men will find this to be a turn-off and manipulative men might see you as an easy target.

I am not particularly comfortable in front of a camera. I had been anti-selfie when I first went online, so I had mostly posed shots that someone else had taken. I didn't like my pictures and said so in my profile. Quite a few men jumped on that as an opportunity to tell me they thought I was very photogenic. I realized over time that was not a healthy approach. I think something like, "I've been told I look better in person than my pictures," (which is true) is a much healthier way to address any insecurities about your photos.

Try to put yourself in the other person's shoes. Would you find someone who was negative and critical to be attractive? Chances are that is not the case. If you start messaging with someone who is consistently negative, it is probably best to cut the connection off quickly. The first messages are generally their best behavior. Imagine how much worse they will get once you have been dating for a while.

Screen Out Narcissists Quickly

You know how I feel about narcissists. I want you to avoid them as much as possible. Some narcissistic men will give themselves away quickly. Keep in mind narcissists think they are perfect. They don't believe that they ever make mistakes, or that they need to work on themselves. As a result, you can often screen out a narcissist by asking a few questions related to personal growth, as follows:

What are you working on in yourself? One man I met gave me an arrogant vibe from his pictures alone. When he started messaging me, the detached manner in which he spoke about his divorce gave me pause. It wasn't final yet, so I had asked him if he was stressed or upset about that. He seemed completely devoid of emotion and said something like, "No, we're just working out the paperwork." He then asked me what I had done to work on myself after my divorce. I noted a long list of all the things I had done, including therapy, EMDR, energy healing, flower essences, tapping, and journaling. I asked him what he had done, and he said, "I'm good." At that point, I was certain he had an unhealthy ego. I told him I was glad he was so on top of things, wished him the best, and let him know we weren't likely a good match.

While I think this question is very effective, I have heard from other women that some men have gotten savvy and have a canned response that implies they are self-reflective when they really aren't. You'll have to use some discernment.

How long was your last relationship? Why did it end? What did you learn from the experience? If the relationship seems especially short, if the man blames his ex entirely for the relationship's failure, or if he didn't seem to grow from his experience, it is a potential sign that something might be off.

Has anyone ever accused you of being a narcissist? I never used this one, but I watched a webinar where two expert therapists said that some narcissists openly admit to being narcissistic. Many narcissists see nothing wrong with their behavior and are brazen about that fact. Of course, you would have to be playful with this question because it could make a nice man angry or defensive.

If the man agrees with everything you say, ask follow-up questions. For instance, if they say they like yoga, ask what style they do and where they take classes. Make them elaborate on what they are saying because agreeing with you could be a sign of manipulation. The additional probing will typically make it clear if they are not being genuine.

Keep in mind some of the other red flags of narcissistic behavior:

* Does he seem "too good to be true?"

* Is he saying all the right things?
* Do you feel overwhelmed by his attention?
* Is he showing an inappropriate level of emotion (i.e., acting head over heels when you only just met)?

Detecting a narcissist is very tricky. These tips are not fool-proof, but they will at least help you screen out the most obvious offenders.

Keep It Light and Fun

Online dating is meant to be fun. Try to make your first online interactions not just informative, but also enjoyable.

Humor is always a great go-to. I mentioned being funny in your profile. I suggest you do the same in your messages, especially when you are reaching out to someone. It is hard to make the first move, but being a bit silly or flirty makes that much easier. For instance, if a man says in his profile that he loves pizza, you could message him and say, "I would kill for a slice of mushroom pizza from [your favorite pizza place] right now! What is your favorite pizza place?"

Asking questions is always good. If you are not sure what to say, put the ball in his court by asking a question. *"Have you seen any good movies lately?"* Or, *"What's your favorite local restaurant?"* are simple ways to get the conversation flowing. One of the best parts of online dating is that you have time to compose your thoughts before messaging. Think of some lighthearted questions that you would want to know about a potential partner. Asking about their favorite things is always a great start. *What's their favorite movie, food, TV show, vacation spot, or hobby?* Try to work from what they have provided in their profile, so it is clear that you took the time to read it.

Stay Engaged

If you are interested in a man, don't let the conversation fall flat by simply answering their questions without asking additional questions in return. I met a seemingly nice man on Match.com a few weeks before I met my partner. He had messaged me with the basic intro questions like "Hi. How are you?" We messaged back and forth for two days with basic pleasantries that had no depth.

I don't think he had a very complete profile, so I had little to work from, and I was tired of making small talk online. Our message chain ultimately went dead. A few days later, he messaged me angrily, saying, "If you weren't interested in me you should have just said so." I was stunned. I replied explaining that his messages didn't give me much to work with, and if he wanted me to interact with him he needed to ask me questions. He immediately apologized, said he was new to online dating, and thanked me for the advice.

The interaction reminded me how awkward it is for both men and women to start and maintain conversations online. Most of us hope that the other person will take the lead. Keep that in mind. Men appreciate when women are assertive and make the first move. You have nothing to lose and it is far more rewarding than sitting back and waiting for men (who might not be your best match) to approach you.

Check in With Your Gut

We've consistently talked about trusting your intuition. The feelings that arise in your body are some of your most helpful tools when first interacting with someone. Do not disregard that information! There is great wisdom in anxiety, fear, or apprehension. A little nervous energy is normal, genuine fear or anxiety can indicate something deeper. I mentioned the man who messaged me using poor grammar. As soon as I received his message, I got a sick feeling in the pit of my stomach.

If you are getting any kind of scary feelings, it is best not to give the man your phone number or to proceed to meeting. Only allow men who make you feel comfortable and excited to gain access to your energy. As a sensitive woman, once you meet someone, that energetic connection is much harder to break.

∞∞∞

Remember, every person you meet is auditioning for a place in your life. They should make a strong effort in those initial communications. Also, be sure you really like the men you meet and that you are not just trying to get them to like you. The initial screening process is a two-way street. You must feel good about those interactions for them to proceed to an actual date.

Chapter 19: Have a Great First Date

I really enjoyed going on dates. Despite my nerves, I always approached every date with enthusiasm. It was so much fun to get to know someone new. Most of the men I met were interested in seeing me again. I think the positive energy I brought to every date was key to that outcome. Of course, not every first date will lead to a second date. That isn't the goal. You only want the most enjoyable, comfortable dates to lead to something more.

Following are tips for setting yourself up for a positive, fun first date.

Prepare for Nerves

It is normal to be nervous. Meeting someone for the first time is intimidating for even the most confident person. It helps to be prepared.

As I previously mentioned, I had some trouble with anxiety when I first started dating. However, it went away the more people I met. Dating provided great practice for getting over that debilitating issue. Anxiety is a fear of fear. The best way around it is through it.

I reminded myself before every date that I was free to leave at any time. It took a lot of pressure off to realize that I didn't owe my date anything and that my health came first. In addition, if I was feeling nervous or on edge, I just told my date upfront how I was feeling. This only happened once or twice. My date always understood and was supportive. These days anxiety is very common and dating is nerve-wracking for everyone. A man who is unable to show compassion if you are experiencing emotional discomfort is not going to be an ideal partner. It is a great test of your date's empathy.

To minimize any nerves before a date, I always gave myself plenty of time to get ready. I generally had dates on days when I hadn't worked a full day so that I had ample energy and time to prepare. This might mean keeping all your first dates to the weekend. Set yourself up for success by honoring what feels best. As I got more confident, I could have coffee dates after work, but they were always a little less enjoyable because we were both typically tired.

If I could, I would do yoga or meditate to feel as balanced as possible. I would also listen to upbeat music to perk up my energy. If I needed additional support, I used natural remedies to calm my nerves. I have used the flower essences Rescue Remedy with great success. You can easily find this online, in health food stores, and in some drugstores in the homeopathic remedy section. Other single flower essences were also very helpful in easing my nerves and providing confidence. Larch flower essence is especially helpful for sensitive women as it supports confidence and strength. The amino acid L-Theanine is also a gentle, natural remedy for anxious nerves. You can take these remedies before a date, or you can keep them in your purse to take should you need them.

Remember that the man you are meeting is likely just as nervous as you are. He doesn't want to make you feel uncomfortable. He wants your meeting to be just as successful as you do, so there is nothing to fear.

Do you remember the exercise we did in Chapter 17 where you visualized your ideal date? Reread that journal entry before each date so it primes you for a great experience.

Plan What You Will Say

Presumably, you already know a bit about any man you are about to meet. You have already spent some time messaging or talking to get a feel for what he is like. You have also found out as much as you can about him online. You probably already know if he has kids, what kind of job he does, and any of his favorite hobbies. These topics give you a lot to work from in terms of asking questions and keeping the conversation flowing. Thinking about what you might talk about in advance helps calm your nerves. If you have thought about topics of discussion and questions in advance, you will never have awkward pauses in the conversation. You could start with very easy, surface questions like:

* *What is your family like?*
* *What do you do for fun?*
* *What are your favorite foods and restaurants?*
* *What are you watching on TV lately?*
* *What is your favorite movie?*
* *What is your dream vacation?*

Then progress to deeper questions if they feel comfortable, such as:

* *What are your life goals?*
* *What is most important to you in a relationship?*
* *Do you enjoy your work?*
* *Who are your favorite people?*

Perhaps you already have some jokes that you have exchanged. Think about that when first meeting and start your conversation with something lighthearted that will get the date off to a positive start.

You don't have to overthink things. Dating is supposed to be fun. Every date I had ultimately took on a direction of its own. I never followed a script or had to resort to pre-planned conversation. However, giving it some advanced thought took a lot of the fear and uncertainty out of a date.

Prepare for the Worst

Expect the best, but prepare for the worst. While planning what you might talk about, you also want to keep your boundaries in mind. Remember your deal-breakers from Chapter 10 and consider how you might handle them if they arise.

Say, for example, that a man talks about how he doesn't want children, while you really want to have children. What will you say? Can you be clear about your intentions? It is certainly possible to enjoy a date even if you realize he isn't your ideal match. But, you probably won't want to continue seeing a man who isn't on the same page with something as important as having a family. You can carry the date through to the end, and when you part just tell the man you had a nice time without committing to a second date if you don't want to.

If a date is sexually inappropriate, making uncomfortable comments, or touching you, what will you do? If he is being playful, you can tell him directly that you feel uncomfortable. However, if he is drunk or acting threateningly, your words are not likely to help. At that point, you can always enlist the help of the surrounding staff. For instance, if you are at a restaurant, you could excuse yourself from the table and tell the manager that you need an escort to your car. Bartenders are especially used to that type of thing and will be sure that you are safe.

I never experienced anything particularly upsetting or challenging on a date, but I was mentally prepared should anything have occurred. Working through worst-case scenarios will help you feel confident about your ability to handle anything a date throws at you.

Protect Your Energy

You can actively protect your energy through some of the practices we previously discussed. If possible, smudge yourself before and after dates using Palo Santo or sage. If it feels comfortable, wear a protective crystal or keep it in your purse. Your mind's intention is also powerful. Establish a mantra that feels empowering to you, like "I am in my full power and energy. No one can take that from me." Or, "I can leave at any time."

Be Grateful

Gratitude is always uplifting energy. It instantly increases your positive vibrations. It is hard to be in a bad mood when you feel grateful.

Of all the women on the internet, this man you are about to meet picked you! Be grateful for the opportunity to meet someone who might change your life for the positive. If it feels comfortable to you, speak out to the Universe. Offer thanks to your Spirit team for helping you find connection, fun, or love. Speaking aloud gives the Universe a very direct message that you are open and ready to receive.

I am always amazed at how powerful this act has been in my life. It brings me joy and seems to encourage more good in my life. You can write about this in your journal too, adding more fuel to the positivity.

Detach From the Outcome

While it is wonderful to be grateful and excited about the new opportunities that a date can bring, it is important to not get too attached to an outcome in advance. Try to take things as they come without thinking too much about the future.

One man I dated, who ultimately ended up ghosting me, had been texting me for almost a month before he finally asked me out. I had decided that morning that if he didn't make a move I was going to give up on him. Interestingly, my horoscope for that day said that I was about to get into a beneficial relationship. My head was spinning with the possibilities that this new relationship could bring.

I knew he had older children and that he lived only ten minutes away. He had sent me pictures of himself on his back deck, and I had visions of us enjoying barbecues there together. I got much too carried away in thinking about how the relationship might progress.

It never occurred to me he wasn't on the same wavelength from the start. After several months together, he never asked me over to his house, nor did he invite me to spend time with his family. Yet, he would regularly text me to let me know how much fun he was having with his kids. It was hurtful. While I originally assumed he was a sweet man because he was a single father, his behaviors toward me were never particularly sweet. It taught me the importance of not jumping to conclusions about someone.

Every date is just that — a date. There is no implied commitment on either side. It is only with time and open communication that you fully realize if someone is a good long-term match for you.

Be Enthusiastic and Engaged

Enthusiasm is contagious. The positive intentions you bring to a date can make a big difference in how you connect. First impressions matter, so do your best to show excitement upon meeting a date.

Most of my dates began with a quick hug "hello." However, that is of course something you will need to gauge in terms of your and your date's comfort level. A handshake or even just a warm smile is perfectly acceptable in meeting someone new.

Be sure to give your date your full attention. Put your phone away and maintain consistent eye contact. Have a genuine sense of curiosity when asking questions.

Men need very clear signals that you are interested in them. Your body language will help to give them clues. If you are feeling comfortable and enjoying the conversation, try to keep a more open stance, with your body directly facing him. Lean towards him to show that you are actively engaged in the conversation. Don't fake it, but if you are genuinely enjoying the conversation, be sure to smile and laugh freely.

When in doubt, or if you are feeling nervous, ask questions and then commit to listening. Put the conversation in your date's hands. As an introvert, I often used this tactic, and it made the dates effortless for me. I could just sit back and listen, which was a comfortable role.

If you are more extroverted and tend to be talkative, be sure you are listening as much as you are talking. Check yourself halfway through the conversation. You can even gauge your date's interest by playfully asking if you are talking too much.

These recommendations go both ways. Your date should exhibit signs of engagement and enthusiasm, asking you thoughtful questions and listening intently to your answers. Pay attention to his body language. Is he making consistent eye contact, leaning forward, or moving closer in any way? These are all signs that he is interested. In contrast, if he is distracted, looking around, or barely listening to what you have to say, you have some strong signs that he isn't that into you.

Be Your Best Self

Given how powerful first impressions can be, your first date is the place where you want to shine. Be your genuine self, but bring your "A" game. It is very similar to a job interview. Your goal, as odd as it might sound, is to convince your date what an amazing person you are. No pressure here, but the reality is you might only get one shot.

I mentioned giving myself plenty of time to get ready before a date. This not only settled my nerves, but it meant I had time to focus on my appearance. I would often do a beauty treatment like a facial mask or a deep conditioner, before taking a long, relaxing shower. Then I would take my time putting on my makeup and doing my hair. Of course, if you aren't someone who wears make-up, you can still put a little extra effort into your appearance by choosing the most flattering outfit or some fun accessories that make you feel good. The effort goes a long way in boosting your confidence.

Once on your date, make sure you keep your wits about you. Be cautious about drinking alcohol. I am much more confident and easygoing when I have had a glass of wine. However, I am also far less inhibited, and probably talk a bit more than I should. I rarely had first dates where alcohol was involved, which was for the best.

Try to maintain your positivity throughout the date. Avoid negative or catty comments and go with the flow. Try not to be critical or argumentative. While you want to talk about yourself and your accomplishments, don't compete with your date. You want to be genuine, but as is true for any new relationship, you need to be gracious too. I have heard stories of women who got into political rants or schooled their date on what they should be eating. That won't go over well with even the most interested man.

Likewise, a man who is argumentative, overly opinionated, competitive, or otherwise rude or negative is showing you clearly who he is. Presumably, he realizes he should bring his best self to the date too. If anything he does or says gives you a reason to cringe, that is important to note.

Trust Your Instincts AGAIN

I bring up trusting your instincts constantly because it is such a vital piece of recognizing if someone will be a good match. You often know right away if someone is right for you.

I mentioned that my worst date was with a "Great on Paper Man." From the moment I first saw him, I knew that there was no spark. It wasn't even an appearance issue. It was the energy he gave off. He didn't seem attracted to me or at all excited to be meeting me. The other men who I ended up dating seriously seemed to light up when I walked in. You can just see it in someone's eyes when there is a spark.

This is where you need to be clear on what is important to you. After having been married to a man who didn't light up when I walked into the room, I knew I couldn't live with that type of partnership ever again. For me, any man I was with needed to show a genuine attraction towards me.

If you feel nothing at first, sometimes the enthusiasm or admiration will grow. After all, some people are just reserved and the connection will build once you recognize shared values, common interests, or a good sense of humor. But, if there is a gut feeling of "no" right off the bat, honor that.

End With Intention

If you have had an enjoyable date, let the man know. Don't hide your positive feelings or be coy. Typically, if the man is interested, he will let you know. However, there is no guarantee here. If a man is feeling insecure, he might wait for you to share your feelings first.

I always preferred a man who was assertive and direct with his intentions. Most of the men I dated said at the end of the date that they had a good time and they hoped to see me again. Several of the shy men, who weren't as open in terms of sharing their feelings and intentions, left things hanging. In those instances, I let them know I enjoyed meeting them and looked forward to potentially seeing them again.

Some men require very literal direction from you. They won't dare ask you out again if they don't think you will accept. It would be frustrating and disappointing for either of you to leave a date not knowing where you stand, so address that clearly.

If you didn't enjoy the date, you can tactfully thank the man for meeting you, without suggesting anything further. Generally, they will get the hint. If they directly ask you if you want to see them again, be honest but kind. If there is a very specific reason you don't think you are a match, let him know. For example, if a man is extremely enthusiastic about travel, and you know you don't want to leave your state, that is an obvious reason not to continue seeing each other. Try not to put blame on the other person, but rather keep things as neutral as possible.

It is not easy to reject or be rejected. Yet, it is far less painful to know right away that a date will not lead to anything more, versus holding on to hope that the person might contact you again. By ending every date with clear intentions, you give yourself peace of mind, even if it hurts at first.

First dates can be scary, but also so much fun! Don't forget why you are dating in the first place. Whether it is companionship, connection, passion, or true love, there is the potential of greatly enhancing your life with every date you have. At the very least, you are growing bolder and more courageous every time you put yourself out

there. Celebrate your first dates, good and bad. They are always a sign of personal growth.

Chapter 20: Assess the Relationship

I had several first dates that blew me away. I was so excited about the new man's potential that my energy swung from giddy to overwhelmed. I was drunk on the possibilities of our future together.

I often failed to ground myself in reality. The feelings of early blooming love were so intoxicating that I fixated on the positive aspects of our first connections and date while denying any red flags or uncomfortable feelings. In retrospect, I wish I had the discipline to assess the pros and cons of the new potential partner objectively. That would have saved me a lot of confusion and disappointment.

I strongly suggest that as soon as you can, try to gain some perspective on what transpired during the date. Write about the experience in your journal, noting your feelings, and detailing the initial positive and negative aspects of dating this new person. Consider the following questions regarding this first interaction:

How did I feel when I first saw him? How did my body feel? (Did you feel light and joyful, or heavy and nervous?)

How did his energy feel? (Did he seem to light up? Did you feel safe with him? Did he seem honest?)

Was he engaged the entire date? (Was he making eye contact? Was he leaning in and focusing on what you were saying?)

Did he ask you questions that matched the depth of those you asked him?

Does he have common interests and values?

Does he have stressful or challenging life circumstances (e.g., a busy job, parenting, or caregiver responsibilities)?

Were there any early red flags (e.g., rudeness, condescension, overly sexual comments or actions, an aggressive tone)?

Were there moments when you felt you were defending yourself or hiding parts of yourself?

As you explore these items, note your emotions where appropriate. Try to remove those same emotions when reviewing the actions and words of the person. Try to be brutally honest about the situation.

Accept the Gift of Bad Dates

In contrast to the amazing first dates, there were a few times when my body and brain immediately told me I never wanted to see a man again. Knowing definitively that someone wasn't a match was a surprising gift. While I had several good dates that didn't turn into anything more, there was one date I considered disastrous.

I mentioned the disappointment of meeting a "Great on Paper Man" in Chapter 7. To refresh your memory, he had wowed me with beautifully written messages for a week before our date. I was so excited about his potential that my hopes were too high.

I rarely got dressed up for dates, sticking with jeans and a nice top. But, for this man, I put on my favorite sundress. I was feeling confident and optimistic. We were meeting at one of my favorite restaurants.

Most of the time, the easiest way to meet someone for dinner is in the parking lot so you can avoid the awkwardness of trying to find each other inside. That was the plan. It had been a gorgeous day, but right before our meeting time, it started to pour. My date texted me to say that he had run inside and was waiting for me there. I had to park quite a distance from the door and ended up running across the parking lot during the deluge. My sandal-clad feet were soaked and despite my umbrella, my hair was a bit wet too.

When I got inside the restaurant, I recognized my date standing near the host stand. I had to push through a crowd to get to him and we had a very awkward, quick hug. In terms of first impressions, I was disappointed. There was no spark whatsoever. His annoyance over the weather and the busyness of the restaurant overshadowed any enthusiasm he may have had for meeting me. Luckily, we had a reservation and were seated quickly. Unfortunately, that only offered momentary relief from the awkwardness.

Shortly after we sat down, I noticed an older man at the booth next to ours had turned his body to face me. His elbow on the table and his chin rested in his hand. He was actively staring at me. I moved further into the booth, pulling my shawl around myself feeling very uncomfortable. I flashed a look at my date. He was clueless. He was yammering nonstop about his life, his job, his family. He barely seemed to notice my presence.

He also wasn't looking at the menu, which meant the server came back to the table three times before he was finally ready to order. At that point, besides the discomfort of being leered at, I was hungry and feeling a little lightheaded. My date just kept talking, only pausing to say, "OK OK OK." like Joe Pesce's character in "Lethal Weapon."

When our food arrived, he realized I had ordered a gluten-free bun for my burger. That sent him into a tailspin. Although my profile said that I had to eat a gluten-free diet, he obviously overlooked that point. It suddenly became an enormous issue for him as he grilled me on my diet.

He asked me if I could have pizza in New York City. I explained that I probably couldn't, but that many places now offer gluten-free options. I also stressed that I have learned to live with my limitations by always carrying snacks and protein bars. He couldn't let it go. He kept saying, "No New York pizza, but I love going to New York for pizza. Are you sure you can't have just a slice?"

It was painfully obvious at that point that he severely lacked empathy and self-awareness and was definitely not my ideal match. Still, he barely took a breath and continued talking at me for the rest of the night. When the check came, I felt such a sense of relief. I just wanted to be home in my pajamas. He wasn't quite through. He whipped out his phone and started showing me old family photos of his parents and him, followed up by the grand finale — several videos of his cat.

At the end of the date, I thought for sure we would just part ways amicably. The pizza issue seemed so difficult for him, and his insensitivity to the issue was a deal-breaker for me. I was shocked when he said he wanted to see me again. I just replied, "It was nice to meet you." He seemed to get the hint.

The crazy thing is that I had recently bought a refurbished iPhone. It suddenly started having strange electrical problems. The day following our awful date, my phone dialed Mr. NY Pizza several times in a row despite my desperate attempts to make it stop. When he called me back, I had to explain that I hadn't meant to call. Everything about our interactions had been so brutally awkward that it made subsequent dates much better by comparison.

This was by far the worst date I experienced. I know other women have experienced much worse. When I shared the details with my mom, she said, "You HAVE to write a book." Of course, the intention at the time was that it would be a comedy. I decided helping other women avoid this type of uncomfortable situation was even more important.

Sensitive women tend to give people the benefit of the doubt, rationalizing, justifying, or minimizing incompatible behaviors, especially when we feel attracted to a person or hopeful of their potential. You must keep reminding yourself that you don't truly know a person after just one date.

In contrast, if your intuition is screaming that someone is not for you, accept that truth. On the most awkward dates I experienced, I knew within the first 30 minutes that the men were not a match. Their energy was scattered, the conversation was challenging, and the date didn't flow well at all. Those dates made me happy to be single. Fortunately, those experiences were not the norm of my dating experience. They gave me clarity, though. They helped me recognize energetically that some men are clearly not a good match.

This again points to how powerful practice and exposure can be when dating. Every date is an opportunity to learn what kind of man lights you up and what type leaves you feeling flat. Try not to let the duds knock you down, but rather see the gift in what they teach you about your relationship needs.

Chapter 21: Avoid Common Mistakes

When you first meet someone, the rush of new energy can be overwhelming. It can be difficult to determine if your new connection has genuine, healthy potential.

Sensitive women are especially prone to making mistakes as relationships progress. We tend to give away our power to the man, allowing him to be in charge of the direction the relationship takes. Alternatively, we get so nervous about the new relationship that we push the man away before even giving him a chance. There is a happy medium. You can find it by avoiding the following most common dating mistakes.

Don't Rush Things

I was the worst at this! My pace was that of an Olympic track star. Most of the men I dated told me within the first or second date that they had taken down their dating profile and were fully committed to our relationship. It was both comforting and flattering to feel supported in that way.

However, that simple declaration meant that everything seemed ramped up from sexual intimacy to the amount of daily communication we had. It was going from being happily single, fully in charge of how I spent my days, to suddenly having someone else to think about all the time. Talk about whiplash!

While I think it is fine to agree to take your profiles down, that does not mean you need to speed up your connection. It just gives you the ability to focus all your attention on one person. Many sensitive women can't date more than one person at a time. The mix of energies is just too challenging. Therefore, being exclusive is a great option to discuss with a man with whom you feel a strong connection.

Again, that does not mean that you have to fast-track the relationship. You can still take things slowly and allow this person to ease into your life without getting carried away by your excitement.

It takes several months to get to know someone. Give yourself that time. If you feel as though you are falling in love quickly, honor those feelings, yet still try to remain grounded and objective. Your heart might be feeling one thing, but you need to give your head some time to catch up. Sometimes what feels like a strong connection is just lust driven by hormones that will ultimately fade.

Remember also that manipulative men like to speed up attraction and connection so that they can lock you down before you see who they are. You can commit to giving a relationship your undivided attention, but that does not mean you must stick with it for the long haul. As soon as things seem to veer off course, you are always free to leave.

Don't Settle

Online dating can sometimes give us a scarcity mentality. If you have reached out to many men with no responses, or if most men who contact you don't feel like a fit, it is normal for desperation to set in. Before you know it, you are settling for communications with men who are not at all your type, or worse, men who are jerks.

It is important to do confidence check-ins regularly. [Rereading Chapter 17 might help.] Remember your worth and your ultimate goal. At the bare minimum, you deserve to be treated with respect and reciprocity. Your interactions should light you up and bring you joy, not evoke feelings of stress or worry.

If you are used to accepting less than you deserve, reframe your mindset to expect more — more attentiveness, more kindness, and more depth. We get used to the rhythms of our lives and sometimes don't even know we are settling. Take some time to think through where you have settled in your life and how you can prepare yourself to ask for, and receive, more.

Be Flexible

Although I don't want you to settle with important things like your happiness and peace of mind, I also don't want you to be too rigid when assessing a new partnership. I know some women focus on surface attributes like money, career, or status. They are looking for the "Great on Paper Man." However, don't forget what we've learned about him. He is often not so great.

Try not to get fixated on perfection in your dates. Keep an open mind with anyone who doesn't quite fit the mold of what you are used to, as he could be your diamond in the rough.

As I have mentioned, my partner is not what I expected. As a biker with an earring and a back covered in tattoos, he doesn't fit the clean-cut appearance of my typical type. Luckily, when he first contacted me, I paid very little attention to his photos, focusing more on the kindness exhibited in his profile. He stated he would do anything for his family and friends, which is an intention I share. Upon meeting him, his warmth and kindness were palpable. He immediately made me feel safe and secure, attributes I believe all sensitive women need in order to thrive.

Our relationship has a natural ease that I never experienced before. After having so many narcissists in my life, I wasn't sure such a state even existed. I believed that chaos and criticism were normal. I thought most men lacked the sensitivity and compassion to support my needs. In all honesty, the majority of men I met online did seem to lack those qualities. However, it only took one. I only needed to find the one man who understood me.

Stay open to the possibility that someone who doesn't seem like an obvious match might be the very person you need. Avoid deciding on a partner based on what your friends or family might think. Choose the person who makes you feel nurtured and supported.

Avoid the Games

We talked about the inherent games that exist in online

dating. Men aren't the only ones playing games. Unfortunately, women do it too, often inadvertently.

There is a belief that "playing hard to get" will make a man want us more. While this can be true, it doesn't lead to a lasting relationship. After all, if the initial connection was based on the chase, what happens once the man catches you, or vice versa? Chances are good that one of you will lose interest. In addition, while being chased can feel exciting, it can lead to resentment and frustration. No one wants to feel like they are being played.

I know that part of my Leo nature is that I like being chased. I don't do well with indecision or unclear intentions. I need to know that a man wants to be with me. However, that tendency to need so much outright attention is why I often ended up with narcissists who are skilled at love bombing. Once I understood and recognized how unhealthy my mindset was around that, I learned to be my own source of love, affirmation, and attention. It made me feel more in control and less prone to resorting to the "hard to get" game to have my needs met.

When I met my partner, he pursued me in such a direct manner that it felt threatening at first. I pushed him away briefly as I tried to sort out my overwhelming emotions. He gave me the needed space, and when we discussed it all openly, our relationship grew even more solid. He asked me early on to always let him know what I was feeling. It shocked me when he truly did welcome my honest input. To this day, we are both committed to consistent, honest communication. It has made everything so much easier.

Honest communication is not the norm for most people. As sensitive women, we have learned to hide our emotions for excellent reasons. Sharing our feelings has typically been met with criticism or complaints that we are too sensitive. We have developed unhealthy coping mechanisms to survive and feel safe. Many of these mechanisms aim to please and placate those around us, which by that very nature makes them manipulative. Yes, even if you have the best intentions of being kind to others, you can end up resorting to manipulative behaviors and games.

One of the most common and unhealthy games that sensitive women end up playing is "I'll make him love me." We know how much love we carry within us and feel as though just showering it on a partner will warm his heart. We can often sense the wounds in others. We feel sorry for the men we meet, knowing that they can't express their emotions because of societal programming or because someone has hurt them before. We get attached to the idea of helping and rehabilitating a man who doesn't want our help.

No one wins in this game. If you feel bad for someone you meet, do not let that bond you to him. Remember, you need a partner, not a project. You can't help or fix anyone who doesn't want to change and attempting to do so on their behalf is depriving them of a path that they must take on their own.

Relationships built on games or manipulation will never be healthy. It is difficult to be honest and authentic when you have built your connection on being coy or hiding your true feelings.

Never Assume

Given how difficult it is for all of us to be completely honest, it is probably obvious that you can never assume anything. My mom always used to say not to assume because it makes an "ass out of you and me." This was some of her best advice for sure. But, wow has it been hard to follow!

As an empath, I can feel energy. I sense when something is off, yet I can't necessarily know exactly what it is. Unfortunately, after years of feeling this uncomfortable disconnect, I have grown to fill in the blanks through assumptions. For instance, when I first met my partner, the intensity of his energy blew me away. He has powerful yang energy. In contrast to my somewhat yin nature, it can feel imbalanced for me. I assumed that what I was feeling from him was anger or discontent. However, when I got brave enough to confront him about it, he was shocked by my assessment. What he was really feeling was excitement and happiness. After years of experiencing negative energy, my gauge was totally off.

Even if you aren't an empath, you might tend to attach meaning to words and actions based on prior experience and your point of view. This will never create genuine understanding. You might get lucky occasionally, but more often than not, you will misread someone's intentions.

The only way through this common pitfall is to be a courageous communicator. Get comfortable asking for clarity as much as possible. If someone is not texting you as often as you would like, don't assume that they aren't interested without asking them first. They may just be busy. If someone seems interested in you, don't assume that you are the only person they are seeing. Directly ask how they feel about you and if you are the only person they are dating.

In my experience, it is better to ask questions in person or over the phone. That way you can pick up other clues like pauses, tone of voice, and body language that can support your intuition in determining if the man is being honest. Unfortunately, you can't even assume that someone is being honest with you when you directly ask questions. You will need to use all of your senses, as well as the evidence of consistent behavior.

It is awkward to be direct, especially as a sensitive person. You don't want to offend, annoy, or push someone away. However, a healthy relationship requires open and consistent communication. If a man can't handle your need for honesty, he is not ready for a healthy partnership.

Don't Forget About Boundaries

We've talked about boundaries and deal-breakers several times already. Similar to always trusting your intuition, setting boundaries is an essential skill sensitive women need in order to protect themselves. I can't emphasize enough the importance of establishing firm boundaries right from the start, especially since it is so dang hard.

You teach a man how to treat you. If you slip and accept behaviors that are disrespectful, dishonest, rude, or hurtful, those behaviors are likely to become the norm.

Every time you forgive or overlook undesirable treatment, you show that you don't value yourself. In contrast, if you enforce a boundary and it causes a man to leave, it is a blessing. Although it feels painful, it is a sign of strength and courage on your part. Congratulate yourself for reclaiming your power and energy from someone who clearly didn't deserve it.

I have heard a similar story repeated in online women's forums. It goes like this; the man tells the woman she is everything he is looking for after the first few weeks of connection. Then, suddenly he texts and says he doesn't think things will work out. Sometimes he gives a vague reason, other times he doesn't explain at all.

The woman then goes into a downward spiral of shame and doubt, wondering if it was because she has children, if she said something wrong, or if it was because she wasn't ready to be intimate yet. It could be for any of those reasons. Regardless, none of those reasons should lead a woman to doubt herself. Those reasons aren't about the woman's value as a person. They are about the man's unwillingness to respect her and participate in a mature relationship.

Setting boundaries with a man like that is saving you a lot of time. I guarantee a man like that was going to leave if the woman didn't have children, if she said all the right things, and, yes, even if she had been intimate with him. Some men just aren't relationship material and the best part of setting strong boundaries is that those men can't waste your precious time.

I know that this stuff hurts. I experienced my share of men who were texting and then vanished. It took some time to get over their unexplained absence. Through experience, I realized that if something I said in a text scared someone away, he was not my ideal partner.

A man should want you to communicate freely with him about your needs. A mature man will honor your boundaries, or explain why something isn't working for him so that you can work on it.

Don't Give In to Fear

Online dating can be scary. You are constantly putting yourself out there, trying to meet someone who is looking for a genuine connection, while most men only seem interested in looks and/or sex.

After being ghosted or rejected without even knowing why you develop a sense of dread. You can't help but worry and wonder when the nice man you are messaging is going to disappear. This is without question a form of psychological abuse. It triggers fears of rejection and abandonment that are common aspects of being human. I fully support you in taking breaks and regrouping as often as needed. However, I don't want you to give in to the fear and deem online dating useless.

The dating apps and websites are simply tools for helping you connect with men you wouldn't otherwise have met. Of course, you are better off never meeting some of those men. Regardless, you have the power and knowledge to weed through those men, giving them very little energy. Even though it is difficult, you are building greater strength and resilience every time a connection ends.

If your single life was like mine, busy with work and never meeting men, your odds of ever finding a partner on your own are low. In contrast, there are many successful love stories made online. Please honor your very normal fears of rejection and abandonment, while also tapping into your inner confidence and courage to continue putting yourself out there. Remember, you are always in control. There is nothing to fear.

Everything we do in life offers us the opportunity for lessons and growth. Online dating provides plenty of both. Don't worry too much about making mistakes. Life hands us the lessons we are meant to learn. Sometimes an awkward or uncomfortable relationship is put

on your path to help you grow stronger. It teaches you how to approach it better the next time. When I look back at the myriad mistakes I made in dating, I can see how much they shaped me into the woman I am today. I am much more confident and comfortable with myself. No matter what your dating outcome, you have the potential to become a stronger, more resilient version of yourself if you commit to honoring your own needs.

Chapter 22: Live Your Life

Online dating can consume your life. It is like living in an alternate reality. It influenced my daily life in confusing and surprising ways. I had a very hard time finding balance.

Even though I had social media accounts and public websites for many years, there was a different energy to being "out there" on the apps. I felt exposed, and I was far too concerned with whether I was getting "likes." The fixation negatively affected my self-esteem.

The best remedy for the confusing, isolating feelings of this alternate world was to be a more active participant in my actual life. I had to re-prioritize what was important to me. I had to remember that my time and attention were better served by connecting with friends and family, snuggling with my cat, focusing on my health, improving my home, advancing my career, and furthering my personal development. I hope you can agree that your time is just as precious.

The following are some healthy activities and mindset shifts that will help you improve your life and provide balance during and between your online dating efforts.

Focus on Health

Most of us are so busy with daily responsibilities that the foundational aspects of well-being fall off our radar. I have been a dietitian for over 20 years, so I would be remiss if I didn't mention the importance of health and the power of nutrition. In my opinion, nothing is more important than health, so I make strong efforts to keep myself as healthy as possible.

What you eat and how you treat your body are core elements of a happy, healthy life. Treating your body well means drinking enough water; limiting junk food; reducing your sugar intake; and basing meals on lean proteins, whole grains, vegetables, and fruit.

It also means watching your alcohol intake. I drank far more wine when I was online dating than ever before. It eased the stress, but my body always felt worse after a night of drinking too much. Limiting myself to one to two glasses of wine, four times per week offered a healthier balance.

Success in life is often based on where we set our focus. Deciding to follow a healthy lifestyle is an empowering way to change your life for the positive. Life can often feel so out of control, but when it comes to the foods you buy and eat, you have a great deal of power.

Exercise Regularly

Similar to nutrition, exercise is a powerful component of good health and greater happiness. Throughout my online dating experience, I took part in some form of exercise every day. On good weather days, I took walks outside in the fresh air and sunshine. I smiled and said, "Hi" to everyone I passed. Although I am introverted and often feel shy approaching others, I also committed to chatting with neighbors, forcing myself to exercise my social skills as well.

As I mentioned before, walking and other physical activity like dancing or yoga helped me feel stronger and more mentally healthy. Exercise is one of the best natural remedies for depression. It served as a surefire tool for uplifting my mood while giving me a consistent, healthy habit to look forward to.

Go Solo

After my divorce, I pushed myself to do activities on my own. I went to dinner, outdoor concerts, and movies by myself. I found safe, public hiking trails I could tackle alone (pepper spray and cell phone at the ready).

There is an inherent awkwardness to going places alone. I worried that people would judge me for being a "loner." However, over time I realized how freeing it was to be by myself. I could come and go as I pleased without having to adjust to anyone else's needs or schedule.

Furthermore, why care what anyone else thinks? If someone is focusing on me, they are obviously not having that much fun with the people they are with. I think most people are impressed when they see someone having fun on their own. It takes a lot of courage.

Shortly after moving into my home, I attended a free outdoor concert in my new town. The music played was a style that I loved, but my ex would have hated it. I thought about how miserable he would have been if he were with me. I would have spent the entire time feeling bad that he wasn't having fun, as had been the norm. Being on my own meant no apologies and no compromise. What glorious freedom!

The following year, I returned to that same concert spot with my current partner. He turned to me a few songs in and said with his typical joyful appreciation, "Wow! This is amazing. Thanks for inviting me." I couldn't help but think I had shown the Universe what I wanted more of, and it enabled me to call in a partner who would enjoy it with me.

Give Yourself Permission to Be

As you know, I love both astrology and personality theory. They offer so much insight into why I behave and think the way I do. My ex-husband had always dismissed them as silly. His negative energy prevented me from embracing them fully. Being on my own gave me the freedom to delve into these fields more deeply. One of my favorite astrologers, Debra Silverman, often says that astrology gives us permission to be who we are. I love that concept!

My entire life I have been told I am too sensitive, that I think too much, and that I care too much about other people's feelings. My personality type and natal chart explain the origins of these aspects clearly. As a Cancer rising, I was born to be sensitive and emotional. Likewise, as an INFJ I am wired to be a helper, putting the needs of others first.

I was destined to think and feel the way I do from the moment I was born. My family members don't share my predominant traits. This has always been a source of sadness and confusion for me. I wondered why I was so different. Now I know I am exactly how I am supposed to be. This is an incredible gift providing tremendous emotional support and increased confidence.

Even if you have trouble grasping these tools for understanding your inner workings, I hope you reach a place where you can accept yourself exactly as you are. When you are comfortable with yourself, you shine without restriction. Exuding an open, genuine, positive energy attracts the people and opportunities that are best for you. This is true in all areas of life, not just in finding your perfect love match. It is as if you are putting out a beacon of light signaling to other people and situations that you are a match. Some may say it is letting your freak flag fly. Please give yourself permission to do so.

I continue to work with astrology and personality theory daily, digging deeper into how they support my growth, and using these tools in my life and health coaching work. If you would like to explore these areas further, please see my contact information in the "Resources" section.

Learn New Skills

Intelligence is sexy! Learning new skills and information helps support your confidence, independence, and personal growth. A full, rich life includes stretching yourself creatively and intellectually.

There are so many ways to expand your knowledge and skills. Take an art class through your community education program. Sign up for a beginner's yoga class at a local yoga studio. Buy a program to learn a new language. Investing in your growth is money and time well spent.

You don't even have to spend money or leave your home to enrich your life. I have used the internet to deepen my meditation practice, expand my yoga skills, learn how to build a WordPress website, figure out how to publish this book, and understand the importance of setting boundaries. Through books and webinars, I have also found greater understanding and healing from the codependent tendencies that have kept me feeling stuck.

What have you always wanted to try? Do it! The more skills and interests you develop, the more interesting and exciting your life becomes.

Come Alive

Life's daily obligations can set us up for a boring, joyless routine. If you are a parent or caregiver, it can be especially easy to lose your inner spark. You end up focused on all the people around you — your children, family, friends, co-workers, and even the men you've met online.

Commit to rediscovering yourself. Working from the "life inventory" you completed in Chapter 14, focus on doing the things that you love most. Eat your favorite foods. Watch your favorite shows. Participate in all your favorite hobbies and activities.

Use all the information you have learned about yourself through the dating process to enhance the most important relationship in your life, the one with yourself. Stop doing only what you have to do. Start doing what you genuinely want to do. Make a conscious effort to do all the things that make you come alive.

Deepen Your Spiritual Connections

Spirituality is a deeply personal and highly individual aspect of life. I know everyone has to find their path and honor their own beliefs around spirituality. I am offering this suggestion knowing that it won't be right for everyone.

Deepening my spiritual connections greatly enhanced my life and personal well-being. My spirituality served as a tremendous source of support during my divorce. It was also a powerful guide throughout my dating experiences.

In addition to regularly meditating, I started to pray daily. Sometimes the prayer was simply an offering of gratitude to the

Universe for everything that I had in my life. In my experience, the more I honored my spirit, the more blessings I received.

I also found comfort in reciting the Lord's Prayer. Reciting prayers gives me a sense of control in a world that often feels chaotic.

I noticed that every time I asked for something aloud, I would receive it. It became a little scary, as I realized that if I asked for what I thought I wanted instead of what I needed, I ultimately ended up with the former. I manifested jobs I thought were perfect but turned out to be a poor fit. The same was true for men who I wanted to date. I asked Spirit to assist in the connection, and while it did often develop, it rarely turned out to be healthy.

This taught me to trust the Universe to deliver what I need without trying to assert my ego. I now ask for what is best for my highest good, recognizing that I don't always know what is in my best interest.

When you open up to your spirituality, synchronicities occur more readily. Synchronicities are meaningful connections that occur despite being improbable. In my opinion, these magical occurrences offer proof that we are in constant communication with the world around us. They are what I have referred to as "You can't make this up" moments.

One example of a common synchronicity that I have experienced for many years is seeing 11:11 on the clock. According to numerology, this is a sign that you are in alignment with the Universal energies, and that you are divinely supported. I was incredibly nervous waiting for my partner to pick me up for my first ride on the back of his motorcycle. I talked to Spirit, asking to be protected. Moments later, I saw 11:11 flash on the clock in my dining room. I knew my motorcycle ride was going to be great, and it was.

I spend my days looking for signs that appear through birds, license plates, numbers on the clock and odometer, songs, and even the messages present in daily horoscopes. The more I appreciate these spiritual signs of connectedness, the more frequently they appear. I can tell you countless stories of experiences that seem unbelievable.

The day I was writing this, I took a break to mow the lawn. Afterward, I stood at the edge of my yard thinking about how grateful I was for my home. Suddenly two hawks appeared seemingly out of nowhere. One swooped down so close to me I heard the swoosh of its wings. It took my breath away.

If you recall the story I shared around meeting my partner, it is filled with synchronicities and signs. We both just kept saying, "You can't make this up." He believes in signs just as much as I do, which has made our partnership even more fun.

One of the major benefits of deepening your spirituality is that it helps you recognize you are never actually alone. Spirits are always surrounding and guiding you, including your loved ones who have left this realm. When you believe this to be true, there is no loss and there is no true loneliness either. For me, it is a comforting and empowering thought.

Deepening your spiritual connection and living life looking for signs is pure magic. It provides so much joy and meaning to even the simplest of things.

In the pauses between online dating, I made an effort to be the best version of myself. I committed myself to falling in love with my life and the beautiful freedoms that came from being single. The more comfortable I got on my own, the happier I became, and the less willing I was to tolerate negative behavior from others. This was a blessing. Sensitive women need to enforce higher standards to protect ourselves. Our positive energy attracts people to us. It is only through discernment and our own strength that we can ensure that only other positive, happy people can bask in our light.

Phase 3: Get Serious About Love

You have prepared for the challenges of online dating, and then sorted out what it is like to put yourself out there. Now we are going to go deeper into what it takes to uncover a great love, one that starts with you.

This section is much shorter than the previous two because it is bonus advice. You could be very successful in having fun, enjoyable dates by following the information in the first two phases alone. This last phase is an extra push toward true love and a successful partnership. It is a bit like rocket fuel to propel you beyond what you thought was possible.

Some of what we are about to discuss is uncomfortable. We are going to uncover some of the harder, more negative emotions that may be keeping you stuck, as they had been for me. We will also delve into more energetic and spiritual practices that will help you heal so that you can welcome in greater love and abundance.

You might need to suspend a bit of disbelief as the more alchemical and spiritual ways of attracting love into your life can seem unusual at first. Please keep an open mind. These are the exact tips and tools that helped me build my self-love and ultimately call in my ideal partner. I'm confident that if you stay open to the process, you too will experience positive shifts in all areas of your life.

Chapter 23: Heal Your Broken Heart

We have all experienced heartbreak. As a sensitive woman, your heart is likely especially battered and bruised. I know for myself that even just five minutes of scrolling through Facebook can hurt my heart — missing dogs, stories of human tragedy, and political injustice. The negativity is unsettling. Energies bombard us daily, causing grief and sadness. Furthermore, when we experience the death of a loved one, a challenging divorce, a painful breakup, or the steady rejection of online dating, these heavy energies can get trapped in the body, particularly the heart chakra, the energetic field that encompasses your heart and chest.

The HeartMath Institute has been studying the power of your heart for over 30 years. They have been able to measure the incredible energy exuded by this organ that does far more than pump blood. Their studies have shown that the heart has a coherent, smooth rhythm when experiencing emotions like joy, love, and appreciation. In contrast, the heart's rhythms are more erratic when experiencing stressful, negative emotions like anger or frustration. As you probably already realize, stress negatively influences the nervous system and the entire body, but it appears to affect the heart in an especially powerful way. [For more on their research and free tools, please see the "Resources" section.]

We will discuss some of the tools and techniques that I have used to strengthen my heart chakra, relieve my broken heart, and release negative emotions. First, I will share how that heart became so broken to begin with. It is a cautionary tale that as a sensitive woman you might relate to.

My Heartbreak Story

Unfortunately, we give little conscious thought to the energetic state of our hearts. I know I rarely did until the magnitude of my grief and loss knocked me out in 2014. At that time, I experienced the deaths of several dear souls: my Grandmother-In-Law, a loving aunt, my cat of 13 years, and my dad. In a span of just a few months, they were all gone. It felt like being buried alive. The grief was crushing. Every day was a challenge.

My husband didn't seem to notice or even care. He refused to take me to the airport when I was traveling for my dad's memorial service and even found it funny to leave me a load full of laundry and a sink full of dishes to wash upon my return.

His cruelty, disguised as humor, had reached an all-time high. Struggling for some relief, I pushed for marriage counseling. However, as he stared blankly at the counselor, refusing to recognize the negative aspects of his behavior, I was forced to accept just how vacant he was. It was as if he didn't even have the capacity for love. I buried my pain further, not strong enough to face it directly at that time.

I had been experiencing gastroparesis since just before my dad's death. This is when food stays in the stomach, causing bloating and pain. After over six months of enduring physical discomfort, I was desperate for relief. I was well aware of the energetic causes of disease. I suspected what I was experiencing was not just a physical ailment, but rather related to an energy block due to my inability to honor my feelings. I was stuffing my feelings down so much that the energy was trapped in my lower chakras, causing all movement in that area to stop, including digestion.

I booked an appointment with a homeopath, who asked me to share all the details of my life. As I spoke of my grief and all the negative people surrounding me, I already felt a sense of relief. She went on to ask me in-depth questions about my personality, personal preferences, beliefs, and lifestyle.

Homeopathy is an energetic healing modality that seeks to treat physical or emotional ailments with a minuscule amount of a natural substance that has the same quality as the ailment. Homeopathic remedies kick-start the body to overcome whatever is keeping it stuck.

I knew homeopathy was safe and effective, as I had used it before. However, what I experienced with that professional appointment was truly remarkable. The Homeopath selected a personalized remedy for me. As soon as I began taking it, I felt an incredible softening come over my abdomen. It felt lighter, as if a knot loosened and released.

When the Homeopath called to check in on me a week later, I relayed the joy I was feeling after finally being able to eat normally. I confided, "I think I have to get a divorce." She sighed and said, "I was afraid of that, although it is likely for the best." She explained that when stuck energy is released sometimes there is no going back. That proved to be true for me.

The last Christmas I spent with my husband and his family was the worst of my life. My husband had given me several thoughtless gifts, including a pair of earrings he had given me before and several bags of candy that contained gluten, even though I had been eating a gluten-free diet for eight years. Before the Christmas meal, my Mother-in-Law yelled at me to cut the bread, twice. Both times, I told her I couldn't touch bread or it would make me sick. Nearly every time I ate meals with that family, I would get sick from gluten. I had finally had enough! Meanwhile, her two daughters were sitting nearby chatting, not helping at all. I snuck off to the bathroom to cry, promising myself I would never set foot in that house again.

On New Year's Eve, I decided I would give my husband one last chance at working on us. I had bought a book aimed at helping couples work on their relationship without the need for a counselor. I approached my husband in the kitchen and asked him if he would consider working through the book with me. As usual, he snapped and said, "I don't have any problems. All the problems in this relationship are because of you." He had said that line countless times, and for the first time, I finally realized how absurd it was. I stood there and started to laugh. I said, "Well, then I guess we are done." Just then, a hawk flew in front of our kitchen window so close that its feathers practically brushed the glass. I said, "What was that?!" Even though he thought my animal signs were silly, he knew what they meant. He said flatly, "It was a hawk. So, I guess we ARE done."

Fully Recognize the Pain

It is very common to deny painful feelings like grief, anger, or guilt. We bury these negative feelings away because they hurt too much. We are often also too busy with life to get sidelined by the painful feelings, so we push them down and pretend they aren't there. Sometimes we can't even recognize the trauma, abuse, or pain because it is such a normal part of our lives. As you know from my experience, feelings can't stay buried for long without wreaking havoc on your health. You must feel them to heal them.

I could finally work through the grief driven by the deaths of 2014. However, the grief and sadness I experienced during and after my divorce were unlike anything I ever experienced. I wanted the divorce, but not really. What I really wanted was for my husband to see how hurtful and unsupportive he had been. I wanted him to work with me on making things better so that the 17 years I had invested into our relationship were not wasted. I also felt intense guilt about having to leave the nieces and nephews who I had watched grow up.

No one really wants a divorce. It is a brutal process. The strange dynamic of asking for a divorce, but not wanting it, makes the grief confusing and especially hard to honor. In addition, people often vilify the person asking for a divorce. That was how I felt. My husband had asked me not to tell anyone about our decision. Then, he attended a party where he told most of his friends. He proudly reported to me the next day how the women, who had been my friends (I thought), cried with him. He always controlled the narrative on things and it was unbelievable to me that, after years of dedicating time and attention to his friends and family, very few of them showed concern for my well-being or my side of things.

I made the mistake of opting to handle all the logistics of the divorce without the use of a mediator, thinking that was a wise way to save us $5000. It meant I had to become a lawyer in my spare time, submitting confusing paperwork, and running back-and-forth to the court that was an hour from where I had moved.

My husband promised he could be fair in settling things on our own. I foolishly believed him. He proceeded to stash money away, claiming he needed to spend $100 a week out at bars. While I was still in the house preparing to move, he was already going out. I encouraged it because I thought if he met someone else he might be less cruel and vindictive. Still, I was shocked and hurt that he was so focused on replacing me before I was even gone.

While he seemed to move on with his life easily, I had to move out of the beautiful, three-bedroom home I had painstakingly painted, furnished, and decorated, leaving many of my possessions behind because I didn't have room for them in the tiny, old townhouse I was moving into. I was terrified to spend money, fearing it might somehow hurt me in court. I lived like a pauper for the nine months of the divorce.

Many people encouraged me to fight for what I deserved. I found it hard to fight at all. It wasn't worth it to me. I just wanted peace. I ultimately settled for far less than the divorce attorney I consulted thought I deserved. I was exhausted and had no fight left.

On the day of the divorce hearing, after already signing paperwork confirming the agreement, my husband claimed to the judge that my figures were wrong. He handed in a revised document. The judge was not concerned with honoring what we had just signed. In shock and on the verge of a panic attack, I agreed to the new figures.

Ironically, the new figure stripped me of nearly $5000, the very amount I had saved us by managing things on my own. Had I used a mediator, I know I would have ended up with far more money and far less stress. Even after everything he had put me through, I still put my husband's needs above my own, to my demise. It was a powerful lesson that took me several more years to process fully.

That night as I was reeling from the shock of that day, I saw a post from my now ex-husband on Facebook saying something about having to walk on in life on his own. I couldn't believe his ability to still play the victim after doing what he had done.

At that point, I didn't realize he was a covert narcissist. That realization painfully set in the longer I was away from his poison. When you are with a narcissist, you get so used to their negative behaviors that they feel normal. Finally recognizing the abuse is part of the healing.

People told me that a man going through a divorce would do things I could never imagine. That proved to be true. Besides the intense grief I was harboring, there was a building rage and disgust for the man who had taken so much from me emotionally, financially, and spiritually.

I never expected to cut ties with him completely. Nevertheless, after his behavior during the divorce, and the way he neglected our cat, which he insisted he keep, I don't want to have anything to do with him. He is not my friend. Sadly, I have had to accept that he never was.

Acceptance is the key to processing difficult emotions. Accept them, feel them, and allow them to pass. This is not easy for any of us.

I still feel heavy emotions arise, sometimes unexpectedly. Something will trigger a memory and a wave of frustrating feelings wash over me. I no longer fight or bury those feelings. I don't minimize or dismiss them. I honor them and give them the attention they need. Fighting and denying your emotions only makes them grow stronger.

I am embarrassed to share the personal details of my experience. I am an intelligent, strong woman. It is hard to accept how I have given away my power throughout my life. The shame and feelings of foolishness are probably the most painful. I know that many sensitive women can relate.

Sarah K. Ramsey talks about the concept of smart-girl syndrome. Through her work in helping women recover from toxic relationships, she has noticed a pattern. The women who are abused by toxic, manipulative men are often smart, successful, and kind. They are "good girls" who wouldn't think of hurting anyone else, which is exactly why they get so hurt themselves.

If any of my story is relatable to you, please know that it gets better. There is a happy ending, and working through your emotions is an essential path to getting there.

Find Peace in Perspective

Shortly after deciding we were destined for divorce, my husband told me I needed to get a full-time job and move out of his house. Of course, that was a ridiculous demand since it was our house together for over 15 years. Regardless, I wanted out. I did not want to be around his toxic energy any longer than necessary.

I had been working as a Communications Consultant with a varied schedule that screeched to a halt after the painful deaths that took place in 2014. I went numb from the loss and had very little energy to devote to work in 2015.

The divorce revelation at the beginning of 2016 sent me scrambling to find a solid job fast. I had been praying for a new opportunity since the end of 2014. I would regularly ask the Universe for, "a supportive group of people who were working together toward the same positive goal." I wanted so badly to work with like-minded, compassionate people. However, I also knew that I couldn't work a 40-hour position, since I struggled with chronic fatigue. Although I am an incredibly productive worker, I could not comfortably commit to a traditional full-time schedule.

I knew instantly that my prayers had been answered when

a 32-hour role at a hospice center appeared in my job search. I literally fell to my knees in gratitude, feeling it was exactly what I was looking for. Despite a long initial commute and an inevitable move away from all of my friends, I accepted the job without even negotiating the low salary. I was just so excited about the mission of hospice.

The medical system failed to treat my dad properly as he declined from Alzheimer's disease. My family didn't know until too late that hospice care could have been a supportive option for him. I wanted to help other families understand the value such care offered at the end of life.

Working in hospice during my divorce was an unexpected blessing. I couldn't feel sorry for myself or wallow in my grief when I was surrounded by families and patients who had things so much worse. The power of that perspective was profound.

At one point, I was struggling with the reality that I would no longer have access to a washer and dryer in my home. The only rental property that fit my budget, and would allow me to have my cat, had a small laundry facility that was three doors down from my townhouse. I was so frustrated and sad thinking about how inconvenient doing laundry was going to be.

As I was wrestling with that challenge, I attended a weekly case review held by the hospice nurses and social workers. During that meeting, one of the senior hospice nurses shared a story of a family who couldn't afford to go to the laundromat. Their dying mother had soiled her sheets, and they had no means of remedying the situation. As I listened to such a dire example of need, I fought back tears. My problems were so small in comparison. That nurse, by the way, used her personal funds to buy the family new sheets. She and I would ultimately become friends, regularly sharing the beautiful synchronicities that were always present around us.

So much about my time at the hospice center was an absolute gift. I met a group of divorced women who I admired greatly. All of them were better off for having left their marriages. Their new lives brought babies, grandbabies, pets, and new loving partners who were beyond what they imagined. Those women gave me hope and strength, as I could see firsthand that I was heading towards a happier, more fulfilling life.

It also deepened my faith. Witnessing the amazing gifts that show up for people at the end of their lives strengthened my belief in a higher power. So many of the nurses I spoke to had stories of unexplained events and beautiful blessings that consistently showed up in their work. One dear nurse who worked with children once stopped by my desk at the end of a particularly draining shift. As I leaned in to hug her, I saw sparks of blue and green light radiate from her chest. It was pure magic.

I'm not suggesting that finding perspective through the suffering of others eliminated my feelings of grief or loss. It did not. However, it showed me firsthand just how strong and resilient humans can be, including me.

It also helped me honor and nurture my strength in storytelling. In my role as the Communications Manager for the center, I had the great pleasure of sharing patient's life stories. It was one of the most meaningful experiences of my career. Prior to that role, although I had been writing professionally for over a decade, I had trouble calling myself a writer. I just never felt good enough.

One dying man, whom I interviewed over the phone for his final story, insisted on meeting me in person. He wanted to tell me to my face how grateful he was for the enduring memory I had given to his family and friends. It was an incredibly powerful moment to have him take my hand in his and say, "Thank you. You are a beautiful writer."

When you are going through challenging times, it is always helpful to pay attention to what is happening around you. In the grand scheme of things, what we see as insurmountable challenges are often just temporary obstacles meant to strengthen us. Sometimes our heart needs to be broken wide open to let more love pour in.

Clear the Heart Chakra

Chakra is the Sanskrit word for "wheel." The chakras are seven spinning discs of energy located along the midline of the body, from the base of your spine to above the top of your head. The heart chakra is at the center of the chest, dividing the upper and lower three chakras. This powerful center is where we process love, anger, and grief. When we focus on clearing and strengthening this chakra, we increase our capacity to give and receive love.

Simply placing your open palm over the center of your chest has a profoundly calming effect. When I was working in hospice, I noticed I started reaching for my chest every time something beautiful and meaningful occurred. It felt like a physical means of acknowledging and locking the loving sensations in. Making a regular practice of placing your hand over the center of your chest and breathing deeply into that space can bring relaxation and comfort.

Many tools and techniques can help clear the heart chakra of negative energy and sadness. These include:

* Spinning a quartz crystal in front of the chest
* Practicing heart-opening yoga poses such as upward-facing dog, cobra, fish, or cow pose
* Chanting the mantra, "Yam" ("yahhmm")
* Using color therapy, focusing on the green and pink associated with the heart chakra by wearing these colors or working with crystals in these colors
* Trying Emei Qigong (see the "Resources" section for more on this powerful healing practice)

Following are several specific modalities and intentions, which are also helpful in clearing and opening the heart chakra.

Use Homeopathy and Flower Essences

I mentioned how dramatically healing my first appointment with a homeopath had been. She helped me release so much blocked energy and heavy emotions. Following the deaths that occurred in 2014 and throughout my divorce, I supported my heart and emotions with a variety of homeopathic remedies and flower essences.

As mentioned before, Homeopathy is a very gentle form of healing that creates an energetic shift in the body. It has been used since the 1700s. Flower essences are very similar and were first introduced in the 1930s.

Homeopathic remedies are typically delivered as small pellets that you dissolve under your tongue. The 30c strength is appropriate for regular use.

Flower essences are tinctures that include tiny amounts of a flower generally in an alcohol base (for preservation). You can put the essences directly on your tongue, add them to your drinking water, or rub them into the skin. Although it is recommended that you take these remedies several times a day until symptoms are relieved, I often only remembered to take them once in the morning or evening, and they were still effective.

Your ideal remedy is often very specific to your unique needs. As a result, if you can find a local professional homeopath or someone trained in flower essences, I advise you to schedule a personal consultation. At the beginning of my online dating experience, I was fortunate enough to find a talented young woman who was studying to be a Flower Essence Therapy Practitioner. She prepared a personalized flower essence remedy that included several flowers designed to build my confidence, relieve my grief, and increase my feelings of self-worth. The remedy definitely helped.

Following are some of the remedies, Homeopathic (H) and Flower Essences (FE), I have personally used with great success:

Ignatia (H) - The most common remedy for loss, particularly when grief is prolonged.

Sacred Heart Formula (FE) - A blend of several flower essences designed specifically for healing and strengthening the heart, particularly in terms of failed relationships and lingering heartbreak.

Larch (FE) - It strengthens self-confidence, courage, and the ability to speak out.

Centaury (FE) - Ideal for empaths or others who have trouble saying, "no," it provides emotional strength.

Mustard (H & FE) - This is the original homeopathic remedy that was suggested when I experienced gastroparesis from holding in my emotions. I have since used it as a flower essence with the same purpose and positive effect. It helps promote feelings of joy.

Self-Heal (FE) - A remedy that supports and empowers your healing by bolstering your belief that you can do so.

You can purchase homeopathic remedies and flower essences at health food stores or by ordering them online. For more information, please see the "Resources" section.

Try Healing Rituals for Release

Letting go can be difficult. Even when we know something has ended for the best, we can still hold attachments to memories, thoughts, and feelings. By taking conscious actions towards release, you can finally let go of the things that are hindering your healing. The following healing rituals are great for release:

Full Moon Release - A full moon is a powerful time for release. Since it symbolizes the end of a cycle, it encompasses an energy of closure. You can set a conscious intention around what you want to let go of by stating it aloud or by writing it in your journal. Any of the rituals that follow can be performed during a full moon to amplify their effects.

Burning Ceremony - I love burning ceremonies. They can be as simple or complicated as you make them. If you have limited space, lighting a candle with the intention that it will energetically burn away all the stagnant and negative energy can be enough. If you have a fire pit, fireplace, or fireproof container, you can perform a more detailed ritual of writing the name of the person or situation on a piece of paper and then setting it on fire, releasing any energetic ties and sending the energy back to its rightful owner as you reclaim any energy that is yours.

Letter Writing - Writing letters to those who have harmed you is a cathartic way to release the pain. You can detail all the reasons you no longer want this person in your life, or even focus on how ready you are to forgive them for the mistakes you both made. As I've mentioned many times before, writing down our thoughts and feelings frees them from our mind and body. After you have written a letter, you can tear it up or burn it as a further sign of release.

Primal Screaming - Rarely do we get to scream freely, but when we can it provides such a deep form of release. If you can find a secluded spot where you won't be heard, let out a scream from the pit of your belly. Even screaming into a pillow can be oddly satisfying.

Shaking - When energies are trapped in the body, the most natural way to release them is by shaking them out. You can do this to fast-paced music, or in the quiet, whichever you prefer. Simply shake your arms, legs, hands, head, and move your hips until your body feels looser and more at ease. Shaking can be done regularly to improve energy flow and prevent energies from getting stuck.

You can treat any effort as a healing ritual if you put intention into it. Think of the activities that bring you peace and reframe them as tools for healing in body, mind, and spirit. This could include drinking tea, listening to music, soaking in a bath, hugging a friend. Think about releasing all negative feelings and replacing them with love.

Use Crystals and Essential Oils

We've briefly discussed the energetic properties of both crystals and essential oils. Like all things on earth, these natural substances have their own powerful energetic vibration, which is what makes them so helpful in healing.

The heart chakra is associated with the colors green and pink. As such, crystals in those colors are thought to support the heart's energy. Rose quartz is one of the most supportive crystals for healing your heart and drawing in love. Following my divorce, and throughout my dating experiences, I kept several pieces of rose quartz in my meditation space. When I was feeling ready to draw in a true love connection, I slept with a large piece under my pillow.

Rose quartz is very gentle, an especially good choice for a sensitive woman. It is also readily available and inexpensive. I suggest visiting a local crystal shop to select the crystals that feel best for you. Buy several pieces of rose quartz so you can carry them in your purse, keep one at your desk at work, have one by your computer, and place one in the relationship corner of your home (the area that is the farthest to the right from your front door.)

Just before my divorce, I purchased a piece of malachite, which is a vivid green color. Malachite's energy is a bit more intense. As soon as I placed it on my heart chakra, I felt my heart and breathing rates increase. I had to work with it slowly, using it for only short periods so that the energetic shift didn't feel too extreme.

I know many people are skeptical of crystals, but those of us who are especially sensitive to energy know firsthand that they can raise our vibrations quickly. Use them at your own pace.

Essential oils work similarly to crystals in that they can raise your energetic vibration and bring ease. You can use them in a variety of ways including:

Topically - Combining them with a carrier oil and applying them to the skin or adding them to a warm bath.

As Aromatherapy - Diffusing them in the air or adding them to a glass container over a gentle source of heat so that the scent is released. *Be careful using an oil diffuser around pets, as many essential oils can be toxic to them.

Through a Porous Medium - Placing oil on a scarf or tissue to inhale the scent, or adding the oil to a piece of jewelry so the scent releases throughout the day.

The following essential oils are associated with emotional relief and are my personal favorites:

Rose - I read somewhere that rose gladdens the heart. I have found that to be true. It is such a gentle, uplifting scent. Pure rose oil is quite expensive, so it is often sold mixed with a carrier oil. This means you can use it directly on the skin. I also love rosewater spray. It offers a nice pick-me-up and is nourishing for the skin.

Frankincense - Known as a spiritual oil, frankincense has a comforting, warming essence, while offering protection from negative energy.

Lavender - Well known for its stress-relieving, calming qualities, lavender is great when used in the bath with Epsom salts. It also aids with sleep and can be sprinkled on your pillow.

Grapefruit - Known to relieve depression and uplift the spirit, grapefruit works well in aromatherapy and even when added to cleaning products.

Many more essential oils can support emotional healing. To learn more, see the "Resources" section.

Practice Metta Meditation

Metta (loving-kindness) meditation is a wonderful way to nurture love within, while also projecting it out into the world. It is a simple practice from Buddhism in which you state loving intentions in a repetitive pattern. It helps to displace negative emotions and promote peace.

Although the actual phrases used can vary slightly, the basic elements of a metta meditation include four brief statements offering peace, love, safety, or ease. To perform a metta meditation, find a quiet, comfortable space and either sit with legs crossed or on a chair with your spine straight and your shoulders relaxed. Take several deep breaths to calm and center yourself, and then repeat the loving phrases you have chosen, first directing them toward yourself (i.e., "May I..."), and then thinking of either individuals or groups (i.e., "May you..."). Keep repeating the phrases on behalf of the person or people you are thinking of. As your closing statement, direct the loving phrases to "all sentient beings" (i.e., "May all sentient beings...").

A sample set of phrases that I have used is:

* May [I, you, or all sentient beings] be safe
* May [I, you, or all sentient beings] be well
* May [I, you, or all sentient beings] be happy
* May [I, you, or all sentient beings] live with ease

You can easily perform a metta meditation on your own. It helps to write out your chosen phrases until you remember them easily. There are also a variety of guided metta meditations available online.

This practice is essentially a prayer offered on behalf of yourself and anyone you wish to honor. One of the more challenging aspects of this practice is offering loving kindness to people for whom you hold negative feelings. By meditating for those who cause you pain or grief, you experience a softening in your heart, which is very healing. It is a wonderful way to bring more love and compassion into your life.

Offer Ho'oponopono Healing

Ho'oponopono (Ho o pono pono) is energetically quite similar to metta meditation. However, it uses a very distinct set of phrases designed to harness the power of acceptance, forgiveness, gratitude, and love. This practice originated in Hawaii, and the word ho'oponopono means "correction" in English. It intends to correct any mistakes that have taken place. Since we have all made mistakes and done things that were not positive and loving, it is a beautiful way to replace any wrongdoings with forgiveness and love.

As in metta meditation, get into a comfortable position, breathe deeply to release any tension, and establish a sense of calm. Then repeat the following:

* I'm Sorry
* Please Forgive Me
* Thank You
* I Love You

You can choose to think of a person or even a particular incidence for which you wish to seek amends. You can also just recite these powerful phrases to raise the collective consciousness and seek relief from the wrongdoings of others.

I have found this simple practice to be amazingly powerful. Shortly after I learned about ho'oponopono in my master's degree program, I had new countertops installed in my home. I am always hospitable to anyone who does work in my home, and I had offered the installers coffee, drinks, and snacks. When they were cleaning up, they asked if they should take my old countertops. I hadn't thought about that, but I realized that would save us some time since we would likely need to cut them up to dispose of them. I said, "Yes," and didn't think much more about it.

The next day, I received an angry call from the owner of the installation company. He accused me of coercing his installers into taking my old countertops and said that I owed him an additional $200. His demands stunned me. I explained that I did not know that would be an additional charge, and if I knew, I would have just handled it on my own. The man was fuming mad and insisted that he would send an additional bill.

I was very upset about the entire interaction. I had errands to run, so while in the car I focused my energy on repeatedly offering ho'oponopono blessings to the owner. I envisioned the man, whom I had never actually met, and repeatedly offered him blessings. I loved my new countertops and felt terrible about this turn of events.

When I returned home about an hour later, there was a message on my answering machine. It was the owner apologizing for responding so harshly. He said he would not be sending an additional bill. His reaction was a complete turnaround and a powerful validation that ho'oponopono works!

I know it seems wild, but I have had other examples of this simple healing tool bringing me peace and softening the behaviors of difficult people. It is a beautiful set of phrases to repeat regularly, as you can never go wrong with their loving intentions.

Break the Spell of Toxic People

A good portion of the heartbreak and emotional pain that many sensitive women experience comes from interacting with negative, toxic people. We must shield ourselves from these individuals if we ever want emotional freedom and optimal health.

One of the most powerful shifts in my thinking occurred during the last week of 2018. While driving to visit my sister's family for a late Christmas celebration, I listened to Dr. Christiane Northrup's audiobook, "Dodging Energy Vampires." Dr. Northrup is a world-renowned women's health expert.

It was validating to hear her explain that, as an empath herself, many narcissists and other disordered people had targeted and manipulated her throughout her life. Her powerful intention to heal and help others had drawn these people to her like moths to a flame.

Whereas many people in the healing field shy away from labeling people in negative ways, implying that it is judgmental, unfair, or unspiritual, Dr. Northrup boldly stated that negative, manipulative people absolutely do exist. Furthermore, she expressed that they are intentionally harming others for their gain. She asserted that empaths and other sensitive individuals must avoid these people at all costs, putting up boundaries and refusing to give them our energy or attention.

At that time, I was still in the mindset of feeling bad for people who were cruel and rude. I went to great lengths to justify and forgive their behavior. For instance, a woman I was working with was always short-tempered and downright rude. People tiptoed around her. I tried to befriend her, hoping she would see me as an ally instead of an enemy. I could see that she was very intelligent and creative. I felt a need to understand why she was always so angry and miserable, thinking that if I knew, I could help support her. Over time, it became clear that she had a difficult childhood filled with criticism and continued to have that same dynamic in her home life. I felt so much pity for her situation that I vowed to praise her and offer support.

Despite my positive intentions, her nastiness persisted. She even actively tried to sabotage some of my work projects and continued to speak so harshly to me that I felt nauseous in her presence. Enough was enough! Emboldened by Dr. Northrup's advice, I vowed to go "gray rock," a technique for giving a person the minimal emotional response, essentially being as boring as a rock.

Many people who have experienced abuse at the hands of narcissists, or other toxic types, go to great lengths to understand everything we can about their disordered behavior. While knowledge does have the potential to help, it sometimes leads empaths to pity these people needlessly.

Narcissism typically occurs as the result of a childhood wound. After learning this, I took it as a call to action to help and support the narcissists I met, hoping it would soften their hearts. As Dr. Northrup and many other experts explain, such positive outcomes never occur. A disordered person is often happy in their dysfunction. They absolutely can't assume the accountability that is necessary for actual change. Any efforts at helping them will only result in further abuse.

Every adult I know has encountered difficult situations. We all experience criticism, bullying, loss, sadness, stress, and trauma to some degree. It is no excuse for hurting others. Some of the most loving and compassionate people I know have had horrific examples of loss, abuse, and tragedy. It is common for empaths to turn their pain into even greater compassion for others. There is never a valid excuse for someone to be cruel or abusive.

Throughout my life, I have consistently poured energy, love, and time towards toxic people. In every case, my efforts only left me depleted and sad. Those individuals rarely even acknowledged me as a human.

There is a phenomenon in business that says 20% of customers require 80% of your effort. I have seen this play out not just in work, but also in all relationships. Difficult people require far too much of our precious resources. We need to cut our losses and give our time and attention only where it serves the highest good of all.

Breaking the spell of toxic people means recognizing they exist and avoiding them at all costs. You do not need to associate with family members who are always controlling or dismissive. You do not need to tolerate a colleague who consistently talks down to you or passes their work on to you. You especially do not need to participate in a romantic partnership where your needs are not supported 100%.

Prevent heartbreak and negative emotions before they can even start by recognizing that the best offense is a good defense. Simply refuse to give toxic people any of your time and attention. Those moths will grow tired of you and fly off in search of another flame.

Be Totally Honest With Yourself

I've already mentioned facing your fears and fully recognizing the pain in your emotions. Both of these actions require a level of acceptance and honesty. I feel the importance of seeing things as they really are, and living in your truth, bears repeating once again.

When I finally shared with my family and friends that I was getting divorced, aside from my best friend who had witnessed the toxicity of my marriage clearly, everyone was shocked. People thought we were the perfect couple. They never suspected anything was wrong. One friend told me she thought my husband was a nice person and implied that I was making a mistake. Another couple reported that our relationship was their role model. It devastated them to realize that we weren't able to make things work.

It was painful to hear these reactions because it showed me how much I had been hiding the truth and living a lie. It embarrassed me to realize I had so many people fooled when I had been deeply conflicted by my husband's behavior from the very moment we met. Rather than acknowledge what I had been feeling, even when I was having second thoughts days before our wedding, I kept telling myself that he was a loving person deep down. I clung to every little crumb of kindness to justify staying, not wanting to hurt him. I told myself repeatedly that he meant well when he said hurtful things. I rationalized that he just didn't know any better. I took it upon myself to parent him in dysfunctional ways.

While completing my master's degree, I met a retired physicist who had been studying the origins of autoimmune disease. I have three autoimmune conditions (Hashimoto's Thyroiditis, Sjögren's Syndrome, and Celiac Disease). As such, I was concerned by his declaration that these conditions are caused by the mind attacking the body. However, it was easy to see that was true. By living a lie and burying my pain, I was emotionally attacking my own body and spirit.

The major ailments I have relate directly to the throat chakra, which is only healthy when we are openly speaking our truth. When I asked the physicist, who was also intuitive, why he thought I might be experiencing disease, he said, "There is something in your life that is not meant to be there."

Although my husband and I were getting along well at the time, I knew immediately the physicist was referring to my marriage. When I confided in some of my colleagues about my revelation, they were uneasy. They warned me of how difficult divorce could be. They feared I could not make it on my own given my impaired health. I agreed with their assessment and continued to bury my beliefs, repeatedly telling myself that my husband was a nice, decent man. Perhaps I was just being too sensitive, as he always suggested?

Oddly, even after leaving my marriage and feeling the immediate relief it brought, I still wondered if perhaps I had been too hard on my ex. My dear, empathic cat assured me that was not the case. She had lived with my ex and me since we adopted her as a kitten. Although she seemed to like him, he often expressed anger that she was far more attentive to me. He would speak to her in a harsh tone, telling her to get out of the way if she walked in his path. I constantly asked him to speak more kindly to her, but he paid no attention. When he came to my townhouse to drop off something related to the divorce, the sweet animal who knew him well hissed at him and ran to hide. I felt bad for him. I now realize that he got the reception he deserved. My cat was a much better judge of his negative energy than I had been. Now that she has lived with me alone for several years, she is a completely different animal. She is much braver and more vocal and affectionate than ever before. I think the same can be said for her human mom.

Similar to how I continued to give my ex the benefit of the doubt, I kept giving the men I met in online dating a pass for unacceptable behavior. If they were sarcastic or insensitive, I would dismiss that knowledge thinking, "Oh, but he is really a nice guy deep down."

I believe many sensitive women have similar faulty programming. We believe people think in the compassionate manner that we do. We feel that deep down most people are good and kind. We want so desperately for that to be true that we ignore even blatant signs that prove otherwise.

Furthermore, we fail to recognize that just because someone doesn't believe us, or agree with our perspective, does not mean it isn't true. It takes a lot of courage to stand firm in your beliefs. This is especially true when you are dismissed as being "too sensitive." However, in order to live fully and authentically, you must honor the truth above all else.

As you seek to heal your heart and spirit, please focus on

accepting things at face value. Please do not make excuses for people. Do not give them multiple chances to keep hurting you. Do not disregard what you know is right. You are not TOO sensitive. You are the perfect amount of sensitivity for you.

This was a tough chapter! I've revealed a lot of my most painful truths here. Please don't let any of my negative experiences drag you down. I share them only in hopes that, if any of them resonate, you will find strength from the lessons. I have turned my pain into a powerful purpose, using a variety of fantastic tools to heal my emotions and myself. Let my comeback story support your growth and awareness.

Chapter 24: Fall in Love With Yourself

It might surprise you to know that after everything I have been through — narcissistic abuse, losing a beautiful home, low self-esteem, and chronic illness — I readily cry tears of joy. I love the life I have recreated for myself. I now live a very simple life in a cozy 2-bedroom home decorated exactly how I always wanted.

There are signs throughout my home containing positive affirmations that remind me of my worth. My favorite is, "She believed she could, so she did!" I have that same saying engraved on a necklace that I wore throughout my divorce.

My favorite things surround me: butterflies; crystals; dried flowers from my hydrangea and past bouquets from my sweetheart; colorful artwork; and treasured photos of friends, family, and my partner. The things we surround ourselves with have the power to lift us up, so I make a conscious effort to fill my home with items that inspire joy.

In contrast, anything that carries negative energy can bring us down. As such, I have gone through every room, closet, and drawer, purging away anything that did not make me happy.

I painted the rooms in my home in my favorite colors. The bedrooms, kitchen, bathrooms, and basement are in soothing shades of blue and green. The living room is a bright, cheerful yellow. There are accents of turquoise everywhere, a color I was drawn to during my divorce, and later learned represents a combining of the heart and throat chakras in a spiritual connection that allows for more loving communication.

You deserve to experience joy every day. Following are just a few ways that you can support and honor love for your life and yourself.

Treat Yourself Well

I am writing this during the COVID-19 pandemic, where self-care has become a bit of a buzzword. If there is one positive to this devastating crisis, it is the recognition that we can't disregard the importance of health in all realms — physical, mental, and spiritual.

Treating yourself well and as a priority is a crucial part of a balanced, successful life. We hear all the time that we can't fill another's cup if we have not filled our own first. You must completely honor this truth and make your happiness a priority every single day, whatever that means for you.

Perhaps it is something simple like splurging for the organic coffee beans that are an extra two dollars a pound or investing in an online yoga app that will help keep you motivated. Even when money is tight, you can still enjoy the simple, free pleasures of life. Personally, one of my favorite forms of relaxation and joy is reveling in the beauty of nightly sunsets. [You can see some of my pics on my Instagram page linked in the "Resources" section.]

You are supposed to feel good! Life is not meant to be all work and sacrifice. Even if you have a mountain of obligations from family, to work, and everything else in between, you still owe yourself joyful experiences. Please work to determine all the little things that bring you peace and joy, and add them to your daily life.

Create a morning routine that starts you off right. I love cold brew coffee and jump out of bed excited to enjoy my first cup. I also love listening to music. I ask Alexa to play my favorite playlist, so I am surrounded by uplifting sounds. I walk around the house, opening the curtains to let in the sunlight. Then, I sit down in my meditation space to smudge myself, say a prayer, pick an oracle or animal card, and give thanks for a new day.

As you start your day, think about what makes you happy.

Consider the following questions:

* *What do I want to do today?*
* *What would make me happy right now?*
* *What would taste good to me?*
* *What does my body need?*
* *Who would I like to connect with?*
* *What exercise will energize me?*
* *What negative emotions am I feeling? How can I combat them with love?*

If you don't treat yourself well, who will? We teach people how to treat us, so make a practice of treating yourself with love and respect. Only then will the Universe be able to offer you more of the goodness that you crave.

Focus on Self-Love

It took me a long time to embrace the importance of self-love. Growing up, I had a close adult who often called me "spoiled." It was a confusing admonishment because I rarely asked for things. My parents were generous and gave my sister and me wonderful toys and gifts, but it wasn't because we demanded them as spoiled children. When I shared my confusion with my parents, they said the person was just jealous. That excuse never made me feel any better. I came to believe that asking for things and even honoring my own needs in self-loving ways was wrong.

As a teen, I encountered teachers and coaches whose words created similar scars. If I dared question them or tried to establish boundaries, they would put me in my place calling me "difficult" or "rebellious." I never wanted to be those things. I only ever wanted to be "good." The emotional conflict was painful and made loving myself feel impossible.

Many sensitive women struggle with self-love for a variety of reasons. Besides having it feel selfish, it is seemingly contrary to how "good girls" behave. We are taught to always think of others before ourselves. We want to be of service and loving ourselves feels uncomfortable.

The problem with this thought pattern is that it sets us up for low self-esteem and emotional abuse. If you aren't able to love yourself, you look to others for that love and support. As we've discussed many times already, seeking that kind of outward validation gives away your power. It becomes an endless cycle, where the more love you give away without receiving it in return, the emptier and more hopeless you feel inside.

To break the cycle, you must recognize the false beliefs that are keeping you stuck and replace them with positive thoughts around your worth. Many of the most effective self-love tools work with your subconscious mind because that is where all those buried childhood memories and beliefs exist.

Often, we aren't even aware of how much negative energy we are directing towards ourselves. Meanwhile, negative thoughts are replaying on a loop. Thoughts like, "You are spoiled," "No one cares what you think," "You are too difficult," "You are such a nag," "Your hair is so frizzy," "You have no friends," are just a few of mine. It is probably obvious that I didn't make up most of these thoughts. Someone said them to me and I locked them in rather than quickly dispelling them as untrue.

One helpful self-love exercise is to write down these thoughts and then counter them in your journal. For example, my marriage counselor helped me counter one thought that burdened me throughout my marriage, "You are such a nag." I always felt bad for harping on my husband to pick up his clothes and help to keep the house clean. I knew I could probably just lower my standards and let that all go if I chose to. The counselor jumped in and reminded me that a tidy house was the ideal. Any responsible adult would recognize that and take steps to correct their messiness, rather than turning the blame on the person who was keeping things clean.

I am sure you can dispel most negative thoughts you have swimming in your head similarly. This exercise can be painful, but it is worth your effort to challenge the negative thoughts keeping you from loving yourself unconditionally. It helps to think of yourself as a child or a dear friend. If either of those people said negative things about themselves, you would quickly jump to their defense. Learn to do the same thing for yourself.

We've already discussed the "I am" writing exercise that I used to increase my confidence and support my self-love. If you recall, all you need to support a positive shift is to write a series of "I am" statements validating and honoring your best qualities. I don't even need to know you to recognize that, as a human, you are filled with countless amazing traits. As a sensitive woman, I know the following wonderful attributes likely apply: "I am compassionate. I am thoughtful. I am generous. I am creative. I am a great listener. I am a helpful friend. I am a loving parent (or Pet Mom)." It will feel awkward at first to write about yourself in such seemingly boastful ways. However, it is important to realize that honoring and recognizing your positive aspects is not arrogant, it is honest. If you can tell yourself terrible lies, why not support yourself with beautiful truths?

There are a variety of other helpful healing modalities that work on your subconscious thoughts to promote more self-love. Following are some that I have found effective:

EMDR (Eye Movement Desensitization and Reprocessing) - This powerful modality works with the brain's natural capacity to heal from trauma. Performed with the support of a trained therapist, it involves replacing negative beliefs with more positive ones. Then, a natural resetting process occurs where you work with tones or move your eyes back and forth. Talk therapy never really made me feel better. EMDR seemed to get to the root of what was keeping me stuck. It removed thought patterns that were making me feel unlovable.

EFT (Tapping) - The best part of the Emotional Freedom Technique (EFT) is that it is free and can be done anywhere. By repeating statements and then tapping on acupressure points, you can change limiting beliefs that have kept you stuck. The tapping process is very soothing. There are a variety of tapping protocols to work on eliminating fears, promoting productivity, and encouraging self-love. You can find tapping protocols on YouTube or through the free The Tapping Solution app.

Clinical Hypnosis - Hypnosis tackles the limiting beliefs that are stuck in your subconscious. Working with a trained hypnotherapist, I could process and dispel negative childhood beliefs. I have also listened to hypnotherapy recordings before bed to improve my health and overall well-being.

Self-Love Meditations - As I have mentioned several times, there are many wonderful meditations available on the internet. The Insight Timer app also has excellent supportive meditations, many of which focus on affirming your self-worth.

I'm grateful for all the excellent, compassionate teachers and tools that have guided my self-love journey. Please see the "Resources" section for more information.

Break Through Abundance Blocks

One of the negative thoughts that plague many sensitive women is specifically around money and general abundance. We come to believe that wanting money is greedy and that we shouldn't ask for, or even accept, the things we want because that is selfish. This has been one of my greatest blocks. I did not know how much it was limiting my growth, in terms of not only financial success, but also regarding self-love and in the love I could receive from others.

I believed I did not deserve abundance so strongly that I married a man who told me I was not worthy of flowers or other simple gifts of affection. He readily criticized me for spending money, when I am by far the most frugal person I know. I only buy things when they are on sale, and I have mastered the art of bargain shopping. It was incredibly strange that despite that obvious aspect of my personality, he still found fault with my spending habits. We were both blocking each other's abundance with our deeply ingrained money fears.

After getting divorced, I felt a sense of ease and freedom in my spending. I was, of course, still very budget-conscious, especially since I no longer had the support of a second income. However, I no longer had the negative energy of someone else blocking my ability to buy the things that gave me joy, especially those things that I didn't technically need. That was the thought that often kept me stuck, "You don't NEED xyz." No matter what it was — a dinner out, a new pair of shoes, a vacation — I always felt the sense that since I didn't actually need it, I wasn't allowed to have it. This meant even minor purchases led me to feel guilty and ashamed.

I have mentioned how needs and wants factor into a healthy relationship. We can want a relationship, but we don't need it. Recognizing the difference between needs and wants is a helpful way to release any strong attachments we may have to the outcome. That being said, we are allowed to want things we don't physically need. This is part of the joy of life. You must honor a healthy balance of both needs and wants to feel fulfilled.

I am certainly not an expert on abundance blocks. They continue to be a challenge for me. However, once I recognized how negatively they were affecting me, I could make conscious efforts to release them. One of the best tools I uncovered was the book, "It's Not Your Money" by Tosha Silver. In it, Tosha promotes a more spiritual approach to receiving. The very week I started working with the prayers suggested in the book, I unexpectedly received two packages in the mail, a mug from a dear friend and some beautiful handmade placemats from my best friend's mom. Add those to the "You can't make this up" list!

I have since also done meditations designed to help me welcome in abundance and honor how worthy I am to receive. These efforts seem to chip away at my former negative blocks around allowing more money, love, and financial support into my life.

Stay in Your Lane

Many sensitive women, especially empaths, tend to get overly attached to the problems of others. We fixate on the co-worker who is going through a rough patch, or we want desperately to ease our close friend's parenting frustrations. We take ownership of other people's emotional issues because we feel them ourselves.

Naturally, this is particularly challenging when we are in a romantic partnership. Our energies get intertwined with our partners, making it difficult to separate from any discomfort they may be feeling. We have to focus on our own problems and energies, disconnecting from those around us. This is much harder than it seems. It requires a very conscious daily intention.

At the beginning of 2020, I kept thinking, "Stay in your lane." I was growing overwhelmed by the ever-expanding responsibilities at work and the constant fear of losing my job because of a reduction in funding. As the pandemic raged, I realized I needed to disconnect from all the negative energies swirling around. There was so much sadness, loss, and anger in the world. As an empath, I felt it all. However, I knew I couldn't do anything to solve the situation other than self-isolating. The act of consciously disconnecting and staying home was a wonderfully healing experience.

Sensitive women need to focus on their own needs and unique way of living. We can't look at what others are doing. The outward-facing manner that most people live simply doesn't support our sensitivities. This means vowing not to compare ourselves to the images we see in social media or pushing ourselves to live in more extroverted ways that don't feel comfortable.

You deserve to live with ease. You don't have to always be striving and doing. That will never be a healthy way to support or harness your sensitivities. Focus on doing less, not more, so that your already overtaxed nervous system can adequately rest and recharge.

For sensitive, empathic women to fall in love with life, we have to allow ourselves to be exactly who we are. We must respect our sensitivities as beautiful gifts that bring more love and compassion to the world. You are here to both give and receive in balance.

One of my favorite sayings is, "Be so happy that others can't help but be happy too." You have the power to raise the positive energy around you. The only way to do that is by honoring what truly supports your happiness while avoiding the negativity of others.

Develop Self-Reliance

Realizing that I could take care of myself was life-changing. I had been a very independent woman before I got married. I always had strong friendships and supportive family around me. I knew that all my needs would be met, and I never felt like I truly needed a romantic partner.

Moving from Rhode Island to Connecticut for my first outpatient dietitian job with a VA Hospital changed that for me. Living alone, in a new state, I suddenly felt as if I did not have anyone to lean on if something ever happened. It was scary. Furthermore, the work of counseling patients affected by PTSD was emotionally draining. I was overwhelmed and felt forced to leave direct patient care for a less meaningful role in a corporation. Shortly afterward, I met my husband.

I recognize now that fear ultimately led me to live with him. Fear then kept me from leaving, even after I realized he was an unsupportive partner. Through his constant criticisms and subtle put-downs, I came to think I was incapable of supporting myself without him. He was quick to remind me that my sensitivity and health conditions made me a liability. *Who would ever want someone with these flaws?*

Even though I was doing the largest portion of the household activities — buying all the groceries, doing all the cleaning and laundry, and paying the bills — I somehow believed I could never manage things on my own. I was ecstatic upon realizing that my life was infinitely easier the second I moved out! I only had to worry about my cat and myself. I was more than capable of handling all the daily tasks of life with ease. It was empowering and eye-opening.

I lived in a rented townhouse for two years, keeping a watchful eye on homes. I was nervous about owning a home, but the cost of rent made it impossible to save. While I worried I wouldn't be able to manage a home on my own, I also knew I had to take the plunge for my financial security.

I took out a map of Connecticut and put in the names of all the helpful friends I knew I could count on. There were only a handful, but that was enough for me to feel safe. I set my sights on homes that were within a 30-minute radius of those friends, ultimately finding the perfect home right in the middle of the state.

The purchase of the home and the move were incredibly stressful. I paid for a moving company to take care of the large furniture and moved everything else on my own through daily trips for over a week. In the meantime, I painted both of the bedrooms, the half-bath, and the living room, trying to take minimal time off from my busy job. I lost five pounds during the process but gained so much confidence in my abilities.

Now that I have been in my home for three years, my self-reliance has continued to grow. As a single woman, if issues came up, there was always someone to call for help. A friend shared the name of a plumber who installed my faucet, other friends offered names for oil companies, and I contracted with a reasonably priced landscaper.

Last year, I upped my game by buying an electric lawnmower and taking care of the lawn on my own. Everything that I tackle independently gives me the mental and emotional strength to recognize that I can survive on my own. Although I now have a partner who helps me with anything I need without complaint, it is a wonderful feeling to know that while I WANT to be with him, I don't NEED to be with him. That shift supports my confidence and freedom.

I encourage you to work on your self-reliance as much as possible. Of course, you don't have to do everything on your own. It is very healthy and wise to ask for support from others. However, as I experienced, every time you complete challenging tasks independently, you empower yourself to achieve even more. We are all far stronger than we believe.

Celebrate Your Strength

Every woman I know is a total badass. You have lived with a rollercoaster of emotions and a seemingly endless list of responsibilities, yet you persevere.

I'm not trying to disrespect men here, but I think the notion that we are the weaker sex is way off base. When I look back on all that I have accomplished in my life, despite the challenges that come from my innate sensitivities, I am incredibly proud. If you knew how much I have struggled with worry in my life, you would recognize what a warrior I am just for getting out of bed every day. I know the same is probably true for you.

Everything in life is relative. The challenges that sensitive women face in our lives can feel like mountains when those with a different temperament only see them as hills. That doesn't mean that we or our perspectives are wrong. It means that we are courageous in ways that some people will never understand. Give yourself the credit that you deserve.

One mantra I used to repeat regularly when working through my codependency issues is "You are enough." I would say that to myself on a loop. Finally, at the end of last year, I suddenly exclaimed, "F*CK that! I am more than enough!" You are too! I believe in you. Please commit to believing in yourself too.

You have this one amazing life. Don't waste it living an existence that is just good enough. Focus on falling in love with yourself and all the spectacular gifts you bring to the world. Give yourself all the

love, attention, and time you have been giving to others. A healthy partnership requires that both parties show up as the best versions of themselves. This is your call to be your best self so that when your partner arrives, he will easily recognize your magnificence.

Chapter 25: Call in Your Life Partner

When I first started online dating, I was hopefully optimistic that I would meet someone amazing right away. I have friends who met their spouses in their first week online. While deep down I knew I wasn't ready for a long-term love right out of the gate, I still fantasized that an intelligent, funny, compassionate man was going to show up and sweep me off my feet.

Thank God/Goddess that never happened! I had barely dated in high school or college, and I married the first man who seemed like a safe choice. I now realize that I needed to experience all the highs and lows of dating before I could be sure I had found my person.

Some people are destined to attract the experiences and people who are healthiest for them early in life. We all know couples who meet each other in high school and end up living blissfully together for the rest of their lives. However, this is not the path for most of us.

I believe there is a life lesson that all empaths and sensitives must face. Society tells us we are weak and meek when we are actually powerhouses. Our inner strength, forged from love and light, is so much stronger and brighter than we could ever imagine. We never truly understand that until we have walked through fire. Once burned, we emerge like a phoenix rising from the ash, accepting finally that we deserve all the love we give.

I'm not suggesting that you must suffer or that I want you to experience abuse before attracting love. I just know that if you have found this book, it is probably because the harsh realities of life have challenged your sensitivities. I want you to recognize that there are lessons in your negative experiences. They have prepared you.

When you have done the work to restore your confidence and reclaim your self-love, you are ready to call in your life partner. So, let's get to the fun part, working on the final push that will help you attract your ideal match.

Let Go of Past Connections

Sensitive women hate cutting ties. We don't feel comfortable ending relationships. We want to be friends with everyone. The idea that someone might be directing negative energy our way feels terrible. There is an interesting phenomenon with my INFJ personality type. We are known to do what is called a "door slam" where we hit our breaking point with someone or with a situation like a job. At that point, we walk away, never looking back. We close the door because we know that we have already expended far too much energy on that path. The trouble is, empathic INFJs never feel good about this decision. We know we have to do it, but we don't want to.

Regardless, slamming the door on unhealthy situations and people is crucial. Our energies are so connected to others that we can't afford to be tied to negativity. It drains us of our power, even just by taking up space in our minds and our hearts.

As a child, I wanted to be an elementary school teacher. I always loved children. When I first went to college, I started out majoring in elementary education. However, at the end of my first year, I was overwhelmed with dread at the thought of standing in front of a classroom filled with kids. I quickly changed my major to nutrition and never looked back. I told myself it would be fine. I would have children of my own one day.

When I met my husband, those thoughts changed. I was diagnosed with Hashimoto's Thyroiditis a year before meeting him. It wasn't a surprise since my mother has this condition as well. Nevertheless, I worried about the fatigue I was already experiencing as a result. My husband didn't want to have children and told me I really shouldn't consider having them since I might not have the energy. My entire worldview changed as I accepted that maybe I wasn't destined to be a mother after all. I opted instead to embrace the nieces and nephews that I was lucky enough to have in my life.

In my 30s, when I was experiencing the peak of my anxiety attacks, I was referred to a powerful energy healer. As soon as she met me, she said there was a piece of my heart dedicated to someone else. She asked if I had a past boyfriend that I was still in love with. That was definitely not the case.

We both concluded that I had been holding a space in my heart for a baby. As she worked on me, it felt as if she was pulling something out of my chest. She warned me that I might have residual pain on the following day. She was right. My heart seemed to be squeezing. If I hadn't been warned, I would have thought I was having a heart attack. Later I felt a sense of expansiveness in my chest.

I had released the attachments to any lingering hope of ever having a child of my own. I no longer regret not having children. As an empath, I can see that would have been an incredibly challenging path for me.

I share this story because it taught me a powerful lesson. Our energy can get tied to expectations, dreams, and people. If we don't sever those ties, they can prevent us from living in our full energy and power.

I've mentioned before that the first man I dated seriously continued to text and message me for over a year after we broke up. I expected we would always be friends. I hadn't realized what a dishonest person he was. I knew he had been dating someone only because he was sharing those details on the social media accounts associated with his business. I was genuinely happy for him.

However, right around the anniversary of our breakup, he messaged me saying that he loved me. I was confused, wondering if perhaps he had broken up with his girlfriend. I got the inclination to look on social media and learned that she had just posted about their one-year anniversary. Turns out, he had started dating her less than a week after we broke up, a fact that he hid from me in an attempt to keep seeing me.

A week after learning that news, there was a Full Blood Wolf Moon Eclipse in my sign of Leo. Eclipses bring out what is hiding from the shadows. In an amazing prediction, two of my favorite astrologers, The AstroTwins, said that some Leos may dramatically end relationships. They also noted, "Learning to love yourself is the greatest love of all."

Both declarations were true for me. I completed a full moon release ritual, cutting ties with all the men I had met and dated online. I realized I couldn't attract a healthy partner if I was still maintaining energetic connections to other men.

Think about all the people and situations that could be draining your love. Make the conscious decision to release all of those past connections and expectations. Remember, anything that didn't work out was never meant to. Reclaim all the love you have been directing outward. Focus it inward, as you prepare for the partner who will give his love in the balanced manner you deserve.

Harness More Crystal Power

I've already discussed using crystals for protection and to heal your heart. This time you are going to use them to empower yourself and draw more love into your life.

At the end of 2018, I purchased a beautiful piece of labradorite. This stone has a brilliant iridescence that just makes me smile. I used it to help strengthen my self-esteem, while also increasing my belief that I could move beyond my past disappointments to claim the love I deserved.

I also focused my attention again on rose quartz. I placed several pieces in the relationship corner of my home. According to Feng Shui, this is the area in your home in the farthest right corner from your front door. It just so happens, that is where my bedroom is located.

One of the pieces had a particularly powerful significance. My best friend had given me a rose quartz pendant when we were in high school, well before we knew anything about the power of crystals. I knew how strongly she wanted me to find love, which magnified its impact. The pendant still hangs prominently in that space.

I also slept with a piece of rose quartz and a piece of amethyst under my pillow. Every night before going to bed, I told my Spirit Team that I was ready for my true love to arrive.

Create a Partner Wish List

I have had a vision board for well over a decade. It is covered in fabric and has sections where I can easily add and remove items. I modify the board at the beginning of every year, removing any items that were fulfilled and adding any new things that I wish to focus on.

When I was looking to buy a house, I had hand-written a note with a list of things that I was hoping for in a new home. One of those things was a view of beautiful sunrises or sunsets.

The very day my house went on the market, I got the impulse to check the real estate listings. I never did that when I was at work, but the urge was especially strong. I had just been with a group of my girlfriends the day before and I had told them I knew a home was coming soon. It was again as if saying my intention aloud had amplified its impact. Scrolling through the listings on my phone, I was excited to find one that looked perfect. I texted my realtor and asked him to get us in to see the house as soon as possible. He let me know we were on for 5:30. As we arrived, the sun was just setting. When we walked out onto the covered porch to a beautiful display of color, we both looked at each other and smiled. The home fulfilled my wishes. It contained all but one item, a garage, which I have since realized I don't really need.

Since I knew how powerful the Law of Attraction and vision boards could be, toward the end of 2018 I wrote out a short list of attributes I was hoping for in a partner. I dated a few men who fulfilled aspects of the list, yet they still weren't quite right.

On February 10, 2019, I revised the list, printed it out, cut it into a heart shape, and placed it on my vision board. This is the actual list:

Please bring me a partner who is:
Kind, Compassionate, Loving,
Affectionate, Handsome,
Generous (with his time and money),
Open-Minded, Intelligent,
Spiritually Connected, Self-Aware
Emotionally Balanced, HAPPY, and
Totally in LOVE with ME!!!!

I can honestly say this list describes the man who showed up just eight days later! Add this again to the "You can't make this up" list. Your mind is powerful. What you set your intentions on you can manifest.

Write Love Letters

On March 31, 2018, we had the second blue moon of that year, a magical and rare occurrence. It was the Full Moon in Libra. Full moons are always about releasing and letting go of what no longer serves us. Libra is about finding greater balance, honoring where you have been, and looking forward to the positive potential that is to come with a wiser, clearer perspective.

At the suggestion of The AstroTwins, I decided to welcome more love into my life by writing two love letters, one to my soulmate and the other to myself. I lit a white candle to attract in the positive energy and sat down at my computer to write.

I began with the love letter to myself. I wrote, *"Someone is coming, someone who truly complements and matches your spirit, mind, and body. He is kind, loving, passionate, committed to you in every way."* The letter went on for a page and a half, and concluded with, *"You will settle into your life finally. You will be able to feel such relief in the fact that you can stop looking, as you will have found it already. The only striving that will take place is to evolve your spirit in a way that helps you both. It will be a beautiful and magical partnership, and it will happen soon. You are loved. You are blessed. You are grateful. So be it. Amen."*

I immediately followed that declaration with a letter to my true love. It was written as a heartfelt "thank you," as if he had just arrived. I started with, *"Dear Love, I am ready for you. I have been preparing myself mentally, spiritually, physically all of my life. I know that you have been doing the same. Together we are going to be an unstoppable force of love, creativity, and intellect."*

I expressed all the things I loved about our life together, noting, *"I love that you make me feel beautiful all of the time. I love that you support my beliefs and my evolution. I love that we can have separate interests and still come together in unity. I love that together all of our needs are met and that we share a collective freedom that allows us space and growth always. I have so much fun with you! You make me laugh and smile. You help me handle hard times and stress."*

I concluded with, *"As a family [with my cat], we share so much love that everyone who interacts with us feels it and feels better about themselves just by being in our presence. I love you completely and unconditionally and I am very grateful that you do the same. We are going to have a long, happy life together and we will complete the beautiful work we were meant to do. I look forward to seeing you soon. Thank you. I love you! Amen."*

Again, I wrote well over a page going deeply into what I cherished about being with my true love. As I read it now, I am in absolute awe over how well it describes the partnership we have enjoyed for the past two years.

With both letters, the words just flew off my fingertips. I almost felt as if I was channeling them from a higher source. I had never really thought that deeply about the man I wanted to call in. The exercise made me recognize what really mattered to me.

It also made me realize that the purpose of the men I had met and dated up to that point was to show me some of the attributes that were possible so that I could narrow them down to those that mattered most. I felt a wave of gratitude for the path that life had put me on. There are no accidents. The hard stuff prepares us for our growth and evolution.

I think the power of a letter-writing exercise like this is in setting your intentions so firmly that you believe it has happened. Conjure up the joy and peace that you know a loving partnership will bring. Then write from that uplifted place.

I know this suggestion sounds wild. I might not believe it if I hadn't experienced it firsthand. This process wasn't quick. It took 11 months for the letters to come true. In the meantime, I would periodically read them aloud before going to bed. The letter I wrote to myself boosted my self-love and confidence tremendously, while the letter to my love gave me a feeling of comfort and hope.

Work on Your Throat Chakra

Many sensitive women, especially those of us with codependency issues, have learned to suppress our voices and not speak freely about our needs. Little girls are supposed to be quiet and agreeable. I know I was often quite rebellious with my words, speaking out when I felt things were unfair or unjust. However, I always felt wrong for doing so. I would typically fight my natural inclination to communicate honestly and with clarity.

The throat chakra governs our ability to communicate. If that area is blocked, you may have health issues with your thyroid, sore throats, or a timid voice. As I mentioned, I have thyroid disease and Sjögren's Syndrome, both of which affect tissues surrounding the throat chakra. These autoimmune conditions occur primarily in women and are quite common. Of course, there are other causes related to genetics, the environment, and viruses, but the tendency for women to block our voices can't be disregarded as a cause.

Why is this important in terms of calling in your partner? Communication is a vital piece of a healthy relationship. If you aren't ready and willing to ask for what you need from a new partner, your chances for a successful relationship are slim. In contrast, if your ability to speak out and talk openly is strong and clear, you will be much more likely to connect with a balanced person.

Healthy, loving men want honest, open relationships. They are just as tired of playing games as women are. They want a woman who shows up knowing what she wants and expressing it clearly and compassionately. If you give a dedicated man your map, he will follow you to the end of the earth.

If communication is a challenge for you, it is worth giving your throat chakra some extra love and attention. Blue crystals like sodalite, lapis lazuli, amazonite, and aquamarine can support your throat chakra. Wearing one on a choker is an especially helpful way to support that chakra.

In addition, chanting the mantra "Ham" (pronounced hahhmm) can help raise the vibrations in the throat. You can find throat chakra meditations online to support these efforts. Writing, or speaking freely with a friend, will also help you work the throat chakra so that communicating is easier.

I hope you can now recognize that being ready to date, and being prepared for the love of your life, are subtly different. You must put in the work to uncover your blocks and heal them as much as possible, while also getting clear on what you are looking for in a partner. Once you have created a life you love and you have let the Universe know your intentions, it is just a matter of time before your ideal partner arrives.

Chapter 26: Recognize a Healthy Relationship

Sadly, we rarely focus on the importance of healthy relationships. So much of our media depicts abuse as normal. Songs focus on heartbreak and infidelity. Movies and TV highlight drama and chaos as the core components of passionate love. When we do see love depicted, it is often with a sticky-sweet tone that feels unrealistic and impractical. This all makes it difficult to know just what a healthy love should look and feel like.

I took a child development course in high school. The teacher was a very compassionate woman. She took a portion of the class to address domestic abuse. She got very serious with us, stating that you can never judge a woman who is in an abusive relationship because there are so many confusing dynamics in place. I couldn't help but wonder, "Why would a woman ever put up with that?"

I told myself that I would never let a man put his hands on me. I clearly didn't understand what my teacher meant about confusing dynamics. Years later, I found myself entangled in a marriage where my self-esteem was eroded so slowly over time I couldn't even see it happening.

While completing my master's degree, I read about the "Boiling Frog Experiment." The premise is that if you put a frog in a pot of water and slowly bring the water to a boil, the frog will never jump out. It grows so comfortable in the warm water that it doesn't even realize it is dying. I was once a boiling frog. As is common in those who have been through narcissistic abuse, I didn't even recognize how dysfunctional my relationships had become.

The truth is a large majority of relationships are dysfunctional. It is common for partnerships to take on a lopsided feel, with one partner carrying more than their share of the work or responsibilities. Even when people feel like this scenario works for them, it often leads to resentment and burnout.

The basis of a genuinely healthy partnership is that the sum of your two lives together is greater than if you were apart. Your lives are easier because you have each other.

The simplest aspects are the most powerful connectors. Do you have fun together? Do you have easy, enjoyable conversations? Do you feel safe, supported, and understood? These are all foundational aspects of a healthy relationship.

Since so many of us sensitive women have been through relationships where we over-give and never reap the rewards of our efforts, it is worth taking some time to think about the healthiest aspects of partnership. They are far more basic and obvious than we tend to believe.

Understand Genuine Partnership

The week before writing this chapter, I picked a daily card, as I usually do. I rotate between three decks, and on this occasion, I picked from the "Seeking Within" deck. I purchased this deck in September 2018 from Joyce St. Germaine after she had provided me with a palm reading.

In that reading, she told me I was supposed to write a book. She also stressed that online dating could work for me, but I had to be especially careful about discernment. In pulling out my notes from that meeting I was amazed to read, "A relationship that is coming will be so comfortable that it will be laughable. It just unfolds and you will not use comparisons because there won't be any." Joyce also affirmed that relationships shouldn't take work. Everything she shared has proven to be true.

Now back to the card deck! When I asked my usual question last week, "What do I need to know today?" I picked the "Partnership" card for the first time. I marveled at how beautifully its message fit into this discussion of what makes for a healthy relationship.

As I typed the words into my journal, which was set to black and white, the text turned a beautiful purple that mirrored the imagery of the card. I knew it was a sign that I had to share the message here.

"True partnership is a shared Love. It goes beyond the physical and familiar co-dependent expectations we all have. In Partnership we can act as mirrors for the other, reflecting back the richness and depths of our souls in freedom, love and acceptance of everything that makes us who we are. In Partnership, we can see we are All One." [Shared with permission from the author, Paula Bush. Please see the "Resources" section for more on these cards.]

I reached out to the cards' creators to ask for their blessing in sharing this. As I was emailing Paula Bush, the author of the cards, I noticed it was 2:22 on the clock. Today as I write this section it is on page 222 of my Word document. We can add these powerful synchronicities to the "You can't make this up" file. Incidentally, the number pattern 222 naturally relates to partnership, love, and being in balance.

See the Green Flags

I have harped quite a bit on the red flags to watch for when trying to find your ideal match. While that is a negative focus, it is important to honor so that you don't get lured in by the wrong man. It is much more fun, however, to look for the green flags of a healthy relationship. Most relate to how you feel when with that person. The ideal feeling states are happy, comfortable, secure, valued, respected, worthy, and understood.

When you are progressing in a healthy relationship, you and your partner are emotionally available to one another. This means that you are both able to recognize and state your wants and needs. In addition, you are both ready to give and receive love. Furthermore, you can give your time and attention freely. There doesn't need to be perfection, but rather a willingness to do the work.

When I first started in my current relationship, I was still struggling to receive love. My partner had to provide me with extra support and encouragement in this area. Healthy relationships include give and take. You are both giving of yourselves 100%, but some days one partner may seem to be giving more, and other days that dynamic shifts. The important thing is that reciprocity is the goal. No one is intending to lean on or take from the other person disproportionately.

Following are some wonderful green flags that alert you to a healthy partner:

* You genuinely like each other. There is a core friendship.
* Your basic needs are met emotionally, physically, and spiritually.
* You feel comfortable being yourself.
* You can communicate openly.
* You feel happy and have fun most of the time.
* You feel safe and secure in his presence.
* You make each other laugh. You share inside jokes that make you feel special.
* You share intimacy, knowing each other on a deep level.
* You are both willing to be vulnerable, expressing your deepest insecurities.
* He is forgiving and supportive.
* He is tolerant of all your moods.
* He is interested in you beyond sexual activity.
* He is willing to help you with the hard things (e.g., daily stressors, house projects, illness).
* You enjoy some of the same activities.
* You feel the same about having children.
* Your life goals and aspirations are in alignment.
* You want the same amount of travel, or don't mind traveling without each other.
* You are affectionate on the same level.
* You get along with their family and friends.
* You have a spiritual connection.

Of course, this list is important to review in reverse. You must be willing to do and be all the things that you are expecting from your partner for a relationship to grow. I know that this list might seem overwhelming and unrealistic if you have never had a truly balanced relationship. Before meeting my partner, I knew I wanted all the things mentioned here, yet I worried that such a man did not exist. I promise you these men are out there! The most important aspect is that you are both willing to work on the relationship. If that willingness is present, there is nothing you won't be able to overcome.

Honor the Traits of a Supportive Man

A supportive man will be easy to recognize. He has a variety of core traits that put you at ease in his presence. He is emotionally intelligent and specifically empathetic, recognizing when you are feeling down. At those times, he offers compassion and kind words.

He is consistent, responsible, and trustworthy. He takes full ownership of his life and honors his word, doing what he says he is going to do.

He respects your boundaries and listens to your requests. If he makes a mistake or doesn't follow through on something, he will own up to it and readily apologize.

He is even-keeled and doesn't get angry or defensive when you have a difference of opinion. He can maintain a sense of humor, even when life is challenging.

Supportive men listen to and honor your concerns. They will be honest and vulnerable even if it is uncomfortable.

A truly supportive man recognizes that no one is perfect and allows you to have bad days, just as you allow him the same. Support is, of course, a mutual need. If you encounter a supportive man, be sure to honor and appreciate him fully. Give him the same support that he is offering so that it can continue to flourish.

∞∞∞

Knowing what to look for in terms of a healthy partnership is a big part of welcoming it into your life. Many of us have never experienced genuinely healthy relationships, so we have a hard time recognizing them, or even believing they exist. Get clear on the core elements that you are looking for in a partner. Perhaps you can now go back to the list on your vision board or your love letter and add to your intentions. Again, focus on how you want to feel around your partner. Those feelings become the energetic spark that alerts you when you have met the one.

A Final Pep Talk

Sensitive Woman, you deserve a joyful, love-filled life. Embrace the possibility that it can be yours. You have the strength, knowledge, and will to make it happen.

Remember the key principles that we discussed. You only need to meet that one special person. Don't get caught up in a mindset of quantity over quality. Conserve your time and energy for a man who communicates openly and welcomes you fully into his life. A committed man will always make you a priority.

Pay attention to how you feel. There is great power in your sensitivity. Your instincts will not steer you wrong.

Your ideal partner will feel easy, comfortable, and safe. He will be consistent, respectful, and supportive. Get clear on the traits that matter most to you. Talk about them. Write about them. Share them with the Universe, so that the energies can align on your behalf. Your person is out there waiting for you.

If you are ready, get on out there into the online world and claim the fun, connection, and love that you are looking for. I am rooting for you every step of the way!

Resources

I am so incredibly grateful for all the books, webinars, videos, blogs, and other forms of free and inexpensive support that are available. My evolution has occurred through the help of many people and the wonderful work they put out into the world. You will find an updated list of the valuable resources mentioned throughout the book on my website:

www.HappyHealthyHer.com/Online-Dating

Afterword / Acknowledgements

Thanks so much for reading! One of the greatest joys in life is being seen and heard. By reading this book, you have given me that gift. I truly appreciate you.

If you have gained anything from what I have shared, please consider writing a positive review on Amazon. Please also spread the word to other women who might benefit from the support.

My heartfelt thanks go out to the friends and family who supported this book's evolution by reading, reviewing, and offering input. In particular, thank you to Chelle Salvucci, Gina Reichert, Monique Gianni, Margaret "Peggy" Barrett, Lauren Sapala, and my mom, Hope Gibeault. I am so very grateful for your friendship, love, and clarity.

To my sweetheart, Ilia Athan, thank you for supporting this work in every possible way. In addition to inspiring and affirming what I know about supportive and committed men, you helped me edit and shape the book with the precision of a master carpenter. I am grateful for you every day.

About the Author

Michelle Gibeault, MA, RDN is a health writer, healing coach, and dietitian with a master's degree in Integrative Health. As a sensitive empath, she helps women harness the gift of their innate compassion in order to live their best lives. She loves all things self-help, including yoga, meditation, astrology, personality theory, natural healing, hiking, and music.

*Follow Michelle at **www.HappyHealthyHer.com** where she shares natural healing tools, inspiration, and empowerment support through affordable courses and coaching services.*

Made in the USA
Las Vegas, NV
30 July 2021